CW00656166

Praise from the Editors

"David Pagel brings a disarming and pragma
[this collection]. He is the prototypical Midw
with a refined understanding of the history and ethos of ascent."

—FROM THE FOREWORD BY **MICHAEL KENNEDY**, LEGENDARY
ALPINIST, WRITER, FORMER PUBLISHER AND EDITOR-IN-CHIEF OF
CLIMBING MAGAZINE

"My high school chums and I graduated in 1983, when Dave's 'Mind Games' appeared in *Climbing* and it blew us away. It was a hugely influential piece of writing in my early years as a Boulder climber—as were his later pieces about the Titan and other subjects. His work has been a guiding light in my own literary progress."

—**CAMERON BURNS**, NOTED CLIMBER, AUTHOR, CO-EDITOR OF
CLIMB: TALES OF MAN VERSUS BOULDER, CRAG, WALL, AND PEAK

"Over the years I had the pleasure of working with David as his editor on features, minifeatures and columns, and I can only say I revere his talent, and *still* remember his lines. From his 'Leviathan,' about climbing the Eiger:

Chicken? I think it's a safe bet that no matter how fiercely Lachenal and Terray disagreed over the prospects of a particular route, the one never resorted to calling the other 'chicken.'"

—**ALISON OSIUS**, EXECUTIVE EDITOR, *ROCK AND ICE* MAGAZINE

And from Readers

"Thanks for putting in writing something that I can personally relate to and say, *We did that!*"

"This well-written piece got me excited to visit Devils Tower."

"Dave Pagel's description of climbing the Matterhorn is a bold and hilarious piece of writing."

"Great job taking a great person/hero…and portraying him accurately—a seemingly scarce journalistic quality these days."

"Hats, or possibly helmets, off to David Pagel…It's nice to feel you're actually being addressed by a fellow mere mortal, not some super rockstar who raised the standards by 10 points and freed everything in record time."

Cold Feet

*Stories of a
Middling Climber*

*On Classic Peaks &
Among Legendary Mountaineers*

THE COLLECTED WRITINGS OF
David Pagel

Foreword by Michael Kennedy

Copyright © 2014 by David Pagel

All rights reserved.

ISBN-13: 978-0692305560

Covers and interior mountain illustrations by
Rick Kollath, **Kollath Graphic Design**, Duluth, MN.

Photo credits:
Page 11: Jim Kennedy; Pages 19, 333: Dean Einerson; Page 20: Kaija Webster;
Page 162: City of Vancouver Archives: CVA 586-504, Photographer:
Don Coltman, Steffans Colmer, Ltd.
All other photographs are from the Author's collection.

For Anderl, who inspired the beginning,

And for Dina, who ensures the ending,
"And they lived happily ever after."

The Lotus Flower Tower, centerpiece of the Cirque of the Unclimbables (see p. 103)

CONTENTS

Epics

Home Turf

Mountain Profiles

Perspective

Verse

Needle's Eye *(5.8 R), Black Hills of South Dakota*

FOREWORD

TO BE A CLIMBER in the Midwest is to dream, and to travel in pursuit of those dreams.

Trapped in a horizontal wilderness of cornfields and cold, gray winters, an aspiring Lynn Hill might discover her personal *Nose* among the graffiti and broken glass of a scrappy urban crag; a flatland Steve House trains for the glories of the Greater Ranges on stadium stairs, Rocky-style, while a nascent Tommy Caldwell finds inspiration in the yellow route in the local gym. Fortunate (read: spoiled) residents of Colorado, California or Washington have dozens of world-class crags, walls and mountains within a few minutes, or at most, a few hours of their doorsteps, but the dedicated Duluth climber will endure 11 hours in the van each way (plus a time change) for a weekend of rock climbing in the Black Hills.

It's no mystery, then, that Midwest climbers tend to be more humble, and can be (dare I say it) more motivated and enthusiastic than their Western brethren.

David Pagel brings a disarming and pragmatic sensibility to each chapter in *Cold Feet: Stories of a Middling Climber.* He is the prototypical Midwesterner, a journeyman climber with a refined understanding of the history and ethos of ascent. I remember well his first published piece, "Mind Games," in which he traces a journey from Minnesota to Devils Tower (via Eldorado Canyon), slyly poking fun not just at his and partner Jim's antics, but at the foibles of the more urbane climbers they encounter along the way and indeed the entire climbing subculture they aspire to become a part of. The tale was a refreshing change from the sometimes transcendent, almost always epic sagas of first ascents on far-off mountains and crags that were stock-in-trade of *Climbing* (of which I was editor), *Rock and Ice*, and *Ascent.*

Self-effacing to a fault, for 30 years David has chronicled his climbs and encounters with heroes, pondering the place of the Everyman in the pantheon of climbing gods and goddesses. Along the way he has continued to dream, and to travel. Let's hope he keeps it up long enough to produce a second volume of his musings.

—MICHAEL KENNEDY

A career takes flight: the Author falling off the Bastille's West Buttress *(5.9+) in Colorado, circa 1979*

INTRODUCTION

(mid·dling) *adj:* of average quality; mediocre

THE FACT IS, I am a writer by accident. It began with a youthful road trip to fabled crags in Colorado and Wyoming. Those places! The climbs! They scared the *hell* out of me—and left me feeling jazzed beyond words. Literally, beyond words. When people asked me about my inaugural western tour, I would ejaculate an enthusiastic but rote narrative of where I'd gone and what I'd done, and they would listen, maybe ask a few questions, and nod with perceived understanding. But they didn't get it. The core of my experience, the runaway locomotive of heady emotions— terror and joy—when compared to the creaky little pump trolley of my previous perspective and passion…this defied description. It was incommunicable, at least by me in conversation. Frustrated by the shortcomings of the clumsy knot behind my teeth and with very little writing experience or aspiration, I put pen to paper. Inexpertly kneading and poking the literary clay, I nonetheless managed to sculpt a story that adequately conveyed my sentiments. In fact, the people who read "Mind Games" seemed to enjoy it enough that, in a moment of uncharacteristic audaciousness, I mailed it off to *Climbing* magazine. I'm not entirely sure what editor-in-chief Michael Kennedy was thinking when he decided to publish it, partly because I'm still amazed that so many readers connected with my stilted little travelogue, and partly because his response was brief and to the point: "A refreshing change from the usual Hardman stuff—I look forward to seeing it in print." I do know that Michael's affirmation was an epiphany. Wow, I thought, if that's all it takes to get published, stories about a middling climber dipping his toes in the Big League and nearly wetting his pants…well, I'm your guy!

I took another trip and had another terrifying and transcendent experience. Flouting the notion that miracles are a one-time deal, I wrote it up and sent it in. "Exodus" was my account of three flatlanders tackling the soaring *Nose* of El Capitan—and getting their butts kicked all the way up. "Better written," was Michael's reply this time. Ignoring the subtext here regarding my first piece, I felt emboldened to milk this cow to the last drop.

What followed was a series of published articles spaced out over the years, essentially expedition reports documenting my career as a run-of-the-mill climber who is either too simple-minded or too pigheaded to be bound by Everyman conventions. In other words, I aspired to estimable routes and mountains I really had little business attempting: the Titan, Mount Kenya, the Eigerwand…the list goes on and on. This isn't false modesty, it's God's own truth by virtue of the fact that I'm not just a middling climber, I'm a middling climber *from Minnesota*. I've lived my whole life on the Great Plains, confined to honing my skills on temperate weekends at a smattering of half-pitch outcrops with little opportunity to work through a proper alpine apprenticeship on lesser peaks before tackling "the big ones." Yet I went for them anyway. Imprudent? Impudent? Both? Perhaps, but as such, the stories collected here represent the aspirations of all the middling, Everyman mountaineers—the anti-Hardmen, as Michael Kennedy has suggested—lived out in glorious and ignominious detail. I suppose this is why I'm so unabashedly willing (eager?) to confess my shortcomings and misgivings, and why there's a lot of near-disaster and outright failure as well as success in these pages. And why I've nearly wet my pants (or worse) on every trip.

Eventually, as a fledgling writer, I branched out further onto a sagging limb by writing about mountain experiences other than my own, notably the 1957 Haramosh disaster ("All That Remain"), and penning profiles of legendary alpinists spanning the generations from Anderl Heckmair to Steve House. Believe me when I say that if you think going out to meet great mountains is intimidating, it is nothing compared to meeting great mountaineers—perhaps because when mountains put you to the test they're not looking you in the eye. Along the way, I've shamelessly tapped some wells twice by writing profiles of the very same routes and peaks covered in earlier narratives, further proof that my mountain experience is limited. In addition, the reader will find a handful of "perspective" pieces included in this collection, interesting or important things I've learned while climbing or about climbing, usually the hard way. I've even thrown in an introduction penned for a special edition of a classic book about the Eiger (another cow I've milked dry) because it offers insight into how and why I became a climber in the first place, and because the piece has never really had a proper airing since almost nobody ever bothers to read an introduction—so the fact that you are reading this one portends that you may suffer *two* before you're done with this brick.

As a Midwesterner, I would be remiss if I didn't include pieces detailing my home turf and that seminal aspect of my climbing experience. Those of us confined to a two-dimensional universe spend our lives trying to scrape up adventure with the meager topographical bones we've been tossed. Our common experience may be a microcosm of the major leagues, but we also share a few things all our own, such as the trials and tribulations of the Road Warrior, recounted here in "The Loneliness of the Long Distance Climber." One of my personal favorites set at my home crag on the North Shore of Lake Superior is "Dust Storm," a satirical piece about the folly and potentially dire results of taking ethical squabbles to the extreme. An unanticipated consequence of publishing this was that at least one of my local brethren didn't recognize it as satire, and/or considered it a reverie of impending violence and sounded the warning bells—providing me a surreal but oddly delicious Orson Welles (OrWellian?) moment.

But as Michael Kennedy asserted in his reply to my very first submission, my forte is the Everyman diarist, whose soul is fueled by exuberant mountain ambition even as the blood is draining from his extremities and the bomb bay doors of the lower intestine are swinging open. My tick list, presented more or less chronologically throughout these pages, is the classics: routes steeped in immense history or of unrivaled quality on the world's most iconic, sought-after peaks. Well, many of them anyway. One in particular is conspicuous by its absence. In my salad days I dreamed of climbing Mount Everest (what pimpled mountaineer doesn't?) yet never fully committed to taking on the second-mortgage required for making that dream a reality. As a result, measured according to the standards of the mass media and public perception, I am an abject failure as a climber. My frustration with society's "Everest bias" is expressed in a Seussian rant titled, "Because It Isn't There." This and the other verse— mostly parody and drinking songs—published here for the very first time are admittedly silly exercises in which I have repeatedly borrowed (stolen) structure and meter from gifted poets and songwriters, usurping their art for my own self-amusement.

Of course, this book is not a product of me alone, and in this regard I am hugely indebted to two groups of individuals. First, my climbing partners: Jim Kennedy, Rick Kollath, Roger Volkmann, Dean Einerson, Jeff Kolehmainen, all the other Daves (Mital, Ostergren, Sohlstrom) and countless others who have led my cruxes, held my falls, and provided reasoned counterpoint to my irrational tendency for retreat (not to mention having endured unwanted celebrity and unwarranted ridicule as a result of their inclusion in these stories); to you I'm grateful, I'm sorry, and I wish we could go back and do it all over again.* Secondly, the editors: Michael Kennedy, Alison Osius, Mike Benge, Duane Raleigh, Tyler Stableford and the other selfless and gifted wordsmiths who have provided opportunity, offered up encouragement, and labored to craft silk purses from the sows' ears I've landed on their desks; I am in awe of your skills and your

---

*Except for that multi-day alpine excursion when I insisted creamed fish would be the perfect bivouac food—for so many reasons, that should never be repeated.

unwavering dedication and largely unheralded contributions to the high art and standards of mountain literature. To you I also apologize if I have in any way lowered the bar, despite your best efforts. Additionally, I must thank Dina Post, Rick Kollath (again!) and Amy Glomski; to them goes the credit for completing the onerous task of reviewing and editing this collection—and, of course, the blame for any typos still lurking within (and now the reader has been introduced to yet another recurring theme throughout my life and these stories: ducking responsibility).

I'll end where I began, by emphasizing the fact that for me, writing was a happy accident. As a climber, nothing I've ever done has been of importance to anyone other than myself. And yet, from the beginning it has all been so significant to me personally that my instinct has been to share…and maybe inspire. Hopefully these pages reveal that with great partners, great luck and great ambition, the average Joe can do alright for him or herself in the mountains—but the mind games are ongoing and universal. If there's one thing I've learned on classic peaks and among legendary mountaineers it is that when confronting fear and uncertainty in the mountains, when toed up to the limit of personal ability and contemplating the necessity of taking just one more step, everyone, Hardman and Everyman alike, faces the prospect of cold feet.

DAVID PAGEL
Duluth, 2014

Cold Feet

*Stories of a
Middling Climber...*

On Classic Peaks

Climbers beginning the epic third pitch of Tulgey Wood *at Devils Tower*

MIND GAMES
Making It in the Big Time

W E HAD SPENT YEARS laboring on the small bluffs of eastern Minnesota under the incredulous eyes of Lake Superior vacationers and St. Croix River valley tourists. "Crazy" they called us, as we clung to ropes the size of their pinkies and disappeared over precipices that loomed all of fifty feet over the spongy ground below. We liked to think of it as training. Two months of our summer dragged once more through this routine until at last, Jim and I decided it was time to pack up the aging Datsun and follow the setting sun. Go west, young man, to the legendary land of multi-pitch climbs.

First stop, the fabled canyon of Eldorado: valley of endless sandstone, stomping grounds of Layton Kor, home of the *Naked Edge*. Our first night there, we walked the entire length of the road in gray drizzle, looking for the climbs. Nothing looked even remotely big enough to fit the visions of this place that our imaginations had conjured. We stood perplexed beneath a large outcrop that offered some shelter from the rain.

"Boy, Jim, this has got to be the place. The sign said 'Eldorado Springs.' You don't suppose there might be more than one, do you?"

"No," he replied, "this *must* be it. We probably just didn't walk far enough up the canyon."

Suddenly, a lone figure toting a chalk bag materialized out of the mists.

"Hey, buddy," we called. "Where would we find the Bastille?" He stared. "You're leaning against it."

Jim and I looked at each other and then slowly raised our heads to the rock wall above. "My God," Jim sighed, "it can't be more than two rope-lengths to the top." We stumbled back to camp feeling cheated.

Foreshortening is a nasty phenomenon, and we soon found out how wrong first impressions made on ignorant flatlanders in the pouring rain can be. A week later (most of which was spent backing off routes that were way over our heads) two enlightened, exhausted, and effectively humbled Minnesota climbers crept out of Colorado.

We coaxed our roadster north into the bleak and smooth, yet warmly familiar landscape of eastern Wyoming. We were headed for Devils Tower, and this time we would start by giving the place the respect it deserved. We agreed to begin climbing 5.7 and then, if we were climbing well, maybe take a shot at some easier 5.8.

Soon the Tower loomed on the horizon, juxtaposed with the surrounding gentle hills like some great corrugated stump. Pulling into the cozy campground near its base, we noticed quite a few sites with mounds of ropes and climbing hardware heaped on the picnic tables. There were even some familiar "Land of 10,000 Lakes" license plates on the bumpers of the vehicles. A merry evening ensued in the company of a large group of fellow climbers. By and by the conversation wandered toward plans for tomorrow's climbing. The party atmosphere had loosened my tongue and apparently a few mental screws as well.

"Oh, I don't know," I drawled, "we were kind of thinking about doing something easy; 5.8-ish."

Jim's eyebrows shot up. "I wouldn't waste my time," someone offered. "Anything under 5.9 is usually pretty wide or dirty; 5.9 and above, though, now that's usually some pretty fine climbing. Say, didn't you fellows mention you were just in Eldorado?"

If I had, I sure hadn't meant to. That was the last thing I wanted to bring up. I resolved to stick to the subject, even though I really didn't like where that seemed to be leading either. "5.9 and above huh? Well, ah…we've got to get used to the rock and stuff first." It sounded like the biggest dodge in the world, which, of course, it was.

"Nothing to get used to," the fellow persisted. "You can jam, can't you?"

"Oh, well…um…of course we can jam, but—"

"Well then, go for it!" He grinned. "You'll never find cleaner jamming than a Tower 5.10."

Jim's eyebrows had now disappeared above his hairline someplace. I needed a way out of this badly.

"What would you suggest for our first climb?" I asked, and cautiously added, "keeping in mind that we're still pretty wiped out from the long drive and would just as soon have sort of a rest day anyway."

"Do *Soler*. It's beautiful. Only two pitches and real easy. It's a great warm-up route."

Easy…warm-up…I liked the sound of that.

"Good protection?"

"The best. You can really lace it up."

My kind of climb.

"Well," I said. "*Soler*, huh? I think that sounds pretty good. Yup, that's what we'll do. *Soler*."

Now that we were publicly committed, I asked, just as an afterthought, "So what's *Soler* rated anyway?"

"5.9 minus."

I had no idea where Jim's eyebrows were now, because his hand was over his face.

I'M NOT QUITE SURE exactly how we got up *Soler*, whether it was luck, biorhythms, karma, or whatever. All I do know is that somehow, astonished but overjoyed, we found ourselves on top. By the time we reached the campground again, we had gotten a little cocky. I perused the guidebook.

"Okay, we've got four days left here…let's try this tomorrow (another 5.9 minus). If we get up that, we'll do this the next day (a solid 5.9), and if we can do that, we'll take a rest day and then do this: *Tulgey Wood*, 5.9 plus." Jim agreed. After all, it seemed quite a safe proposal because neither of us believed for a moment that we would ever get past day two of this scenario. And 5.9 plus? That was pure fantasy. We didn't think anymore about it as we concentrated on celebrating our newest conquest, and initiation into the world fringing on 5.9.

Thus, it was a bit disturbing when, two days later, we were still going strong. Our attempts on *Gooseberry Jam* and *Walt Bailey Memorial* ended with the same unlikely success as on *Soler*. Something was not right here and I attempted to reason it out. These climbs had been hard, but not at the absolute limit of our abilities like they should have been. Surely one of us should have fallen, at least once. I began to sense the hand of something or someone far greater than Jim or I in all of this. Somehow we were being led into a fateful rendezvous with the fourth day of our game plan. Then again, perhaps we had just been lucking out. Whatever it was, I slept uneasily that night because now that I had to take it seriously, I had begun to fear *Tulgey Wood*.

7

We spent the first part of our rest day engaged in one of our favorite Devils Tower pastimes, "tourist baiting." We first discovered this game while hiking down the trail that circles the Tower, after climbing *Soler*. Fully clad in ropes and hardware, we were obviously quite a novelty to the countless tourists who also wander this path. Enthusiastically they questioned us about our climb, our gear, and the inevitable, "What's it like on top?" We laboriously answered their questions and then graciously offered to pose for photographs with their daughters.

It quickly became apparent, however, that no matter how carefully and meticulously we described our activities, these people had absolutely no grasp of how rock climbing worked. We had run into this problem before, but Devils Tower vacationers seemed a breed apart. They had mastered the formidable skills necessary for piloting vehicles that were size, mass, and fuel consumption equivalents of the space shuttle, yet they were incapable of understanding even the most fundamental principles of roped climbing.

We soon tired of repeating our tedious and apparently fruitless explanations and began to make things up. The game quickly evolved. Whichever of us could tell the most outrageous lie about climbing the Tower and still be believed was considered the winner, and thus earned the prestigious and envied title of "Master-baiter." I currently held this honor for convincing an elderly couple from Ohio that the summit was littered with ruins and had, in fact, been the site of a Druid temple and observatory to which access had once been gained via an intricate network of cedar scaffolds and ladders.

This particular morning the game was not much fun, however. It was hard to have a light heart while standing in the shadow of *Tulgey Wood*.

Around noon we flopped down in the talus to watch a party from Montana who were engaged on the route. This was their second try. Their attempts on the previous day had climaxed with a nasty twenty-foot peel out of the crux on the first pitch. Now they had just reached the stance on top of the column that forms the short second pitch. We watched for over half an hour, and they didn't move. It was clear that they were both exhausted. We decided to leave for a while and run some errands. After driving the thirty miles to town and back, we returned to the talus. The two climbers were still on the ledge.

Later than evening, we ambled over to the Montana campsite with the intention of pumping them for some information. I was a little apprehensive and not at all sure that it was in the best of taste to bring up *Tulgey Wood* in light of the way that these guys had spent the past couple of days. It seemed a little like asking Mrs. Lincoln what she thought of the play. As it turned out, we should have stayed at home. For over an hour the "Big Sky" boys cussed and cursed and expounded on the terrors of *Tulgey*

Wood. They had reached a point only about twenty feet above the spot where we had observed them before being once again, and this time conclusively, defeated. Psyched out, fed up, and all in, they backed down.

"I have absolutely nothing good to say about that route," one of them warned. "It's scary and sustained and a hell of a lot harder than any 5.9 that I've ever done."

His partner, though not much of a talker, seemed to agree. "It sucks," he muttered.

Jim and I had just about made up our minds to chicken out when a group of the local hardmen showed up. Before we could slip away, our more talkative host introduced us as "the Minnesota guys who are gonna have a crack at *Tulgey Wood* tomorrow…they gotta either be pretty good or pretty bold trying that bastard after watching us die on it."

"Balls," his partner grunted, "real balls."

One of the locals gave us a crocodile smile. "*Tulgey Wood,* huh?" he grinned. "That's a real nice climb. Unique, that's for sure! Good luck, guys."

Something about the smirk on his face reminded me of the way Sitting Bull might have smiled at Custer the night before the massacre. Somehow, we had just gotten roped into doing another route that was way over our heads and that neither of us really wanted to do.

Back in our tent, we discussed our options. As I saw it, we had three choices: quit climbing forever, change our names, or try the route. Jim liked climbing, and his name, but didn't want to do the route. Thus, he came up with another solution.

"You can lead the first two pitches," he said. "That's where the toughest stuff is, and it's your turn to lead the crux pitch anyway."

"Shouldn't we flip a coin or something?" I protested weakly.

"Now look," he continued, "it was your offwidth mouth that got us into this mess in the first place. Besides, if we get an early start, we can probably back off in time to pack up and get a good head start on the drive home."

There is usually a clear boundary separating optimism from pessimism, but this skillful blending of the two left me somewhat confused in regard to his true disposition. My own bordered on despair.

AND SO, shortly after sunrise on a beautiful August morning, when I could have been climbing any one of a dozen easier routes and really enjoying myself, I found myself tied to the front end of the rope, trussed up in enough clinking hardware to anchor a battleship, staring up at a climb that I knew would probably maim me for life. I turned to Jim. He was anchored securely to a little bush and was grinning, probably in anticipation of the bloodbath that was sure to follow. At that moment, he would have bet an orphan's crutch that he was never going to have to leave the ground.

"You know," I snapped at him, "if I crater, it's going to be on your conscience."

"No," he smiled, eyeing his position relative to the crack above, "I believe it'll be on my shoes."

I hoped that the shrub he was tied to was poison ivy.

The crack started out real nice. Fingers in, twist, toes on nubbins. The protection also seemed pretty reasonable.

Voices drifted across the talus from the Visitors Center. "Look, Martha! There's a man going up right there...no, lower...down near the bottom... climbing up that red rope." I winced.

The crack got smaller and entered a dihedral. Boy, would this be a great spot for my #7 Taperlock (my favorite piece because of its pretty yellow cord), but it's still a long way to the top. I better save it till I really need it. I made do with a wired Stopper cammed sideways. Slowly I inched upward. Before long the crack became almost too thin to work my fingers into. Another little pocket appeared, perfect for the #7. The yellow cord tempted me, swinging back and forth on my rack like a hypnotist's watch, begging to be wedged into the bombproof groove. No, my friend, I better save you for when it gets really desperate up above. I rigged another imaginative wired placement and continued on.

The crack had all but sealed up by the time I reached an awkward rest stance right below the crux. I looked up and saw ten feet of bulging dihedral with no crack. I slipped a #2 wired Stopper into the seam and recalled that my last two pieces had also been pretty marginal. I despaired at my frugality with my precious #7 and vowed that if I lived through this, I would mercilessly hammer that damned Taperlock into tinfoil. I thought once more of Jim, grinning and safe and laced to that plant. I yanked hard on the #2, sealing it deep inside the seam. With any luck, he'd have one hell of a time trying to get it out.

I hooked my fingertips up and onto some very obscure holds on the right wall, planted my feet on the left, and began to layback. With the intense effort the surrounding world faded out of my perception and was replaced with a universe consisting of the two feet of rock surrounding my face and the magnified tom-toms of my racing heartbeat. My skull became a vacuous container rocking with the echoes of fragmented voices and imaginary noises:

Cigarette or a blindfold?
(a siren began to wail)
Our Father, who art in heaven...
(warning buzzers)
Impact force equals mass times the acceleration of gravity.
(Pop! And the second stopper below spun lazily earthward)
Next, please.

Coming to grips with the first pitch of Tulgey Wood

(bells tolling)
...Thy kingdom come, Thy will be done...
(weeping)
Ashes to ashes...
(bugle Taps)
So young...
(snapping perlon)
...so much to live for.
(twisting aluminum)

Suddenly my hand was on a jug. My feet were on a small ledge. I was confused. I looked down, and the hellish dihedral bulged out below. I looked up, and a ladder of cracks and knobs led ten feet to a belay stance. Slowly it dawned on me. *I did it. My God, I did it!*

And yet something was wrong. I felt dizzy and began to see spots. Only as my head began to spin did I fully realize what the problem was. I wasn't breathing! Judging by the ringing in my ears, I had probably been holding my breath through the entire crux.

I reinflated my lungs with gluttonous gasps. Fully conscious again, I hastily reconciled with my #7 and popped it into a slot, my first good piece in miles. A quick scramble and I was at the belay, where I let out a whoop so unique in tone and intensity that the tourists below fled eagerly to the telescopes in the hopes of spotting either a spectacular injury or a dangling corpse. After making myself secure, I sat back against the wall and relished the level ledge. I closed my eyes and smiled.

An impatient tug on the rope reminded me that Jim had yet to undergo the ordeal. As I took in the slack, I yelled words of advice and encouragement. Secretly, of course, I hoped he would find it a bitch. I leaned out of my perch to watch him make his preparations to follow. I chuckled with uncontrollable delight when at last he removed the sling between himself and the bush, thus severing his last tenuous connection with the horizontal. I slumped back onto the ledge when at last he began to climb, as I much preferred imagining him pawing and thrashing to watching him dance up in a style that would rob me of my hard-earned feelings of superhuman ability. By the time he reached the crux, however, the rope was coming in unusually slow, and I began to hear vague curses amidst remarkably labored breathing. By God, old Jim really was having trouble!

It never crossed my mind that he was a good foot shorter than myself, and that the crux holds had been just within my reach. I had also temporarily forgotten about the wired stopper that I had bitterly jammed deep within the hairline crack. And it didn't occur to me that Jim's crack-ravaged hands were stiffly bound with more tape than Tutankhamun's. Consequently, I interpreted each grunt and gasp as a genuine compliment of my fine lead.

When he finally heaved himself onto the stance, I quickly stripped him of the gear he had cleaned and announced that I was ready to tackle the second pitch.

Actually, it wasn't much of a pitch at all. Approximately twenty feet long, it appeared to consist of four identical moves of 5.9-ish liebacking. By standing on tiptoe I could place a nut almost halfway up the pitch, and so it was also well protected.

All that was in my mind, however, was that this would be my last hard lead and that it was rated easier and was infinitely shorter than the pitch I had just finished. The crux was below us and to me, deluded by my success, this pitch looked trivial. To Jim it meant everything. It represented his last chance and hope that I might fail and he might be spared the opportunity of leading the only remaining crux of the climb: the endless third pitch.

I was determined, however, that any failure on this route would not be mine. After all, I reasoned, hadn't I just led the crux pitch without a fall? Furthermore, hadn't I done the hardest climbing without oxygen? (The difference between gasping above 8000 meters on a Himalayan peak and holding your breath out of terror on a prairie rock climb did not seem significant as my ego blossomed.) And wasn't I now embarking on my second consecutive 5.9 or harder lead in order that my second might rest himself for one paltry pitch of less or equal rating? The fact that his pitch would be longer than all of mine combined also escaped me in my slightly "touched" state of mind. I believe psychologists call this "delusions of grandeur." It is an accurate term, for at this point I had become mentally equivalent to the greatest alpinist on earth.

I seized the crack with iron fingers, and with a lusty roar I informed a pale Jim that "this shouldn't take long, it's only 5.9!" I leapt catlike onto the unsuspecting dihedral, where after two feet of upward progress, attained by some impressively overdone moves exhibiting classical liebacking techniques, I slid with a thump back down onto the ledge.

The fog in my brain began to clear. I was not the world's greatest climber, either mentally or obviously physically. I was, in fact, a mediocre toproping specialist from an area known geographically as the Great Plains. I further realized that I was damn lucky that I had gotten up what I had so far, but I optimistically reasoned that what I had done once I ought to be able to repeat.

I decided that the key to a pitch this short was momentum. I knew I would have to discard the textbook techniques for my own more comfortable and effective personal style.

My method of climbing is based on a little known principle of physics called the Sub-linear Vector Axiom. It is basically an inversion of all the known laws pertaining to the conservation of energy. Reduced to its simplest form it states, "A climber in motion tends to seek rest." How Newton missed this one is a real mystery. In practice it involves an initial output of massive quantities of energy. As the supply is rapidly depleted, a sort of coasting effect takes over that will hopefully carry you to some kind of ledge. If not, you're screwed. Less educated climbers, upon observing this technique, often remark that it looks suspiciously similar to uncontrolled thrashing and lunging. This is the price I pay for introducing high-powered science into the relatively Neanderthal world of athletics.

I launched myself off the belay ledge, alternately swimming and clawing my way upward. My initial surge gained me an almost instant ten feet. Inertia propelled me another five. Sure enough, a rest stance appeared just as gravity decided that this had gone on long enough. My #7 dived deeply into the bowels of the crack. You could have hung a truck on that placement, and I didn't even flinch at using up the piece. I'd be damned if I'd make the same mistake two pitches in a row.

Looking up, I was confronted with a bulging rounded slab. It appeared to be the last obstacle before the belay, and Jim was going to get his pitch because the anticipation of success had triggered a mental relapse and I had become Reinhold Messner again. I humped my way upward and was soon confronting bolts, old runners, and a ledge you could roller-skate on. I was exuberant and built a delirious belay. "Let's hear it for good anchors! Three cheers for a safe and comfortable stance: Clip-clip-hooray!" Finally, lashed to enough points to moor the USS Nimitz, I sat down and reeled in my little fish. When at last he arrived, Jim was pretty bummed out and not just a little scared.

"Well, James, the ball is in your court now." Nothing like rubbing a little salt in an open wound, I always say.

He eyed my belay setup. Unceremoniously, he began to dismantle it, mumbling something about needing the gear. The pieces were all finger size, and his pitch was all fist and offwidth, but I was still anchored to bolts and so I allowed him this small retribution. I draped him with the rack, and the baton was passed.

When God built Devils Tower, He smiled graciously upon rock climbers. When He chiseled out the third pitch of *Tulgey Wood*, He was either in a hurry, a particularly unpleasant mood, or making a very bad joke. A single wide crack runs its entire length. Though the first pitch is the technical crux of the route, the third pitch is vastly more difficult physically. The first pitch has many reasonable rest positions, and the real difficult section is brief. The third pitch is moderately hard but incredibly sustained, almost impossible to rest on, and hard to protect. It certainly represents as great a barrier to successfully completing the route as the first pitch.

Of course, at this point we knew little or none of this. Certainly Jim was closer to guessing the truth than I was, because after eyeing it for a few minutes and tentatively feeling out the first ten feet, he suddenly sagged back onto the one and only nut that he had placed and said, "No."

Still basking in the glory of my performance, this caught me quite off guard. "What?"

"No," he repeated.

"What do you mean *no*?" I demanded.

"No," he shouted. "N-O. It's a short adverb used to communicate denial, refusal, or dissent, and in this particular case it means all three. Basically, what it boils down to is that I don't think I want to do this."

Well, if this didn't beat all. And after I had gotten us so far! Through the crux (or so I thought), without a fall (an event as unlikely as the repayment of the French war debt), and without ever once considering the possibility of retreat (this, I believe, marks the point where I finally lost all touch with reality). What's wrong with him anyway, the sissy! What kind of an attitude is that, saying "no" and just giving up? Who does he think he is, uttering negatives while dangling so close above the belay that if I only had a bat I could reach up and smash his spine except that he doesn't seem to have one.

I leaped to my feet, shook my fist, and roared. "Now listen here! I upheld my half of the bargain! I climbed my ass off to get us to this point, and now that we're almost there and past the hardest part and have one crummy 5.9 pitch left to go, nobody in this party is going to hang up here and shout *no*!"

"Do you want to lead it?" Jim asked.

"No!" I shouted.

We were in a fix.

I knew Jim was capable of climbing this thing, but a climber in the grips of a psych-out is as hard to budge as mercury in a Duluth winter. I quickly realized that the key to resolving this crisis did not lie in physical threats. Jim, although considerably shorter, could undoubtedly mash me to a pulp at will. Nor was the answer to be found through verbal abuse (for the same reason). Psychology seemed a safer and more logical alternative.

I resolved to subtly prod him with guilt by reminding him of the sense of duty that partners have to each other, and of the trust and faith that we place in each other when we bond ourselves with perlon. The relationship is unique to climbers and trapeze artists, but we don't use nets. Yes, friends are special, and climbing partners are special among friends. Jim would see this and realize that he owed me his best shot.

"Jim?"

"Yeah?"

"I've always been proud to call you my climbing partner. And I want you to know that, well, if you're not feeling well we can rap off right now and, heck, it won't change a thing…old buddy."

"Stuff it, Dave, it's not going to work."

So much for Plan A. Plan B involved playing on his ego. I figured I could caress it to the point where his head would swell as big as a balloon and he would float right up the crack.

"Jim?"

"Yeah?"

"I don't know if I've ever told you this, but I've always admired the style and fortitude you exhibit when you climb. It's damn impressive. You are one tiger. Grrr."

"Thanks. Dave. You want to lower me back down to the stance now?"

I was rapidly running out of cards to play. One avenue remained with which to compel him, but the result if it failed was even more unthinkable than simply backing off the route. I hesitated for long moments, but at last, a true gambler at heart, I elected to pursue it.

"Say, Jim?"

"Yeah?"

"If you're still willing, I think maybe I would like to take a crack at this thing. Why don't we switch places?"

He was climbing!

ONCE HE got under way, Jim never even looked back. He looked like one of those machines they use to hammer in railroad spikes: chugging along at full steam and then, bam!—in goes a piece of metal and then chug on again to the next one. He never even really broke stride. Every foot of rope that fed out raised my spirits one full notch. We were actually going to do it! I leaned back, relaxed, and smiled.

I was still smiling when I noticed that Jim was nearly out of rope. The guidebook said 160 feet for this pitch, so Jim must be there. I looked up. Either the guidebook or the people who made my rope lied, because he was still below the overhang at the top of the pitch, and that meant at least ten feet left to go.

The rope was now taut between us, and from high above came a faint stream of seemingly meaningless babble: "More...wrote...you...trick!" I deduced from this that Jim was near his wits' end and firmly gripped in the iron hand of panic. But then I considered that that didn't seem like Jim at all—which led me to a simpler truth: The wind and distance were making all of his p's sound like t's.

Thus it was that in less than ten seconds time, I left the world of supine bliss and total relaxation and was returned to the vertical struggle unwilling, unprepared, and relatively unbelayed. Daydreaming one minute, nightmare the next. I thrashed up ten feet, but the alarming loop of rope that dangled below cautioned me to slow down and let Jim catch up. In order to at least create the illusion of a good belay, I was going to have to match his pace.

Why wasn't he moving? I glanced up. Miles above, Jim was coming to grips with the final overhang. Slowly the loop of rope below me inched up. I tried to preoccupy myself with prying loose the big Hex he had hung on. At last the rope drew tight again and I moved on.

The crack was getting wider, and in order to jam, my arm was crammed in up to the shoulder. Soon the good jams receded even deeper, and just as I gave them up and slipped out and into a much more strenuous and infinitely less secure layback, I received a long-distance call from Jim: "Off belay!"

Now, rationally I should have realized that he was the one who was "off belay," but rational isn't exactly the word I would choose to best describe my state of mind at that particular moment. After all, if you were right in the middle of some pretty desperate moves, and the guy at the other end of the rope suddenly yelled "off belay," whose neck would you assume was on the chopping block?

Pulling up and in again, I managed to stuff both feet into the crack. Side by side they just spanned its width, but I knew that it was one of those situations where taking too much weight off my arms might cause my feet to pop through, and this dark crack would drop me like a gallows. The difference would be that here, there might not be a sudden tightening of the rope before I slapped the pavement. I was just aiming my jump for the belay ledge when Jim called back: "Belay on." I realized then that the only danger in my falling was the possibility of jerking Jim off his stance before he got any anchors in. As it turned out, this would have been unlikely because his belay ledge was so huge that you could have played golf on it.

The really awkward offwidth only lasted thirty feet or so, and then the crack closed back up a little. This was fine for the moment, but there was still at least 120 feet of fist jams capped by an overhang left to go. Very few details of the rest of the pitch stick in my memory, for indeed, each ten feet seemed a carbon copy of the ten feet before. Also, I can't be a hundred percent sure that I was conscious the whole time.

A general impression does remain, however. Physically it was a lot like running a marathon with a pillow tied around my face. Mentally, it was incredibly dulling—like staring at checkered wallpaper. I remember almost falling a lot, but I do that on every climb. I was particularly impressed by the quantity and quality of Jim's protection. There was very little and it was very poor—just a few big Hexentrics seeming to defy gravity in the parallel-sided crack and some large T-tons cammed into place only under the weight of their own slings.

When at last I found myself plastered under the final overhang, my needle was on empty. I was grateful to be free of the fist-crack treadmill but was unsure if I could cope with this last obstacle. My brain was a sponge in an ocean of adrenaline, and it was clear that this chemical was the only fuel that remained with which to propel me in the direction I needed to go. With every muscle fiber and neuron firing sparks of protest, I reached up, jammed, pulled, and kicked. And then again, and again, until I flopped like some great beached tuna onto Jim and the eighteenth green.

We spent a great deal of time recuperating on that ledge before we felt able to move on. The remaining two pitches seemed quite trivial in light of what we had just done. They consisted mainly of stemming blocky and weathered chimneys that were choked and spattered with guano and quite typical of the upper part of many of the routes at Devils Tower. The only move that was at all memorable was actually pulling onto the belay ledge at the end of the fourth pitch. The technique required seemed awfully similar to that used when getting into a top bunk without a ladder.

At any rate, we flashed these pitches running on a rich mixture of euphoria and adrenaline. At long last, and in defiance of all the known laws of probability, we stood on top of *Tulgey Wood.* Jim and I raced and danced through the summit prairie, and life was never so good.

I marveled at the transition we had made this day, finally smashing through the formidable barrier beyond 5.8. We had done a multi-pitch route, consistently climbing 5.9 or harder, and without a fall. We would not be eating quiche this night.

With great pride we carefully and legibly printed our names and the route title in the summit register. Then we zipped down the four rappels to the base of the Tower at speeds that left our friction gear sizzling and popping as we spat to cool them down.

As we trudged the footpath back around the Tower toward our car, I felt a great need to express the deep and moving feelings I was experiencing from our adventure. I wanted to communicate to Jim my personal joy in our achievement and thank him for his role in it as partner and friend. I had to make sure that he was sharing my delight at our triumph.

And so, as we walked the narrow trail, myself in front and Jim at my heels, I made a speech. The exact text is not important, but let us simply say that for me it seemed quite eloquent. I told him that this had been one of the greatest days of my life, certainly of my climbing career. I said things that climbers rarely share after the route is done, like how petrified I had been on my leads and how impressed I had been by his. I confessed the emotions I had felt on the route, feelings that all climbers have but that even the closest partners usually keep hidden. Things like envy and jealousy of the other's skills, or delight when the other slips where you didn't, and disappointment when they don't where you had trouble. I admitted that the statements I had made in my ruse to get him moving on the third pitch had, in fact, been true—except for the one that had finally worked.

When I finished, I waited for some word in answer, but there was only silence. Surely after such a baring of my soul the least he could do was

The summit of Devils Tower

reciprocate just a little. Hadn't he heard a word I had said? I turned and discovered that he hadn't.

Jim was about two hundred feet back, near the telescopes. He was engaged in vigorous conversation with a man in baggy khaki pants who was harnessed to the world's largest Nikon. I ambled back a little until I could make out his familiar voice.

"That's right, hollow. The thing's as hollow as a rotten log! And filled with rainwater...there's a lake on top. That's why we don't hammer in spikes here like you see 'em do on TV. The Park Service is afraid we'll bang 'em in too deep and drain the damn thing!"

I smiled and turned and clanked back down toward the parking lot in search of my own tourist to play with.

Originally published in CLIMBING, *No. 85, 1984.*

Author's notes: Not long after our climb, the first two pitches of Tulgey Wood *were upgraded to 5.10a—and that would have been the end of it for me; my fledgling mindset would never have contemplated attempting a climb that was double-digit hard. Even so, the sustained 5.9 fist crack that Jim led (third pitch) is still generally regarded as the greatest hurdle to topping out. Today, most parties that start up* Tulgey Wood *plan to rappel after the second pitch rather than subject themselves to the rigors of this awkward and insecure squirrel cage. In short,* Tulgey Wood *"in total" is a climb that appeals to unique types. For further proof, read "Seeing Is Believing," page 283.*

Other climbing adventures at Devils Tower are recounted in "Hanging by a Thread," page 71, and "Devils Advocate," page 271.

Bugaboo Spire; the Cooper-Gran *route ascends the sheer wall right of center*

EAST FACE OF BUGABOO SPIRE
Tapping Hidden Reserves on an Alpine Bivy

MINE WAS THE TORMENT of the Ancient Mariner: surrounded by water, dying of thirst. True, most of this water was in the form of solid ice, hemmed up in the thick glacial skirt that surrounds the Bugaboos—the famous granite spires that rise like moon-washed citadels amidst the sedimentary ruins of the Canadian Rockies. But even that was beyond our reach. From the bivy ledge high on the East Face of Bugaboo Spire, Rick and I could only fantasize about the thirst-slaking potential of the asteroid-sized popsicle spread out below. Not carrying any water was the crowning boner in a long list of mistakes we'd made on Bugaboo Spire. I say "we," but in my defense, I was still in big wall diapers: The 1300-foot *Cooper-Gran* route on the East Face of Bugaboo Spire (V 5.9 Al or 5.11) was to be my first multi-day rock route as well as my first alpine bivouac. And so I approached it as a learning experience, deferring the packing decisions (such as our provisions and gear) to my older, more seasoned partner.

Unfortunately, one of the essentials I had not yet learned was that Rick is a minimalist maniac. For example, he insisted that we lighten our load by carrying only one set of crampons between us. Of course, the minute we reached the tilted hockey rink leading up to the wall, he appropriated these for himself, leaving me to hand-over-hand up the rope Batman-style to where he stood planted on the ice. As a result, we'd belayed more horizontal pitches on the approach to Bugaboo Spire than we would climb on the face itself.

Once we hit vertical terrain, however, the deficiencies of our kit were forgotten as I reveled in the clean cracks and knobby friction of Bugaboo granite (thankfully, Rick hadn't ditched our harnesses or rack). Bugaboo Spire's east face has exfoliated into a series of stupendous flakes and corners and the *Cooper-Gran* links a superb, right-angling line directly up the center of the wall. In fact, the climbing—mostly a 5.8 to 5.9 jamfest—was so good and our packs were so light that I'd all but forgiven my miserly

High on the East Face of Bugaboo Spire

quartermaster. That is, until we reached the bivy ledge, where I discovered that our water bottles hadn't made the cut.

It was just beyond this ledge that Seattle climber Ed Cooper had been forced to throw in the towel during a remarkable solo bid to make the first ascent of the face in 1960. Cooper had been well stocked to deal with the short, blank section above (his bag of tricks included a bolt kit and a seventy-foot aid sling), but when the bit of his drill jammed and his hammer fell apart, it must have seemed like Fate itself was ordering him down. Although Cooper eventually returned to complete the route with Art Gran, he'd doubtlessly shed some tears here. I, on the other hand, couldn't have wept a drop if a puppy's life depended on it. Panting all day in the alpine air had left me drier than a popcorn-and-rice cake sandwich.

To make matters worse, melt-water from a snowfield high on the face was percolating with a tantalizing gurgle through the recesses of a nearby crack. I tried in vain to reach the maddening trickle, first wadding my shirtsleeves into the crack in a futile attempt to wick it out, and finally, pathetically, probing anteater-like into the gritty fissure with my tongue.

Then, just as hope itself evaporated, Rick plucked a baby-angle piton from the rack and fitted it into the crack. Like a modern-day Moses, he delivered a mighty blow, and a jet of water issued from the rock, piped from the depths by the hollow, U-shaped plumbing of the pin.

On the East Face of Bugaboo Spire, I learned that you cannot squeeze blood from a stone, but it is possible to survive on the marrow of the mountain.

Originally published in ROCK AND ICE, *No. 125, 2003.*

Author's notes: After languishing for decades in a box of old notebooks and other college-era artifacts, the journal I kept during my trip to the Bugaboos recently came to light. It begins: "Doubts about my ability plague my mind…and thoughts of Death." Sounds like it could have been written yesterday.

In fact, Bugaboo Spire was the first in a long line of mountain obsessions I've courted over the years. And as my first, it encompassed a far amount of fumbling, bewilderment, and loss of innocence. This included pulping my thumb with a pin hammer, having to climb back up a jammed rappel line, and, of course, my introduction to partner Rick Kollath's tendency for alpine-Amish frugality. For more on this last topic, see "Mind Over Matterhorn," page 37.

The soaring South Face of El Capitan; the Nose route traces the line between sunlight and shadow

EXODUS
Plagued on the Nose *of El Capitan*

"A BUS." The tone of Jim's voice exhibited none of the apprehension that the situation would have justified. The statement was, in fact, so bland and utterly devoid of any emotion that I felt a great reluctance to wrench my eyes from the spectacular view out the driver's window and return my attention to the road. In the back seat, similarly transfixed, Chuck chose to ignore him altogether.

I knew Jim, however. I had climbed with him enough to know that the calm, matter-of-fact timbre of his speech rarely varied. If Jim said "duck" he could be trying to communicate anything from a passing mallard to a nuclear attack. Knowing this, I regretfully refocused my concentration upon the road ahead.

There was indeed a bus. The massive motorcoach had come to a stop mostly in my lane, since the shoulder of the narrow one-way barely accommodated even one set of its gargantuan tires. Furthermore, the doors were open and it was disgorging hordes of bespectacled, camera-clicking Asian tourists out onto the highway, eager to document the wonders of Yosemite.

A combination of mashing the brake and mangling the steering wheel enabled me to narrowly avoid ruining their vacation. Utilizing the bus like a huge offensive lineman, I skidded through a flanking maneuver around the rubbernecking mob and came to a stop in the touring barge's protected shadow. Chuck looked back and winced at the vulcanized streaks that equaled about three years wear off his car's tires. Amidst the unusual aroma of fragrant pine mingled with hot brakes, we disembarked.

The object of our fascination and thus the cause of our near disaster loomed above us in a magnificent facade: El Capitan. The pictures in a thousand books were at last put into some sort of perspective, and yet not much. It was simply too unbelievably immense. Standing and staring in awe, craning our heads back farther and farther as we followed its sweeping line, each of us finally toppled over backwards into the grassy meadow.

JIM AND I wanted to climb El Cap's *Nose* route, the 3000-foot crown jewel of Yosemite wall climbing that meanders directly up the majestic central prow of the monolith. Chuck was not a climber, but he owned our transportation and so he delivered an ultimatum: one week. He would be content to hike and swim and laze in these splendid surroundings for seven days. Then he was headed east. Since the only reason that we were in Yosemite in the first place was because we had been able to convince Chuck to make this "little detour" while on the way from Salt Lake City to Minneapolis, we knew we were in a very weak position to protest his decision. So we had one week, which for us meant one crack at a big wall. We didn't have nearly enough gear to attempt a gigantic grade VI route like the *Nose*, but now that we were here and had seen El Cap, anything less seemed negligible. Nevertheless, we were about to surrender to our frustrating lack of tackle and do some modest climb for which we were still woefully under-equipped, when Dave showed up.

We grew up climbing with Dave back in Minnesota and we were overjoyed to see him because on top of being an old friend and a familiar face, Dave had gear. Lots of gear. More gear than the climbing shop. He had been in Yosemite for four months and in that time his car had become a rolling locker for seemingly every climbing bum in the Valley. Crammed into every nook and cranny of the sagging Ford Pinto there were duffels of racked gear alongside crates brimming with carabiners, pulleys and pitons. Mortared into the cracks between were great mounds of ropes and slings. He had a flotilla of water bottles, countless etriers and Jumars, and more Friends than a sweepstakes winner in a crowded bar.

We gazed upon these treasures with wide eyes. Incredibly, Dave seemed to regard his situation as something of an inconvenience. "I haven't been able to get into my car for two months now," he complained. "I don't even know who it all belongs to or when they're coming back to get it. Everybody's gone up to Tuolumne to try and escape the heat." He seemed oblivious to the two fellow Minnesotans hovering over his vehicle like a couple of vultures circling a bleeding pig. "I can't even get at my own stuff that's buried way down deep," Dave sighed. "I sure do wish I could get rid of some of this junk for a while."

Jim and I, with our noses crushed flat against the glass of his wind-shield, broke into grins that cut our heads from ear to ear.

NOT ONLY was Dave able to completely outfit us for the *Nose*, but he decided to come along as well. He had hopes of soloing an El Cap route later in the summer and viewed a chance to do another big wall before then as further opportunity to hone his fitness and technique. We were more than glad to have him because besides being a strong and experienced climber, Dave had already done the *Nose* twice before and would be able to

"We gazed upon these treasures with wide eyes."

steer us with practiced efficiency through the complexities of its various back-and-forth traverses. The only problem that remained was the midsummer heat, but we elected to ignore this in a burst of positive thinking. Across the vast expanse of El Capitan there was not a single climber to be seen anywhere; routes that in cooler months would normally be teeming with parties were now utterly deserted. Luxuriating in the moist shaded grass, dabbling our feet in the icy waters of the Merced, it was easy to reason that a little warm weather was a small price to pay for having this iconic mountain all to ourselves.

The following day we fixed ropes up the first four pitches to Sickle Ledge. I was the last to arrive atop this crescentic perch, and was surprised to find the others sitting quietly, munching cookies and drinking coca-cola. My astonishment stemmed from the fact that we had only brought one tiny daypack and it had not contained any treats or canned beverages.

"Where'd that come from?" I asked.

"Found it," Jim croaked, spraying sugary crumbs into the void. "Manna from heaven."

"Abandoned," Dave said. "Probably left behind by someone backing off." Lucky us, I thought, reaching for a warm Coke. I popped the tab and triggered an explosion of carbonated foam into my lap that drained down my legs and pooled in the watertight recesses of my rubber climbing shoes.

After rappelling to the valley floor we took stock of the weather. The sun had been bad but not unbearable. We were, however, back on the ground and into the shadowy forest well before the real heat of the day. Our haul bag, weighted with food and water for three persons, already felt like a wrecking ball, but with a thought toward staving off dehydration and a newly acquired taste for sugary drinks, we cautiously added a can of soda per person per day to our provisions. No sense taking any chances. No sense at all.

The next morning Chuck hiked with us to the base of the route to retrieve our fixed lines as we cast them off and set sail upon a vertical ocean of exfoliated granite waves. Being a non-climber, he freaked out watching us zip up the ropes using our Jumar ascenders, and after gathering up our gear he wandered away into the woods hooting something about James Bond and Batman. Looking down, I noted with a frown that we had neglected to school Chuck in the practicality of neatly coiling our ropes and carrying them out. Instead, he was dragging them in loose, loopy bundles through the dirt and pine needles, but before we could reprimand him, he and his tangled train had processed off into the trees.

From the beginning, the elephantine haul bag almost killed us. I kept waiting for the pulley to explode under the extreme forces prying at its innards. Dave—now in full training mode—did the lion's share of the grueling work raising it to Sickle. A magnificent effort, but I feared we might have to give him a sky burial then and there. Dave has more lives than conjoined cats, however, and when his locomotive breathing finally slowed to a less frenzied chug, he insisted that the ordeal had actually given him a degree of confidence for his soloing aspirations. For Jim there was no silver lining. His compact frame (he's quite sensitive to "short") made him a pitiable counterweight for hauling. Even with his most vigorous exertions the bag would only sluggishly yield inches. For all his efforts, it was never really clear what was hauling who. Thus, for the rest of the day, hauling became a group effort. Pitch by pitch, we got the job done, but even working together we could have really used about three more guys.

The air temperature had spiked from unpleasant to alarming by the time we finished the pendulum swing into the Stoveleg Cracks. In the foundry-like heat, the name seemed a bit of an understatement. I kept waiting for the fissures to start oozing molten granite and I began to wonder at what temperature shoe rubber melts. The only relief we had enjoyed so far from the punishing glare was the belay within the shadowy niche of the Dolt Hole, spent pressing our lips to the relatively cool rock and slaking our thirst with whatever meager saliva could be raised from sucking the tart lemon candy we kept tucked in our socks.

Dangling on the exposed face that is split by the Stovelegs, there was no reprieve. Here, even the convection-driven breezes that scour Yosemite's granite trough offered little more than a fan to the fire. Somewhere along this stretch the heat drove me mad, for in my memory the rest of that afternoon is a steaming blur. I do recall stretching violently as I pulled over the top of Dolt Tower, and then bewilderedly looking around to see its blocky summit already occupied by an English butler proffering a moist towel and a French maid seated upon a cooler of frosty beer. Had this not been a mirage, I fear I might have tossed the poor couple from the ledge in a frenzy to get at their ice.

Sunset found us perched on the luxuriously flat crown of El Cap Tower. With the shade, mental, and to some extent, physical equilibrium had been restored. We optimistically reasoned that the worst was certainly behind us. The bag would be lighter and the wall steeper beyond this point, and so the hauling should be infinitely easier even if the heat continued unabated. "At least," I assured my companions, "we can relax for a while now." Jim passed me a Coke, and I detonated another sticky-sweet grenade into my shoes.

DAVE'S SCREAM ripped through our heads like mortar-fire and in seconds we were all wide awake. The night was well along but the full moon was still high and illuminated our surroundings like a cold, white sun. I looked toward Dave's end of the ledge half expecting to find it empty—his cry had been precisely the kind one might shriek while being plucked from the wall by a giant bird of prey. He was still there however, and was shaking his head from side to side like a wet dog.

Jim, unfazed as ever, was taking it all in. "What seems to be the problem?" he yawned.

"Rats!" Dave hissed. Surely, I thought, this was an unrelated expletive rather than a reply indicating that there were large rodents afoot. I was wrong.

"A big rat just crawled through my hair!" he moaned.

"Pretty gross," Jim had to admit. "Hey," he frowned, "I hope they didn't get into the food."

Dave was more concerned with what they might have been "getting into" on top of his head, but a quick check revealed that we would indeed be on half-rations for the remainder of the climb: An entire loaf of bread and half its plastic bag were missing. It was difficult, not to mention disconcerting, to imagine platoons of thieving rats scurrying up and down the cracks and flakes of El Capitan, carrying out commando raids on groups of bivouacking climbers, but evidently this is just what happens. We had seen photographs, taken during the first ascent of the *Nose* in 1958, of Warren Harding's rodent-chewed sleeping bag, and now we knew that at least a few of the descendants of those furry vandals were still carrying on the family tradition.

One final casualty was not discovered until the next morning. The evening before, Jim had removed his decidedly ripe stockings and placed a loose rock over them to smother the odor and keep them from blowing away. The foot of one sock was left protruding from beneath the rock and the rats—apparently ravenous beyond all reason—had devoured it. All that remained was the elastic cuff. To keep the sun from burning his pale ankle, Jim wore it anyway, like a tiny cotton gaiter.

We climbed as quickly as possible in an attempt to get a good chunk of wall under our belts before the furnace kicked in. A short game of "rock, paper, scissors" decided that Jim owned the largely unprotected lead up the widening chimney behind Texas Flake, and Dave got the gravity-defying mukluk of the Boot Flake. I led the exhilarating double-pendulum called the King Swing, rocketing back and forth in great metronome arcs like a fly riding a hypnotist's watch.

Getting three people and the bag past the enormous lateral jog of the traverse was complicated, even though Dave had worked it out in his head the night before. Despite his impressive logistics, by the time the four of us had crossed and reunited, the heat had returned at full blast. We fought it for several more pitches, but after crawling up the dung-spattered slabs below the popular bivy ledge called Camp Four, we finally succumbed. Shortly after noon and only a few hundred vertical feet above our previous day's highpoint, none of us felt capable of climbing another inch. Instead we lay sprawled upon the cramped shelf that comprises Camp Four, panting and choking on our swollen tongues, praying for an eclipse. We were trapped on an oven rack, like three green bananas at the mercy of broiling heat that quickly roasted us from ripe to rotten. At some point we discovered a small slot just large enough to accommodate a human head, and every half-hour we rotated so that each might have a chance to at least momentarily escape, ostrich-like, from the sun's fury. Even the crazy swifts, who normally seem to derive such pleasure from dive-bombing climbers or whistling past in a fair and frightening imitation of stonefall, were nowhere to be seen. Nothing seemed to be moving, especially the sun, and certainly not us.

At long last, evening came and we made preparations to sleep. Camp Four was a miserable, lumpy bunk barely large enough for one person, impossible for three. Jim and Dave seemed to have found a sort of compromising arrangement which allowed them a degree of comfort, and since I had a reputation for slumbering deeply in almost any circumstance I built a nest some ten feet above them and settled down with one cheek occupying a rounded shelf and the remainder dangling in slings.

My dreams alternated between being cooked alive and clips from the vermin-as-predator horror movie *Willard*, and so it was not terribly irritating when commotion on the ledge below awakened me. Fully expecting some

Jim Kennedy sweltering at the belay atop Texas Flake

new rat epic, I groggily rolled over to peer down at my friends. Weirdly, they were standing and brushing one another like a couple of grooming chimpanzees. The real eye-rubber however, was the way their bodies glistened and shimmered in the moonlight, as if they were soaking wet.

"What's going on?" I called down. The reply curdled my blood into cottage cheese.

"Bugs!" Jim sobbed. With mounting horror I began to understand. My companions were both covered with thousands of tiny crawling insects. The silvery moonbeams reflecting off countless wings and carapaces were causing Jim and Dave to sparkle and glitter like crystal statues. It was an alien scene that belonged in a Poe short story or Stephen King novel, but certainly not fifteen hundred feet up the vertical face of El Capitan.

"What are they?" I shuddered "Where did they come from?" Bone-white in the moonlight, the fabric of my friends' insect pajamas looked to be woven from threads of squirming maggots.

"Springtails or silverfish…" Dave moaned. His voice was filled with the disgust of someone who has just stepped in something loathsome. "From out of the cracks. They don't bite, they just crawl…everywhere!" The full implications of this were driven home by the sounds of him clearing his throat and Jim snorting air out his nostrils.

My partners passed the night shaking out their clothing and brushing one another in futile attempts to rid themselves of this scourge. Thankfully, the attack seemed confined to their ledge, but I also spent a sleepless night trembling in the fear and anticipation that the swarm might migrate upward in search of new meat.

Shortly before dawn the insects retreated back into their lair within the cracks. It chilled me to think of the previous afternoon and taking turns thrusting our dozing heads into the same shadowy cleft, unaware of the crawling secret it harbored. We held a council. After this latest ordeal, Jim and Dave were adamant: They would not spend another night sleeping on this cliff. We must climb out, all thirteen pitches, even if it meant finishing in total darkness. I agreed that liberating ourselves from this strange wall, with its infernal days and bizarre nights, was of the essence. It seemed as though the plagues of biblical Egypt had descended upon us: heat, rats, famine and insects; prudence dictated that we effect an exodus lest we wake up tomorrow to find that the remainder of our water had turned to blood.

Fueled by our resolve to escape and our fears of what other unknown terrors might lurk within the cracks of El Capitan, we sprang to action. In my mind, it seemed not only possible but entirely likely that where rats and glittering hordes of insects dwelt, hairy spiders and deadly snakes could not be far behind.

Soon after negotiating the vaulted overhang of the Great Roof, we found ourselves immersed in the healing shade of the *Nose*'s upper dihedral.

Although the air temperature was still in triple-digits we felt remarkably refreshed to be protected from the sapping effects of direct sunlight. Since we were determined to top-out, there was no need to conserve water, and so we kept our bottles accessible near the top of the sack and steadily nursed them at every belay. With each gulp gravity further loosened its grip on our silent companion and this, combined with the now overhanging wall, made hauling trivial, almost delightful compared to the labor it had once been.

Jumaring in free space was another matter, and again it was Jim who bore the brunt of the discomfort and indignity. His borrowed ascenders were rigged for a Goliath. Thus, for him, every upward inch was a pull-up, and whenever he stopped to rest, the daypack that he wore slowly upended him like a capsizing schooner.

The day matured and the sun finally caught us, but soon enough it mercifully disappeared again behind the other wall of the dihedral. The water and shade allowed us to make remarkable progress, and it seemed possible that we might indeed escape that very evening. Belaying in the stench of Camp Six, with one eye nervously glued to the reeking, anaconda-sized crack along the back of the triangular ledge, I was truly grateful that at least we wouldn't be spending the night here.

So it was a great relief when just as the sun dropped below the valley rim, Jim led off up the final bolt ladder toward the summit. From below, watching him make each of the agonizing reaches between the remarkably spaced protection, the logic in sending our most compact individual to deal with this obstacle seemed—like the fixed hardware—strained. The ancient bolts were rusted and fatigued with age, and we shuddered to contemplate our unthinkable predicament should one suddenly pull loose, cutting us off within meters of El Capitan's summit below a crackless and overhanging lip. Jim soon disappeared from sight, however, and our fears were quickly replaced by an impatient anxiety. As the gloom thickened, it was all too easy to imagine the skittering whisper of spiders' feet. Finally, the haul bag began to creep up, signaling that the ropes were secure and ready for us to follow. With one final shivering glance into the darkening abyss, Dave and I clipped into our ascenders and scurried up to join our friend.

OBLIVIOUS TO the irony with our previous sufferings, we built a blistering fire and sat baking in its cheery glow. The scrubby crown of El Cap, littered with enough dry wood to fuel a moon shot, lends itself well to post-climb pyromania. Lying about the fire, we reflected on our experience. Dave had hit the jackpot in terms of beefing up his fortitude and grit, and was already looking forward to another, more technically demanding El Cap adventure—albeit in cooler weather and without all the critters. Indeed, his big wall confidence and ambition would be largely responsible for his participation later that summer in an extremely complex rescue on *Tangerine Trip*. It took them two days to get him down.

For the present, we were all in agreement regarding our stupidity at pooh-poohing Yosemite's midsummer heat. We admitted that even if we had never discussed retreat, while we'd been frying in the pan it had crossed all of our minds. And although our unnerving encounters with El Capitan's nocturnal creepy-crawlies had in fact catalyzed us on to success, they had also seriously unspooled us and compounded our fatigue—maybe even to the point of sealing our defeat had not most of the upper dihedral been shaded from the crippling sunshine. The fact that we had succeeded made it hard to fully appreciate just how close we'd come to blowing the *Nose* by being unprepared to deal with these factors.

Yet I had no fascination with extremism or love of discomfort, and so I silently vowed that it would be some time before I would again allow myself to underestimate potential risks or be caught off guard by something that experience and common sense dictated I should have seen coming.

Rummaging in the firelight through our deflated haul bag, Jim came up with our last can of soda. He offered it to me, but I smiled and waved him off, reaching for a water bottle instead. For the moment anyway, I was done shooting myself in the foot.

Originally published in CLIMBING, *No. 90, 1985.*

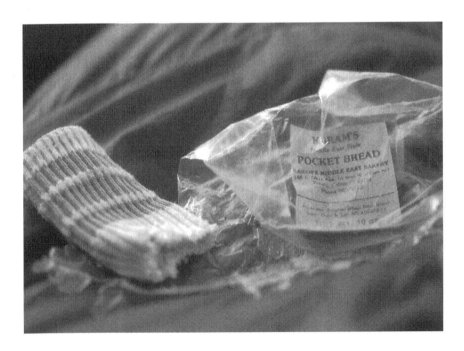

Author's notes: A few days after this story first appeared in print, I was having breakfast in a diner near Devil's Lake, Wisconsin, a major climbing center in the Midwest, when I overheard climbers at the next table discussing the latest issue of Climbing *magazine. I nearly snorted out my ice cream (breakfast of champions) when one of them remarked, "Did you read that weird story about the guys fighting rats on El Cap?" I held my breath, anticipating comments along the lines of: "I guess they'll print anything…" and "What a load of crap!" But before anyone could say another word, my climbing partner leaped out of the booth and shouted, "That was* this *guy!" The din of conversation and clinking silverware abruptly ceased as everyone in the restaurant fixated on me with expressions ranging from suspicious frowns to doubtful incredulity. Finally one of the other climbers piped up, "Dude, that story was* hilarious!" *Whereupon they dragged me over to their table, assailing me with kudos and questions, and they even paid for my meal (I knew I should have ordered the deluxe banana-split!). It was my first brush with positive feedback from readers outside my circle of friends as well as my first taste of something bordering on celebrity—a heady moment indeed. That is, until later in the day, when everyone at the crag jostled to watch the Famous Writer climb, expecting an acrobatic flying squirrel, but encountering something more akin to a clutching hedgehog. That was the day I learned that nibbling quietly in the tall grass is vastly more preferable to falling from a pedestal.*

Since its original publication, this story has been lightly massaged in terms of some word choices and phrasing.

Finally, the details of Dave Mital's epic rescue during his solo attempt on El Capitan's Tangerine Trip *are recounted in "Strange Trip on 'the Trip,'" page 189.*

Below the Matterhorn's Hornli Ridge

MIND OVER MATTERHORN
Leaving My Mark on Hallowed Ground

T O MOUNTAINEERS, the ground surrounding the village of Zermatt is holy. For generations, this soil has borne silent witness to great events in alpine climbing's history. It has felt the hob-nailed and crampon-shod boots of heroes, received their pitons, their axe strokes, and, on occasion, their mortal remains. Whymper, Mummery, Bonatti, and others have battled the gods here, and through triumph and tragedy have left their marks upon the flanks of the Matterhorn.

And now, in my ignominious but distinctive fashion, I was leaving mine. In the shadow of the most awesome and recognized alpine profile in the world, I lay face down, retching uncontrollably into the immaculate Swiss sod.

From heartland America, I had arrived in the Alps in an unusual state: physically fit. Several months of manual labor had swelled my pockets and slimmed my waistline. I was therefore eager to begin my alpine season before bodily inertia could reassert itself. Now, finding myself in a culture where draft beer is sold by the liter, I was a sitting duck.

There was a problem, however. My climbing partner had not arrived. Rick is a frugal lad, and was determined to make his way to Europe as cheaply as possible. He was probably crated up in the belly of a mail plane or hitching a ride with some third-world smuggler. God only knew when or if he might show.

In the meantime, I found myself surrounded by more horns than a stumbled drum major. The compelling topography of the Matterhorn, Weisshorn, Ober Gabelhorn, and Zinalrothorn were assembled about me, and I could hardly wait to strike up the band. I decided that an outing to the Rothorn hut, a high mountain refuge centrally located among these peaks, would be the perfect reconnaissance. This hike promised a significant altitude gain as well as spectacular views of the Matterhorn.

Eager to be above treeline, I raced out of Zermatt like a scalded cat. In seemingly no time I encountered a trail sign announcing "Rothorn Hütte: 3."

Being a worldly sort of fellow I quickly calculated miles from kilometers and marveled at my physical prowess as evidenced by the remarkable proximity of my goal. In my light running shoes and gym shorts I pulled out all the stops, confidently sprinting past the scores of clompy-booted, well-bundled Europeans snailing up the steep switchbacks.

Unfortunately, distances in the Alps are flagged in neither miles nor kilometers, but in a more universal increment—hours. I came to this realization after an eternity of uphill running produced nothing more than altitude sickness, hypothermia, dehydration, and another sign proclaiming "Rothorn Hütte: 2." The stalwart European hikers gave me wide berth, and a few smug looks of amusement, as I puked and stumbled my way back toward Zermatt. On hands and knees I crawled into the campground and collapsed upon the grass near my tent. Sometime that evening Rick arrived, but all he could get out of me were moans and the contents of an occasional gastric spasm. I didn't even notice he was there until the next day.

As SOON as I could sit upright, we got down to planning our Matterhorn assault. Which route should we tackle? Clearly, my lack of proper respect for these mythic peaks had offended some higher power. I did not need another butt-kicking to get the point. The *Schmid Route* on the north face was out. As one of the Three Great North Faces of the Alps, it was simply too overwhelming for Rick or myself to contemplate. This attitude was re-inforced by the discovery that the local churchyard was filled with bones that had once possessed far greater mountain skills and experience than us.

That left one of the four ridges. The ridges of the Matterhorn radiate down from its toothy crown with pyramidal symmetry, each quite unique in character and challenge. Viewed from Zermatt, the Swiss ridge, called the Hornli Ridge—or *Hörnligrat* in the local parlance—bisects the mountain's most classic perspective. It is the path of least resistance and the scene of Edward Whymper's initial triumph and subsequent disaster. It is also the cattle trail up which the Swiss guides routinely herd hundreds of well-paying Whymper wannabes. To facilitate this, the Hornli sports a hotel at its base, fixed ropes, and a comfortable hut known as the Solvay at two-thirds height. We were green, but we were pretty sure we weren't that green.

The Italian ridge, known as the Lion Arete, is more challenging, but situated on the opposite side of the mountain. The Lion was in the right league, but the wrong country; we needed something that could be approached from our basecamp in Zermatt. That left either the steep and technical Furggen Ridge, a climb that many guidebooks rate even more serious than the North Face, or Albert Mummery's masterful mixed route, the *Zmuttgrat*.

Clearly the Zmutt was the one for us. Situated on the Matterhorn's right skyline, an elegant snow ridge, rocky towers, and a final soaring buttress

Grave reminder: the tomb of Michel-Auguste Croz, killed while descending the Matterhorn after the first ascent

combine to make this climb one of the most classic on the mountain. But our lack of experience in these particular alps still made us uneasy. A solution, in the form of a lone Dutch climber, soon presented itself:

"I am Peter. Perhaps the two of you need me to climb with you on the Matterhorn?"

Well, perhaps we did. Having climbed for several alpine seasons in the Zermatt district, and with a couple of impressive-sounding routes under his belt, Peter did seem to have what we lacked. But how was it that after spending so much time in this area he had never managed to tick the centerpiece summit?

"Good heavens!" Peter exclaimed, with what would prove to be his trademark expletive. "The Matterhorn must not be taken lightly! Many climbers are still killed each season because they underestimate the difficulties. I have waited, slowly gathering experience, until now I am ready for such a climb."

Well, that clinched it. Such deference could not help but pacify the mountain's spirits. Peter was on the team.

THE APPROACH to the Matterhorn, once an arduous slog, has been utterly domesticated by the Swiss in their dogged pursuit of the tourist dollar. Pay your francs and a cable car now whisks you from the edge of town right up to the lower slopes of the mountain. Rick, of course, would have none of it. Not only was the idea of mechanical transport offensive, he also steadfastly refused to put so much as a nickel into the Swiss coffers when there existed a free alternative.

From our seats in the tram, Peter and I marveled at Rick's tiny figure laboring up the trail far below. I couldn't help but admire both his frugality and his sense of fair play. My guess, however, is that Whymper would have paid for the ride.

Once Rick finally joined us at the Schwarzsee station, we took our place in line on the trail to the Hornli hut, a Ramada-sized building situated at the base of the Hornli Ridge. But while most of the other traffic consisted of guided parties heading for a night in the hut before an ascent of the Hornli, our plan was to bivouac nearby and, in early morning darkness, traverse over the Matterhorn glacier to the Zmutt Ridge.

A peculiar thing about the Matterhorn is that the closer you get to it, the less appealing it appears. From a couple of miles away it is a stunning monolith, the epitome of mountain form and symmetry. As one approaches the peak, however, its sharp lines begin to erode into indistinct towers and furrowed walls. But it isn't until you're on it that the mountain reveals its true nature: teetering mounds of shattered slate, heaps of rotting shale, and decomposing gullies spitting out new bits of scree with assembly-line regularity. The celebrated Matterhorn is, in fact, a great pile of rubble.

We soon learned that Peter was an engineering student in Amsterdam, when he insisted upon engineering a monumental bivouac platform in the loose debris above the Hornli hut. Rick and I watched in amazement as he went about chopping at the dirt and prying up boulders in an attempt to create a perfectly flat surface. We tried to pitch in but each time we so much as moved a rock or smoothed some gravel Peter scowled, "No, no, good heavens, no..." and pushed us aside. He was clearly a do-it-yourselfer.

When at last our bunker had been prepared we snuggled into our bags and watched as the waning sunlight lit the swirling clouds with vivid shades of orange, pink, and finally purple. Though spectacular, I could not help but consider whether these mists might portend a change in the weather. It did not take long to find out.

The snow began in earnest at about midnight. By morning, both mountain and mountaineers were blanketed beneath six inches of heavy white slush. "Good heavens, what is this!" Peter sputtered. The guy slept in a coma and had wakened to discover that his bivy sack had been wide open to the elements throughout the night. Moreover, Peter's masterful sleeping platform had proven to lack one crucial feature—drainage. Water had pooled everywhere, permeating every zipper and seam until sleeping gear and clothing clung to our bodies like wet newspaper. The gods had not smiled on us; in fact, they seemed to have pissed all over us.

Climbing was out of the question. In these miserable conditions, it took most of the day just to pack up and make our way back down the valley.

IT STORMED for the better part of a week. We lingered in the smoky beer halls of Zermatt, commiserating with other climbers and formulating a new plan of attack. Rick was like a tiger straining at the leash and favored an immediate and all-out assault as soon as the weather cleared. He dreaded the thought of devoting another entire day to the approach. His idea was to hike up in the early morning and then climb through the afternoon, bivouacking as high as possible, perhaps even near the summit.

"Good heavens," Peter said doubtfully. "This is a bold strategy. It means you are entirely committed to the mountain."

"Exactly!" Rick grinned.

I could see things both ways. On the one hand, it is my nature to always know where the exits are, but I had also been in Zermatt for nearly two weeks now and had yet to do any actual climbing. Perhaps a certain amount of boldness was just what was needed to climb this mountain. This was, after all, a peak known far and wide as the very symbol of human triumph. If Whymper and the others had remained in the valleys, confined by prudence, the Matterhorn might still be unconquered. Throwing caution to the wind; seizing the bull by the horns; damning the torpedoes—these are the ideologies of victory and the mechanisms by which a mountaineer may measure his true potential. And if ever a mountain represented a worthy yardstick for making such a measurement, this Matterhorn was surely it.

I banged down my mug with so much conviction that even people outside on the street flinched. "I'm in!"

IT'S EASY to philosophize about grabbing a bull's horns and the like while tanking up in some cozy mountain tavern, but it's quite another thing when you're actually looking the beast in the face. Dodging a cannonade of afternoon stonefall while crossing under the *Schmid Route* a few days later, I was having serious doubts about this whole idea. Rick, however, was in his element, cruising across the glacier like a missile targeted on the Zmutt Ridge—and even Peter seemed to have stowed any reservations once we'd actually started climbing. I resolved to get myself more into the spirit of things, providing I didn't catch a brick off the North Face.

Soon enough, we were out of the shooting gallery and at the foot of the great ice wall beneath the ridge. Our guidebook suggested traversing the base of this wall and accessing the Zmutt at the far end, where it drops to within a few rope-lengths of the glacier.

"Seems like a pretty indirect route," Rick frowned. "Why not climb straight up here, and save on all the doubling back?" Nobody seemed to have a good reason not to give it a go, and so up we went.

An hour later I was brimming with good reasons not to give it a go. First of all, the ice face was much larger than it had appeared from below. After a thousand feet of strenuous front-pointing and step-kicking we were still nowhere near the ridge. Furthermore, and even more significantly, the afternoon sun had quickly transformed the face into slush. Our crampons balled and slipped from every step, and though we buried each axe pick to the hilt, we could get no real purchase. Every inch was gained only through the most desperate exertions. Falling was always a real possibility, and protection never was. When at long last we crested the ridge, all three of us were ready to call it a day.

By climbing the ice wall direct, we had bypassed the snow ridge section of the Zmutt, and so we now found ourselves only a short distance from the rocky towers known as the Teeth. Nestled snugly against the base of the nearest outcrop was an old bivouac site that someone had thoughtfully shoveled from a snowbank. We each gravitated to our most habitual behavior. Peter went to work improving, enlarging, and leveling the site. Rick sorted gear and studied the guidebook. I lay slumped against the secure rock face, vomiting from the day's potent combination of altitude, exertion, and frayed nerves.

Thanks in large part to Peter's efforts, it really was a splendid bivouac. Perched under a cozy rock overhang, we could anchor ourselves to solid pitons and stretch out in comfort on the flat, snow-packed floor. The only drawback was that the perimeter beyond our feet featured a sheer drop thousands of feet to the glaciers of Italy. For all Peter's work, the thing we could have used most was a railing, since by the time we broke camp the next morning we had sent the Italians a helmet, a mitten, and our cooking pot.

No sooner had we gotten under way again, when we found ourselves in the company of two other parties. Having employed more conventional tactics than ourselves, including a comfortable night in the hut and tackling the initial snow slopes in early morning when everything was still nicely frozen together, they had ascended in only a few hours the same ground we had battled for the better part of a day. I couldn't help thinking there was a lesson here somewhere.

The first group consisted of two Austrian guides and their client, the second were a pair of Swiss. Though amiable, these fellows dogged us as we rock climbed through the devious Teeth, yet refused all opportunities to pass. For the moment, even the guides seemed content to let us lead the way. The logic behind this was soon made clear.

Conditions on the Zmutt were considerably less than ideal. The steep buttress beyond the Teeth was supposed to be a straightforward rock climb, but any rock was now entombed in verglas, snow, or both. More and more frequently we were called upon to throw down a line to the parties below until finally we were all more or less connected as a single rope. As morning turned to afternoon and we inched our way up the icy rocks, both the climbing and the protection became increasingly precarious. Things finally

Cresting the snow ridge on the Zmutt

came to a climax as Rick led a long snowy slab midway up the buttress. Fifty feet out he skeptically tapped a single pin upside down into a crumbly pocket. Forty feet beyond that he fell.

With a high-pitched wail, Rick tobogganed down the crest of the ridge and dropped out of sight over the sheer precipice of the Italian frontier. Instinctively, everyone grabbed onto the rope or the rock and all eyes riveted to the lone piton which had seemed so contrived and upon which so much now depended. Waiting for Rick to hit the end of the rope was like the split-second before a car crash—Peter, myself, the three Austrians and two Swiss stared helplessly into the oncoming headlights. Miraculously, the other car swerved at the last second. The pin held.

"Good heavens!" Peter gasped.

Once Rick had been reeled safely onto our stance, the Austrians announced that they had had enough.

"*Gott im Himmel!* Ve moost go down!"

Apparently the Swiss concurred, as they were already rigging a rappel. Shaken by Rick's fall and assailed by such urgent warnings from genuine European mountain guides, we began another epic descent back to Zermatt.

I WAS BEGINNING to hate this mountain. It had already consumed more than two weeks of my European holiday, yet I could not bear the thought of leaving without standing upon its legendary pinnacle. Rick and I were about to acquiesce to a climb of the Hornli and be done with it, when a new opportunity arrived.

"I understand you're a party of three," the stranger said. "I don't suppose you'd fancy a fourth and a crack at the *Furggengrat*." His name was John, and he introduced himself as an American expatriate, now a resident of Scotland. I'd never met an expatriate before, in fact the term had always sounded a bit seditious to me. But John seemed likeable enough, and his invitation to climb the Furggen Ridge was intriguing. We informed him that we had dismissed it as too severe for our limited experience, a perception reinforced by our failure on the Zmutt.

"You underestimate yourselves," John responded, "and you exaggerate the Furggen. Look, the Zmutt's got a northern aspect that favors wintry conditions. And with all that fresh stuff lying about from the recent storm it's little wonder that it spit you off. But the Furggen's another story; lots of sun, quick to clear; sure, it may get steep up top, but it's good rock, free of snow or iced-up cracks. Aye lads, do the Furggen with me and you'll agree that you've already done your hardest bit of climbing on the Zmutt!"

Rick and I were swayed immediately. John's charisma and subtle ego-stroking easily overpowered our collective common sense. Peter was more hesitant. Like most European climbers we had met, he suffered from a crippling awe of any of the "harder" routes in the Alps. Moreover, his alpine paradigm was founded on the sensible theory of progressing gradually to more difficult climbs. For him, switching abruptly from the Zmutt Ridge to the Furggen was like suddenly asking a dog trainer to tame a lion.

"Good heavens," Peter fretted, "this is a serious proposition." He reminded us that Mummery himself, that brilliant architect of the Zmutt, had been foiled by the steep upper section of the Furggen. We had made up our minds, however, and so for him it came down to a simple choice: tempt Fate and step up his game, or see the three of us continue on without him. Whether his decision reflected any confidence or respect he had gained for us on our previous attempts, or a simple reluctance to be left behind was unclear, but the fact is that when at last we departed for the Furggen Ridge, it was as a party of four.

EVEN RICK'S miserly habits were no match for the rugged cliffs and glaciers that bar the approach to the east side of the Matterhorn. We all rode the tram to the Trockener Steg station, and then enjoyed a straightforward march over the relatively flat and dry Theodule Glacier to the base of the Furggen Ridge. John had certainly been right about one thing, the southern flanks of the mountain had much less snow on them than either the Hornli or Zmutt ridges. The rock, however, was by no stretch of the imagination "good." In fact, it was looser and more rotten than anything we had experienced. Holds and ledges simply disintegrated in our hands or crumbled away underfoot. Our saving grace was that the climbing was neither steep nor difficult. We moved together, mostly scrambling, occasionally stopping to spot one another on short, steeper sections. In this way we made steady progress up the indistinct margin of ridge bordering the east face. By late afternoon we had climbed several thousand feet—to a point level with the Solvay hut on the Hornli Ridge—when the wall above us steepened precipitously.

"Right, that's it then," John said. "We bivy here."

"Here?" I was incredulous. "Sleep here? A bug couldn't lie down here."

Indeed, the entire face was inclined at about 50 degrees and was composed of the foulest stone yet, more compressed dirt than rock. Rick had been idly pecking away at it with his hammer while we discussed our situation when suddenly he brightened and remarked, "I think this'll be all right." With that he began chopping away at the face and in no time at all had excavated a niche big enough to set his pack. The rest of us quickly unsheathed our axes and with blades and adzes blazing hacked away at the rock until we had fashioned ledges large enough for sleeping. As I settled into my trench for the night, I noted with some concern that Peter-the-engineer's ledge was neither spacious nor aesthetic. Apparently he was still a little rattled about being on the Furggen.

Approaching the Furggen Ridge

Considering that I wasn't really anchored to anything, I slept remarkably well—although I could have done without the wake-up call: As soon as the sun hit the summit pyramid the next morning, stones of all sizes and descriptions began hailing down. In record time we were packed up and moving onto steeper ground.

The crux of the route soon presented itself. A line of weathered pitons angled left across an awkward, bulging traverse. To move as quickly as possible on the upper mountain, we had previously decided to climb as two parties of two. Now, Rick and I took point. The rock had improved markedly by this time and Rick made the most of some good incut holds to move gingerly between the airy pegs. With seemingly no thought whatsoever to the eye-popping exposure beneath his boot soles, he levered over the bulge and manteled onto a fine belay shelf. I was soon on my way up to join him, but not before John sheepishly inquired whether I might carry his rope across as well. Well, so much for functioning as two independent groups, but as John seemed to be finding the technical difficulties of the climb somewhat stiffer than anticipated, and with Peter looking increasingly frazzled ever since we left the ground, I could hardly blame them for seeking this unification.

Beyond the traverse, a short vertical step brought us to a long ledge at the base of the massive summit pyramid. While John and Peter rested, Rick and I tried to sort out the proper exit. On the Zmutt, ignoring our route description had nearly proved disastrous, so we were determined to stay on course here. Yet nothing we could see made any sense relative to our description: "Make a thirty foot traverse, then up." After fruitless hours of head-scratching and false starts, we finally determined that the guidebook printer had omitted a digit—*one hundred* thirty feet of traversing revealed the correct line, and yet another unpleasant surprise. The key slab leading upward off the ledge was running black with meltwater. On this attempt it was my turn to make the most of it, which I did—taking perhaps three times longer than most.

By the time we reached the summit chimneys it was late in the day, and the demons that had plagued Peter since the first suggestion of this climb had completely overwhelmed him. He shrieked hysterically for tension at every move. I found myself belaying him from a single loose peg in a water-soaked chimney, and the drenching I was taking had made me both hypothermic and short-tempered. Rick and John had continued up the next pitch to escape the deluge, but Peter was out of sight somewhere below, hanging on the rope and not moving. Because of the dubious belay, I was supporting his full weight.

"God damn it, Peter," I screamed into the void. "You're killing me—you've got to climb!"

All I got back was a plaintive request: "Jumars?"

I admit that all afternoon I'd been concentrating so hard on the climbing that I hadn't really been paying much attention to Peter. I certainly hadn't grasped just how far out onto the limb he had crawled. As a result, not only was I not cutting him any slack, I was inclined to start cutting his rope.

"Jesus Christ," I thundered down, "the belay sucks! This pin won't hold shit! I'm freezing to death and you're pulling me off the mountain. Now move!"

"Jumars!"

Shaking with cold and straining against Peter's weight I somehow managed to unshoulder my pack, clip a pair of ascenders onto the rope, and send them sliding down into the gloom. As the anxious minutes passed my core temperature continued to drop, my legs began to buckle, and still nothing seemed to be happening. What could this guy's problem be? It was getting dark, for God's sake, where was he?

With the swish-click of an ascender stroke, Peter suddenly appeared.

I recoiled in horror. His eyes were unfocused and corpse-like, his nose and forehead were mashed and bruised, and blood drooled from his gums where he had broken out several teeth. Lacking the strength to put out a hand to protect himself from swinging against the wall, Peter had used his face instead.

"Good heavens!" I shuddered.

With some effort I managed to keep Peter from kissing the rock again, at least until we got him up the final pitches and onto the summit. I arrived last and found my companions crouched in a howling wind, already preparing for the descent.

"There's a big iron cross over there if you're interested," Rick smiled grimly. I squinted toward the Italian summit, but John's chattering teeth and Peter's disturbing lack of them seemed to dictate an immediate descent. We roped Peter to a short leash ahead of Rick, John acted as a human crutch to help guide and support his weight, and I went out front to scout the way down the Hornli.

Probing the dark, snowy ledges below the summit of the Matterhorn, I admit to some apprehension regarding the Whymper party's fatal plunge from these same rocks. But that was before I discovered the ropes.

At the very brink of the north face the beam of my headlamp suddenly fixed upon a grouted steel spike. Dangling below, like braided ladders, hung a series of colossal hawsers. I shook my head in wonder at the sheer size and girth of the things—fully three inches in diameter—and I reflected that in their zeal for safety and efficiency, the Swiss guides have made climbing the Hornli Ridge of the Matterhorn a lot like gym class.

On this particular night, however, I was grateful for these fixtures. As I gripped the fat strands worn smooth from countless hands, I could not help thinking about the generations of mountaineers who had passed this way.

Most, like us, had come and gone, climbing the mountain unheralded and without celebrity. And the closer I looked, the more evidence I saw of these passages: polished holds, crampon scars, the occasional bit of gear or scrap of clothing—mute testimony to the countless untold adventures, epics, and mysteries that have occurred on this peak. One of these seemed to me particularly poignant and baffling:

A short distance above the Solvay hut, I found a solitary crampon impaled on one of the protruding anchor spikes. I could not in my wildest imagination comprehend a reason why someone would leave such a thing behind at this place. While I pondered this enigma, the rest of the party caught up to me. Peter was half-dangling zombie-like on the end of Rick's tether. John was cursing.

"What's wrong?" I asked him.

"Look," he muttered, lifting a naked boot. "Straps must've loosened up. Stupid thing just disappeared a couple pitches up."

I stared at John's single remaining crampon, and then with amazement at its perfect match, hanging like a horseshoe on the stake beside me.

Sensing that we had come to a halt, Peter suddenly came to life. "Bivouac?" he mumbled hopefully through his broken mouth.

Why not, I thought? Clearly, at last, the gods were with us.

Originally published in CLIMBING, *No. 160, 1996.*

Author's note: The morning after our bivouac high on the Hornli, I was startled from slumber when somebody used my knee as a handhold. It was the vanguard in the daily conga line of climbers strung like colorful beads down the length of the ridge. For me, climbing the Matterhorn, with its foul stone and guided throngs, was a once-is-enough experience. That being said, I would never discourage anyone from seeking to achieve this historic and iconic summit. Indeed, the world-famous Matterhorn should top everyone's tick list if for no other reason than having climbed it greases potentially awkward conversation at parties with non-climbers. Conversations that invariably go something like this:

"So, you climb mountains, huh? Ever climbed Everest?"

"Nope."

"Well…how about the Matterhorn?"

Glenwood Icefall: *a sun-rotted house of cards*

MELTING MOMENTS
Feeling the Heat on the Glenwood Icefall

THE FIRST ICE CLIMB I ever did fell down on top of me. Well, that's not exactly true. It more or less brushed past me and landed on my best friend. He and I were lost boys—directionless square pegs adrift in the adolescent doldrums between conventional sports and hooliganism. We eventually filled our sails by imagining ourselves as mountaineers, even to the point of scraping together enough paper-route money to mail order a set of starter ice tools and crampons. The gear arrived on the crest of the spring thaw, but even a heat wave couldn't deter us from cutting our alpine teeth, and so we eagerly boarded a city bus for the Mississippi River valley, the closest topography to our homes in the Minneapolis suburbs. We spent the day sniffing and probing a labyrinth of sodden sandstone gullies until at last we ferreted out a sickly, thirty-foot icicle. Somehow, the rickety pillar held together long enough for me to make my maiden voyage, but my buddy wasn't so lucky. His enthusiastic chopping elicited a shudder, then a groan from the slushy behemoth; the torso-sized pedestal supporting its base buckled, and then the whole mass came crashing down like a condemned building with its foundation suddenly blown out from beneath it. After enduring a jaws-of-life extraction, several pins in his tibia, and a thorough lambasting from his parents, my friend's ice climbing career was over before it ever began. But I pressed on, despite a reprimand from my own next of kin, who made it clear that the lack of judgment evidenced by this affair was a poor reflection upon the family genetics. "Climbing ice!" my mother glared, "Aren't you smarter than that?"

I'd like to think I am—or rather, I'd like to think that ice climbing itself is not inherently the result of damaged or missing chromosomes, and that a lesson learned is wisdom earned, and that disastrous mistakes are not likely to be repeated. And yet, I can't help thinking that perhaps there is something wrong with me. Maybe I do have frayed genes, but not because I nearly squashed myself under tons of collapsing ice in my youth—that was

51

pure adolescent stupidity. The reason I worry that I might be defective is because later, as an adult, I did it again. For some reason, I thought climbing the *Glenwood Icefall* was a smart idea.

By the end of the second Reagan administration, the Cold War was over and "trickle-down" was the country's economic motto, but I wasn't paying attention to these portents. By this time, I really was a climber, with rock, ice, and even whole mountains under my belt. In fact, my friend Paul and I had just come off of a thoroughly alpine winter thrashing in Colorado's Sangre de Cristo range, and we drove through the night to investigate the high-country ice climbing along the I-70 corridor. With the memories of bitter cold and steep, backcountry approaches still throbbing in our brains and extremities, even climbs like the *Rigid Designator,* the Vail-area hyper-classic located in a shadowed amphitheater only a short hump above the highway, seemed too much like work. We kept driving, in the hopes that eventually the vertical ice would land right in our laps. Finally, in the vicinity of Glenwood Springs, where the canyon narrows so precipitously that the roads, river, and rail line are virtually stacked on top of each other, we found our prize: a towering, multi-stepped icefall that in warmer months must keep windshield wipers working overtime. Pulling over to scope the formation, we were practically parked on its apron.

"Christ almighty," I exhaled, my eyes tracing the pale veins stair-stepping off ledges and other features not yet visible in the predawn murk. "That bastard must be at least 400 feet tall." Paul sighed; as a devout and spiritually centered individual, he bristles at vulgarity—and sacrilege in particular. For him, traveling with me must be like chaperoning a dockworker at a wine tasting. But for once, he didn't wince. His gaze was fixed even higher, where the stars were quickly giving way to the emerging cobalt of a crystal-clear morning. "It's going to be a lovely day," he said. Then, eyeing up the climb's position relative to the gathering daylight, he added cheerfully, "We might even see some sun." Somewhere, deep in my gut, childhood memories stirred and fired a warning shot straight through my bowel, but I dismissed it as pre-climb jitters.

As Minnesotans, Paul and I hail from a hinterland midway between the North Pole and the equator. We have real summers and real winters, but the two never mix. Once the mercury dips below freezing we're in the meat locker until spring. Throughout the long winter months, the sun is little more than a low-wattage light bulb, emitting feeble, oblique rays that generate little or no heat. Even so, among Midwestern climbers, ice exposed to direct sunshine is prized for its plastic consistency—if we're lucky, it may accept a tool placement without exploding like shotgunned peanut brittle. On the other hand, Colorado is blessed with a more temperate latitude, well out of reach of polar air masses. Even the Rockies are subject to schizophrenic seasonal variations—in January, temperatures can suddenly soar into T-shirt territory. In Colorado, ice exposed to direct sunlight is living on borrowed time.

By the time Paul and I were racked and roped, another party had arrived and looked to be hot on our heels. We were relieved, then, when they selected a line on the same formation but well off to the side of us. "Howdy," we yelled across, in a friendly attempt at good ol' fashioned farm-country etiquette, "Say, do you fellas know what the heck this is we're climbing?" After a long pause, they shouted back. "*Glenwood Icefall,*" and then, "Where *y'all* from?" There seemed to me a note of affectation in their query, but I gave them the benefit of the doubt. "Minnesota," I hollered, "You?" There was an even longer pause, some muffled snickers, and then one of them choked out, "Co-lo-ra-do," with every vowel expanded in an unmistakable parody of our pseudo-Canadian accents. Any further communication from them consisted of fits of laughter interjected with the occasional, sardonic, "Yup, yup, yup!"

"Fuckers."

I bit my tongue, but only out of pure reflex; it was Paul, remarkably, who had given voice to what we both were thinking. Even with temperatures conspicuously on the rise, hell had frozen over.

In fact, the local boys seemed to be all talk. They paced us neck and neck for two moderate pitches, but just as we were coming to grips with the serious ground, they turned like rabbits and hightailed it for the valley. Fifteen feet above Paul's belay, I paused to set a screw and contemplate this sudden and unexpected evacuation. "I guess they're afraid of steep ice," I smirked, watching as the pair retreated back down into the gloom. Reveling in the warm sun that had finally broken over the canyon rim, Paul suggested, "Or their own shadows." It was about then that the dripping began.

The *Glenwood Icefall* is broad enough along its base to offer a number of climbing variations. Higher up, however, all paths narrow to two distinct finishes: Exiting via the left-hand variation is steep and sustained WI5, while the right-side pillar is a little easier at WI4. Between the two formations a protruding nose of rock juts sharply outward and from its nostril a great dagger of ice hangs over the lower pitches like God's own cruise missile, its launch code keyed to the thermal trigger of the naked sun.

While I was climbing, the persistent patter on my helmet barely registered, particularly in light of the alarming fact that with every passing minute, the ice underfoot and beneath my tools was becoming more liquid than solid. However, once I established a belay (if two tools thrust into vertical mush qualify as anchors) I had ample time to contemplate the rising tide of meltwater cascading from the menacing stalactite's tip. Here was the nightmare from my childhood, resurrected, reconstituted, and relocated directly over my head—only this time it was also all around me. The entire

"It was about then that the dripping began."

formation was streaming, sloughing, and creaking. Now fully exposed to blazing sunlight, *Glenwood Icefall* was rapidly being transformed into simply Glenwood Falls.

For Paul and me, it was a race against basic chemistry—the most fundamental phase change in nature: ice versus water (with a little sweat, adrenaline, and piss thrown in to boot). Retreat was now unthinkable since building solid anchors was impossible. The only way off was up, and it was going to have to be fast; the streaming dagger alone threatened to thump us at any moment. Paul barely paused at the belay, as there was no need to re-rack screws that could be stabbed in up to their hangers. Instead, he immediately threw himself at the right-hand variation, punching and swimming up the soft pillar. His axes raked for purchase, and beneath his crampons whole sections of ice broke away, exposing dark, streaming rock. As I stared wide-eyed into the air pockets beneath these open wounds, it was suddenly clear to me that the entire formation was detached from its foundation, suspended, rather than fixed, upon the cliff face. Our climb was a hollow and collapsing carapace.

And yet even as the world around us was falling apart, Paul kept it together. His life is rooted in faith, and so I guess it makes perfect sense that he was able to lead this pitch and deliver us from evil relying on little else. Then and there I resolved to watch my language around this guy— now that I'd seen him walk on water.

But the question remains: What's my deal? Having survived this sort of thing twice now, why haven't I learned? In my defense, it is not unheard of for spectacular bad luck to return for an encore. At least sixteen people who survived the Hiroshima atomic bombing were nuked a second time at Nagasaki. A woman who survived the sinking of the *Titanic* was also on board the White Star Liner *Britannic*, *Titanic*'s sister ship, when it exploded and sank a few years later. Of course, if it happens to me a third time, I'll at least have to consider the other possibility—the one that sometimes keeps my mother awake nights, wondering whether or not the hospital sent her home with somebody else's baby.

Originally published in CLIMBING, *No. 231, 2004.*

Author's note: So far, so good.

Chamonix: alpine Mecca

CHAMONIX DIARY

Mont Blanc's Evolving Alpine Game, Viewed from the Cheap Seats

*A*UGUST, 2000 - BOARD GAMES

I am laboring, positively toiling, up the north face of Mont Blanc du Tacul, a glacial rampart of icy meringue that looms over the French village of Chamonix like an impending pie in the face. This wasn't supposed to be a difficult climb. Granted, the line is fairly steep and threads among gaping crevasses and jutting seracs, but it was first ascended way back in 1855 by men dressed like English butlers who clawed their way up using little more than pointed sticks. Now, nearly a century and a half later, despite the latest microfiber clothing and state-of-the-art axes and crampons, I am moving with all the ease and grace of a pig on ice. My only excuse is that it is late. Really late.

My companions and I are victims of the twin frailties that, for me, seem to define the alpine start: lack of preparation and excessive breakfasting. As a result, we have barely begun the route by the time most parties are reaching the summit. Where others climbed with surefooted security over firm snow, we now find ourselves mired in sun-soaked mush that makes each footstep a balling, sliding ordeal. The slopes are heavily loaded from a week of bad weather and are inclined at an angle that is textbook for avalanche. Sure enough, as if on cue, the sound I have been dreading—the slithering, hissing white noise of moving snow—erupts above us. I cower, bear-hugging the slope, braced against the cloud of white death that I'm certain is freight training toward us. When I risk an anxious glance upward a spray of snow slaps me squarely across the face—but it is hardly the vanguard of disaster. Instead, a snowboarder carves a loping end run around our rope, and then jets downward, a rooster-tail of wet snow erupting in the wake of every lazy turn. Sixty seconds later he is skimming across the broad basin of the Vallée Blanche, breezily crisscrossing the track over which we slogged nearly an hour and a half before.

Slack-jawed, I consider that innovation has always been central to the business of moving in the mountains above Chamonix. The Mont Blanc massif is arguably the place where serious alpinism began, and it is certainly here that the techniques, tools, and attitudes of mountaineering have been redefined again and again over the centuries. But as my rope-mates and I return to the discouraging business of sweating bullets on what for some guy is merely a quick schuss in the hills, I reflect that even in the 20 years since I first starting coming to Chamonix, times have changed.

AUGUST, 1980 - BABY STEPS

Nose squashed to the window glass, I am straining to get my first view of the French Alps. When at last my train enters the deep valley carved by the river Arve, an icy torrent springing from the highest and most complex mountain mass in Western Europe, I cannot help being disappointed. Most of the needle-sharp granite peaks—the famous Chamonix *aiguilles*—are visible, but a puffy cloud layer is obscuring the greater bulk of Mont Blanc. Mont Blanc is a mountain that seems out of place in the Alps; formed of the finest granite and mantled with a thick layer of ice, it is more akin to Denali than the Matterhorn. At 15,771 feet its gleaming, basilica-like dome soars well over 12,000 feet above the cobblestones of Chamonix. Far from being just a high point, however, the Mont Blanc massif is a range unto itself. Thrusting for 20 miles along the French and Italian frontier, this bulwark of crystalline summits and jagged glaciers forms the most formidable European border since the Berlin Wall.

At present, however, with everything shrouded in cumulous, I have no way to truly gauge these proportions. It turns out I'm just not looking high enough. Tracing the puffy outline of clouds to their zenith, I am puzzled by a thin, ragged line etched horizontally across the face of one lofty thunderhead—until my skin prickles with recognition. I am thrilled, and a little unnerved, by the realization that what I'm seeing is a bergschrund splitting a snowfield so impossibly high that it has merged with the uppermost clouds in the atmosphere. I'm beginning to think that I could get into some serious trouble here.

An hour later I have decided that these mountains won't get a chance to do me in because just getting to a campsite is going to kill me. Over the last century, Chamonix has evolved from a pastoral mountain village to a major tourist center and, as such, the town offers a wide range of convenient and comfortable accommodations—for people with money. Climbers, on the other hand, have traditionally set up camp in one of several squalid nylon slums that are tolerated by the local folk because they are located out of sight, and out of town. Straining under the burden of two bulging packs, I find myself creeping along a country lane feeling an odd kinship with the fat slugs clinging to the surrounding rocks and fence posts. I'm about to belly flop into my own trail of slime when I finally arrive at Pierre d'Orthaz. The Orthaz climbers' campground is nicer than most; it features a famous

The Aiguille de Chamonix (right to left): Midi, Plan, Blaitiére and Grands Charmoz

bouldering rock, semi-level ground, and an old shed with a square hole in the floor that serves as a pit toilet. The reason Pierre d'Orthaz isn't overrun despite such amenities is that a modest fee is levied to stay here. The amount varies unpredictably and is collected infrequently, so a two-week stay can actually end up costing about the price of a pint of beer. For many climbers, however, this is too dear a trade. The really frugal set up camp in nearby Snell's Field. Over the years, Snell's has hosted some of the greatest names in mountaineering. Perhaps not so coincidentally, many of these people have died young—maybe it was something they caught here. Snell's is part refugee camp, part opium den, and, during heavy rains, part Love Canal as scraps of old noodles and bits of used toilet paper float out from the surrounding woods and raft among the sodden tents. Camping here is free, but so is malaria. After scoping Snell's Field from the road, I pitch my tent at Orthaz.

I have come to Chamonix, like so many others, to touch greatness. The mindset among the overwhelming majority of climbers here is to repeat the landmark routes of Walter Bonatti, Riccardo Cassin, Joe Brown, and the legendary French guides, Lionel Terray and Gaston Rebuffat. In fact, Rebuffat's 1973 photo-essay guidebook, *The Mont Blanc Massif: The 100 Finest Routes* (informally referred to by climbers as simply *Rebuffat*), has become the unofficial tick list for the area. The prevailing sentiment seems to be that if a route isn't in *Rebuffat*, it isn't worth doing. And in fact, these climbs (arranged by increasing difficulty from one to 100) are among the world's great mountain classics.

Throughout the 19th century and well into the 20th, when routes like the Grands Charmoz-Grepon traverse, Mont Blanc's *Brenva Spur,* and the *Walker Spur* of the Grandes Jorasses, were put up, Chamonix was the cutting edge. Indeed, the very concept of pursuing new routes up mountains that had already been ascended by less arduous paths can be traced to climbs on Mont Blanc and the nearby Aiguille Verte. Right up through Bonatti's 1955 solo first ascent of the stunning rock pillar on the Dru that bears his name, climbing in the Alps—to the point of giving a name to this type of climbing—defined alpinism. More recently, however, the avant-garde has shifted to higher and more remote ranges of the world, and the Mont Blanc massif has come to be regarded as a training ground, a place for alpine apprenticeship and résumé building, a whistle stop for climbers on a track to the last great problems of Patagonia or the Himalayas. I am here to plant seeds with the hope that someday, in the greater ranges, I might pick plums.

Within a few days I have rendezvoused with my partner from home. Like me, Rick is eager to enter the alpine arena with swords in both hands. Confidently confining our choices to the final pages of *Rebuffat,* we quickly settle on number 98: the *American Direct* on the west face of the Dru. The Petit Dru is without peer in the Alps, perhaps in the world. A striking 3000-foot tower of flawless symmetry, it is El Capitan rolled into a slender cone. And like some of El Cap's finest routes, the *American Direct* was first climbed by Royal Robbins and represented a groundbreaking shift in techniques and attitudes by introducing Yosemite-style, big-wall climbing to the Alps. Rick and I have both climbed in Yosemite, so we figure we've got a leg up on this thing right from the start.

We soon learn some hard facts related to the sheer numbers of climbers who annually pilgrimage to Chamonix: With the vast majority flocking to Rebuffat's *100 Finest,* overcrowding is inevitable. Secondly, for the same reason, whenever a rock falls or an avalanche occurs, someone is squarely in the line of fire. We arrive beneath the Dru to find 18 parties strung out over the initial 20 pitches of our route. Before we even have time to register discouragement, a nasty looking couloir off to one side burps out a half-ton of shattered stone and two unfortunate climbers. Yosemite this is not.

By the time we reach the scene of the accident another party has already extracted the pair from a deep bergschrund. Miraculously, they are still alive, but their rope, chopped into nearly a dozen pieces, has come through in better shape than its owners. One, whom we dub "The Moaner," has a multitude of serious injuries including a likely concussion and several nasty compound fractures. His partner, "The Sleeper," never regains consciousness during the 12 hours that we sit vigil over him. Throughout the long, cold night that follows we do our best to keep the two warm by wrapping them in our jackets and sleeping bags and brewing cup after cup of hot tea for the one who can drink. For The Sleeper, however, our ministrations are limited to periodically monitoring the almost imperceptible vibrations of his pulse. At first light, a rescue helicopter clatters up to our ice ledge and the two are quickly bundled inside it still cocooned in our warm clothing. Things happen so fast that before we can reclaim our gear the chopper takes flight. Physically and psychologically spent, and now sorely under-equipped, Rick and I watch it—along with any remaining hopes we might have of climbing the Dru—dwindle to a speck and then vanish.

The lesson we take away from this experience is one of embracing moderation. We can now see the wisdom in testing the waters, rather than diving in headfirst—after all, a wader may stub his toe, but he almost never breaks his neck. Patagonia will have to wait; the rest of our trip is given over to less prestigious but infinitely less traumatic outings in the bristling granite playground of the Chamonix *aiguilles.*

AUGUST, 1984 - FORWARD, SONS OF FRANCE!

I think I am starting to get the hang of the Chamonix scene: two- to three-day bursts of hard activity in the mountains punctuated by concentrated bouts of revelry in the campsite or at one of the rowdy watering holes in town. These include the *Alpenstock*—the scene of a legendary window-shattering brawl between French and English climbers—and the even more notorious *Brasserie Nationale,* where a one-eyed bartender named Maurice Simond dispenses endless mugs of local ale to a decidedly non-local clientele. Primarily a British climbers' hangout, it seems that anyone who speaks the Queen's English, has a knack for table soccer, or holds enough francs in his pocket to buy a round is welcome—but pity the French tourist who blunders unknowingly through these doors. Anglo-French enmity is legendary in Chamonix, particularly these days.

There is a revolution taking place in the mountains around Mont Blanc, one encompassing boldness, speed, and innovation—and the names being spoken in hushed tones, names like Cristophe Profit, Patrick Berhault, and Jean-Marc Boivin, are distinctly Gallic. The proponents of this new wave are blitzing up the classic testpieces like cats on fire. Routes like the *Dru Couloir,* the *American Direct,* and the *Great Peuterey Ridge*—climbs that normally encompass several days—are being done in a few hours, often solo. Even more incredibly, these visionaries are rumored to be enchaining routes—flying like comic book superheroes from the summit of one mountain to the base of another so they might polish off a second major climb the very same day. The grumbling coming from shadowed booths in the *Nationale* and around the kerosene bonfires in Snell's Field seems to center on topics only peripherally connected to these amazing feats, i.e. fair means versus the use of paragliders and helicopters, the folly of record breaking and celebrity seeking, and the absurdities of Continental fashion (the French, it seems, are fond of neon jumpsuits). Even the staunchest traditionalists, however, are quietly lifting a pint to the sheer audacity and incomprehensible deeds of this new breed of mountaineer.

As an American climber of mediocre talent, my idea of enchainment is to order the full menu deal—appetizer, entrée, and dessert—at one of the excellent bistros in town. But the fact that the French are leading a movement that hinges upon thinking way outside the box does not surprise me, not since I first laid eyes on the Aiguille du Midi anyway.

The Midi is the tallest of the granite pyramids that stand like a dam between the forested hills around Chamonix and the ice world of Mont Blanc, so much so that in the places where these sub-peaks are absent, glacial ice has oozed down almost to the valley floor. All of these *aiguilles* sport pencil-point summits, but the Aiguille du Midi is in a class by itself. To the naked eye, its peak seems positively hypodermic, a sliver of rock so thin it defies nature—in fact, it is completely artificial. Binoculars reveal this to be the metal mast crowning a man-made fortress that is a hybrid of medieval architecture and science fiction. Also visible under magnification are a pair of gossamer threads that loop in mile-long uninterrupted strands between this impossible edifice and the forested bench at the mountain's foot. This is the Aiguille du Midi *téléphérique,* the world's premier cable-car system and a project of such grand ambition that—like the Eiffel Tower or Panama Canal—it could only have been engineered by the French.

The *téléphérique* visible from Chamonix is actually only part of a much larger scheme that spans the entire range. From the summit of the Aiguille du Midi, the cables continue across the Vallée Blanche and the Glacier du Géant, and then down toward the Italian village of Courmayeur. It is the amazing station high atop the Midi, however, that has rewritten the nature of climbing in Chamonix by providing even the laziest mountaineer ready access to the heart of the massif. This is my kind of outing.

Shortly before first light I gingerly pick my way among the shadowed tarps and snoring flotsam of Snell's Field to fetch my partner. He is an Englishman, cut from the same cloth as Don Whillans, and as such he has put in a long night on the stools and does not rouse easily. Once he is upright, however, and everything is "right as rain" (meaning he has successfully made a trip to the "bongo pit" at the edge of camp) we are off down the gravel lane leading into town. Despite our early start, the line at the *téléphérique* station in Chamonix has already swollen out into the streets. I'm lucky to have a graduate of the English juvenile reform system in my corner, someone who knows which of the side doors is usually unlocked, and how to open ones that aren't. Soon enough we are inside the station, and jammed along with nearly a hundred of our fellows into a tram cabin the size of a cube van. The ride up takes 15 minutes, a few more to switch cars, and then another quarter-hour to the Midi station. This second leg is

Climbers thronging the ultra-classic Rebuffat Route *(5.10), Aiguille du Midi, South Face*

guaranteed to cause some shifting within the intestine; no skimming of the treetops here. Instead, the view is a bird's eye tour up the 4000-foot north face of the Midi—a cliff as cold and forbidding as any Eiger nightmare. Once on top, however, a warren of catwalks and tunnels soon leads to a slender snow ridge that wraps down around to the base of the sun-baked south face, a steep but friendly slab that is yin to the north side's yang. Unpacking my sack beneath our chosen line, well over 7000 feet higher than where I woke up only a few hours ago, I have yet to take a single step uphill. The vista is a fairytale kingdom of snow and rock, my route is a warm and perfect granite crack, and at the summit there is a snack bar. *Vive la France!*

AUGUST, 1986 - THE APEX OF EUROPE

High on the flanks of Mont Blanc I am cowering like a baby in a dingo's den. I have timed a few hours of sleep during a solo attempt on Mont Blanc's standard route to coincide perfectly with a vicious spate of evening thunderstorms. Digging a bivy trench on this snowy crest seemed like a good idea at the time; the afternoon cloud build-up looked to have peaked as isolated pockets of benign cumulous. But no sooner had I zipped my sack over me when the air was transformed into a hissing, snapping, snake pit of electricity. With the first salvos of lightning I tossed out my axe and crampons; now, with enough energy to light a city arcing around my head, I'm wishing I had kept them long enough to pry out the metal fillings in my teeth.

Oddly enough, it was a similar lonely bivouac—minus the fireworks—almost 200 years earlier that led indirectly to the first ascent of Mont Blanc. By the mid-18th century, tourism and scientific curiosity, not to mention the substantial cash reward offered by a prominent Geneva physicist, had combined to make trying to reach the highest summit in the Alps a worthwhile venture. For decades the Chamonix guides spearheaded numerous attempts to breach the mountain's upper defenses. In every case, however, the summit bid was started from the highest rocks before the glacial ice cap, a point well over 7000 feet below the top. The conventional wisdom was that a night spent out upon the ice of Mont Blanc's highest slopes would be a person's last.

In June of 1786, yet another reconnaissance ended in defeat at the foot of the Bosses Ridges, a steeply exposed crest of ice barring the way to the final dome. As the older guides turned back, their sights now fixed on the safety of a high camp below the snow line, a young tag-along named Jacques Balmat lagged behind to hunt for rock crystals. By the time Balmat began to retrace his footsteps, darkness was upon him and he was forced to pass the night in a shallow snow hole. Two important things resulted from Balmat's forced bivouac: First, the bogeyman of spending the night out upon the upper mountain was dispelled. Secondly, it introduced Balmat to Michel-Gabriel Paccard, the doctor who treated Balmat for "severe indisposition" resulting from his ordeal. Paccard was also an enthusiastic mountaineer, keenly interested himself in bagging the first ascent of the peak. Dr. Paccard admired Balmat's fortitude and proposed that they join forces. Less than two months later, Paccard and Balmat planted a flag upon the highest European ground west of the Caucasus.

Today, the "ordinary route" up Mont Blanc is not the one followed by these pioneers. Whereas their route traced a meandering line among the complex seracs and crevasses directly above Chamonix, the path upon which I am camped follows the right skyline from the dark triangle of the Aiguille du Gouter, across the rounded shoulder of the Dome du Gouter, and up the impressive spine of the Bosses Ridge. This route, although technically more difficult than the *Ancien Passage,* exposes climbers to far less objective danger. Of course, by the standards of the 1700s, the modern climb has been equipped with a number of "improvements" that have tempered a great deal of the hardships. These include a cable car and train that eliminate an entire grueling day of switch-backing up through the steep forests and moraines below timberline, a system of hotel-like refuges for passing the night in comfort, and steel cables fixed over the steepest rocks—not to mention the invention of crampons and the use of ropes, both of which are conspicuously absent in the engravings of 18th-century mountaineers.

But there are still challenges and perils aplenty on this, as well as the myriad of other routes that now penetrate every wrinkle and fold of Mont Blanc's alpine veneer. The rapid ascent facilitated by modern means often positions people dangerously high with little or no previous acclimatization. Altitude sickness is a common affliction, and it is especially dangerous in this place where storms can develop, seemingly out of nowhere, engulfing climbers in vicious wind, arctic temperatures, and whiteout precipitation. Not to mention electric death. Cringing in my hole, waiting for God to throw the switch on Old Sparky, I am painfully aware of how two centuries after Jacques Balmat's solitary bivouac, a climber can still pass a terrifying night of abject misery high on the slopes of Mont Blanc.

AUGUST, 1989 - CHANGING TIMES, CHANGING CLIMBS

I have a score to settle with the Dru; the same Dru that derailed my very first attempt to climb in the Mont Blanc massif by spitting two busted-up mountaineers into my path. The same mountain that upped the ante several years later by dangling a corpse in front of me—the smashed body of someone I had gotten to know only the evening before. I mean to slay this dragon, even though the escalation of its taunting seems to indicate that the next time I have a go at it, it will try to slay me.

There have been some changes over the last decade, however. A free-climbing movement, spearheaded by the Swiss climber Michel Piola, has taken the Mont Blanc massif by storm. New, bolted routes seem to be springing up daily on the flanks of venerable formations like the Grand Capucin, Grepon, and Aiguille du Plan. In addition, some of the old classics are being transformed. On some big walls, free-climbing enthusiasts are eschewing the summit in favor of climbing fast and light up only the portion featuring the best rock and the cleanest cracks. These climbs have been equipped with rappel anchors so that what once was a major chunk of a multi-day excursion is now a popular day climb. The *American Direct* on the Dru is one of these routes. The *American Direct* follows a plum line of cracks and flakes to an enormous jammed block at two-thirds height. Most consider these pitches the meat of the climb, since not far beyond, a series of overhangs forces a traverse onto less aesthetic terrain. Amazingly, the first 20 pitches up to the block go free at a sustained but moderate level of difficulty. My buddy Roger and I are hanging out at one of the sanitized campgrounds that have recently supplanted the infamous tent ghettos of the past decades. We are spinning our wheels waiting for conditions on the *Walker Spur* to improve. The *Walker,* a 5000-foot granite north face in a league with the Eiger, is the carrot holding us here, but an evil and persistent glazing of ice is preventing us from sinking in our teeth. In the meantime, all the *pains au chocolat* and *biéres grandes* I've been indulging are threatening to ground me for good. I need a brief, challenging adventure to get me out of town and away from all my dough-boy vices. Roger suggests the *American Direct* in the new style. A bit of a stick-in-the-mud by nature, I normally bristle at any suggestion of climbing with a nontraditional bend—especially if it means pulling up short of the summit. But twice now I've humped a haulbag full of iron to the base of this mountain and both times I've been chased off with Death nipping at my heels. An opportunity to trivialize my old nemesis—lose the wrecking ball, lighten up both the load and the atmosphere—is just what I've been looking for.

The approach to the west face of the Dru is all downhill, God bless the *téléphériques.* Settling into a cozy bivy below the face, we turn in early so we can get a jump on things in the morning. Unfortunately, our jump is completely off route. Futzing around by headlamp on a face festooned with history—old pegs and pieces of tat nailed into every nook and cranny—we have definitely crossed the border into the state of confusion. Soon it is a state of war. Roger is certain we go left; I'm insisting it's right. We practically have our hands around each other's throats when the sun comes up, and, of course, the correct line is somewhere else altogether.

Once we are back on track, however, the gears have never shifted more smoothly. We discover pitch after glorious pitch of cracks so clean they might have split open only yesterday. The friction is like that of sandpaper,

*The embodiment of alpine symmetry: West Face of the Petit Dru
(the* American Direct *ascends the vertical shield of granite left of center)*

The famous statue (left) of Horace-Bénédict de Saussure, who made the 3rd ascent of Mont Blanc, and guide Jacques Balmat in Chamonix; and an equally determined Author with Roger Volkmann

the protection couldn't be more solid if it was welded. The crux, however, is an offwidth flake, which throws me a curve since we have no big cams.

Instead, I manage to sling a rotting wooden wedge so old it could be a splinter of Noah's Ark. Eventually, as the morning slips away, clouds start to build on the face, but there's no malice here; they are fleecy sheep bumping and rubbing a granite post. We reach the top of the jammed block by mid-afternoon. Other than a few hours of groping around in the dark, it has been an idyllic day: 20 uneventful, perfect pitches on one of the finest walls in the Alps. As we rig our first rappel, I remark to Roger that the Dru has let me off easy. And then the doors of Hell fly open and a thousand screaming demons try to tear out my soul.

Somewhere high above us, huge sheets of frozen rock have pried loose in the warm sun. They are peeling from the wall, one after the other, like granite dominos toppling into space. To us, it is as if the dome of the heavens is collapsing around our heads. The sky is alive with debris raining down, exploding off ledges, whizzing past like rifle fire. Throughout our descent—all 20 rappels—our adrenal glands are pumping like lawn sprinklers as the air is infused with the purring hum of plummeting blocks and the acrid stink of bruised stone. After two hours of playing dodge ball with the Grim Reaper, we stagger from the Dru as shell-shocked as any trench fighters during the Great War. Some things, it seems, never change.

AUGUST, 2000 - CLUCK, CLUCK, CLUCKIN' ON HEAVEN'S DOOR

I am climbing solo up the northwest face of the Petite Verte, an easy mixed route on an inconsequential peak (lowly number 10 in *Rebuffat*). Still, as I maneuver past roped teams of novice alpinists who are swarming the climb, I find that they regard me—the Solo Man—with a degree of reverence and awe. Sadly, this has nothing to do with me and everything to do with perspective: To newborn chicks still moist from the egg, the rooster must seem god-like in all his strutting, crowing glory. But to the eagles soaring high overhead, he's just a big chicken. I know where I fall in the Chamonix pecking order.

It is a social structure that has evolved in step with Chamonix's shifting role on the stage of world climbing. Each time the theorists have proclaimed the Mont Blanc massif to be climbed out or passé, some combination of new ideas, new gear, or new attitudes have emerged to reinvent the place. When I first started showing up here, the *créme de la créme* were people who could recite from first-hand experience the latter chapters of Rebuffat's *100 Finest*. Today, the top echelons are spread out across a number of mountaineering disciplines. These include the flamboyant soloists, who rip through *Rebuffat* as if it were a comic book, striving to shave ever more minutes from the great classics and enchain ever more improbable combinations for the record books and the TV cameras. Meanwhile, both in and out of the limelight, hard-ice specialists and cutting-edge alpine technicians have continued, year after year, to ferret out radical new lines throughout the Mont Blanc massif, most recently amid the ephemeral smears and ghost couloirs that come and go with icy sleight of hand. Now, however, the rock climbers who slumber in the huts for hours after the mountain men and women have stumbled out into the frozen darkness, and then trade this luxury for grappling with some of the hardest technical moves imaginable, must also be counted among Chamonix's climbing elite.

And then there are the rest of us. A vast barnyard of roosters, busily pawing and scratching away for our kernels, and every once in awhile managing to uncover a pearl. For me, the view from the summit of the Petite Verte is such a gem. Below, in a deep wrinkle of mist, the villages of Chamonix and Argentiére are still shrouded in the dewy shadows of early morning. But soaring above me, the steep rocks and summit *á la mode* of the Aiguille Verte are blazing with the golden light of a new day. I am happy and jazzed just to be back in Chamonix. With any luck, thanks to the *téléphérique*, I will be back at the campsite about the time my friends are just waking up. And then I'll have something to crow about.

Originally published in CLIMBING, *No. 200, 2001.*

Author's note: The terrifying hail of rockfall that we encountered on the west face of the Dru in 1989 was nothing compared to what happened in June of 2005 when the entire southwest shoulder—the center third of the mountain depicted on page 66— collapsed, displacing an estimated 265,000 cubic meters of rock and erasing the most iconic route on the mountain, the Bonatti Pillar. In short order, French guides from Chamonix forged a new route up the shattered and unstable scar.

The southeast aspect of Devils Tower; The Window *is the overhanging feature right of center*

HANGING BY A THREAD
Nearly Curtains on The Window

THERE IS LITTLE DEFENSE against the charge that anyone who goes aid climbing at Devils Tower is a moron. "The Tower" is, after all, one of the world's premier free-climbing venues. Its perfect fissures define a standard: Climbers of every nationality travel here to calibrate and measure their crack-climbing skills. The monolithic stump is raked with testpieces; scores of continuous fractures offering up everything from limb-torquing offwidths to ultra-modern, tip-tweaking seams.

And then there is *The Window* (IV 5.6 A4), first climbed by Royal Robbins and Doug Robinson in 1964 and an unholy aberration in this 5th-class paradise. The route encompasses several pitches of a plumb, butt-smooth, fingernail seam capped by a massive, double-tiered overhang. The odds of anyone ever scaling this anomaly by fair means are slim to none, and so it is the province of misfits—aid climbers, people who choose to dangle in slings while everyone around them is jamming heavenly cracks. People like X and myself. Morons.

I refer to my partner as "X" not to shield his reputation—he threw that to the wind the moment he agreed to attempt *The Window* with me—but because I honestly don't remember his name. I only met him the day before our climb, and I've not seen hide nor hair of him since. Because X was a stranger, he was unlike anyone I'd ever partnered with before—especially for something as grave as *The Window.* There are so many things about climbing that are beyond my control that I cling like a barnacle to the few I can, which is why, up till then, I'd made it a rule to stick with partners I knew and trusted. There comes a point in nearly every life, however, when, against better judgment, caution is thrown to the wind. In my climbing career, X marks that spot.

Aside from being the only climber who wasn't incapacitated with laughter at the mere suggestion of attempting *The Window*, X oozed confidence. He had the self-assured bearing of a commando, and the physique to match—his back muscles rippled beneath his T-shirt like the wake from a battleship. He was also funny: "Any fool can monkey about on rock overhangs," he hooted across the campground at climbers triple racking for one of the Tower's assembly line free routes, "but it takes craft and cunning to beat *The Window!*" (I later discovered that he lifted this phrasing from Scottish climber and humorist Tom Patey). Finally, his stories of past big-wall glories seemingly confirmed that he had the résumé to back up his bravado (although I've come to suspect he may have borrowed these as well).

To anyone paying attention, our approach to the base of *The Window* was plagued with enough bad omens to turn a Roman army on its heels. Lugging our massive aid racks, swarmed by mosquitoes, X and I struggled through the predawn gloom, soloing precariously up loose, brushy ledges, lush with poison ivy. We were so intent upon these labors that the sun could have risen fully eclipsed and dripping blood and it wouldn't have registered.

At last we collapsed in a weary heap on the shelf at the start of the technical climbing. But before I could even catch my breath, X announced, "I defer to you, my squire. The first pitch is all yours." I registered this with alarm, since we now had a headrest view straight up the rails of the guillotine. The geometry of the sweeping columns that comprise Devils Tower is always surreal, but this clean corner rising to a series of jutting hexagonal roofs seemed particularly unnatural—and menacing—like the throat of a massive pile driver. Withering in the shadows at ground zero, I don't think either of us believed we had a chance of reaching even the first hanging belay, much less the inverted A4 terrain. And I couldn't help feeling that by volunteering me for the opening sortie, X was already hedging his bets.

Thankfully, the first pitch wasn't so bad. Mostly slam-dance gear punctuated by the occasional question mark but nothing hairy enough to freak me out. In fact, once I found my rhythm, I even started to enjoy myself. The whole experience was made richer with the knowledge that by batting at the top of the order, I could look forward to kicking back in butt-bag splendor while X came to grips with the truly hair-raising aid on the crux pitch.

To his credit, X did indeed make an attempt on the crux. He actually managed to push the route another twenty or thirty feet before lowering back down to my belay, where he scrambled for the anchors like a thunder-phobic dog diving under the bed. His nerves were shot; he wasn't coming out again until the storm was over. Of course, he'd also neatly managed to commit me to the crux pitch, as a fair chunk of it was now plugged full of my expensive micro-nuts and cams. (His own gear, he explained, had been held in reserve for "higher up.") And so up I went, thrust once more into the breach, trying desperately to rekindle the flame of confidence, now all but X-tinguished.

Approaching the imposing A4 double overhangs of The Window *on Devils Tower*

Trembling in the footsteps of Royal Robbins, I tried to calm myself by focusing on the movements and methods of the first ascent party. From the pin scars I encountered, I deduced where Robbins had managed to tack his way up and through the jutting double overhangs using only conventional pitons (I, on the other hand, had pitons, nuts, and cams at my disposal, and I was still going to need a trouser change when this was finished). But when at last I drew near to the very lip of the final roof, I was baffled; the seam suddenly closed up tighter than a clam in ice water. In desperation, I probed the rock for some hidden crevice that would unlock the mystery of how Robbins had turned the corner. Finally, twisted like a balloon animal, stretched to the point of nearly toppling from my aiders, I managed to peer around the edge of the overhang...and I saw it.

When Robbins and Robinson first unlocked *The Window*, the pinnacle of aid climbing gadgetry was the RURP, an acronym for Realized Ultimate Reality Piton (which has never made sense to me; I think it more likely that the name originated in Camp 4 where it was belched into being after a zesty supper of bean burritos and cheap beer). Unlike peg-style pitons, a RURP's blade is designed to hatchet into shallow, hairline cracks. If a climber is lucky, the putty knife tip of the RURP may penetrate 1/4 to 1/2 inch. If a climber is blessed, that may be just enough to support body weight—*the* criterion for A4.

Craning over the final lip, I glimpsed an ancient RURP, buried to the hilt inside a flaring pocket. Contortionist hammer blows had long ago mashed it into little more than a mangled, rusty blob—I might have missed it altogether were it not for the threadbare loop of weathered tat welded within the wreckage. The RURP had been Robbins' salvation; my own deliverance was tied to even less—literally.

I tried searching for another placement, raking my fingernails back and forth across the rough porphyry, clawing for any nubbin or shard of purchase alongside the old relic. I even considered driving my own pin directly into the heart of the iron sliver, but nothing less than Excalibur would have penetrated more than the few remaining threads of nylon still looped within the joint. There was nothing left but to face up to my own "ultimate reality." By pulping the RURP so completely, Robbins had sealed the only bit of texture, and my fate. I was going to have to clip that tattered sling.

There is something about hard aid climbing that is conducive to an out-of-body experience. Perhaps the fact that the mitochondria aren't firing on all eight cylinders (in fact, the muscles themselves are largely garaged) while the brain is being redlined with anxiety and dread, makes it easier for the mind to take a little drive in the country. This is my only explanation for how I can recall the details of the groping carabiner, pinched cigarette-like between my two extended fingers, nosing back and forth against the stiff, closed loop of the decades-old fragment. Bunched beneath the overhang, I'd have needed a periscope to see the sun-bleached fibers, dry as balsa, popping and shedding dusty filaments when at last I pinned the loop against the rock and forced the biner through. And how else could I remember how, as I finally eased my weight out and onto the shabby sling, the threads crackled like a dry leaf, stretched taut as a bowstring—and held. Like watching an egg stand on end, my instinct was to remain utterly motionless, lest a single breath or twitch suddenly upset the applecart and bring everything to ruin. But having once again fused body and mind, I knew that in this case the exact opposite was true: This rickety RURP was a time bomb, dangling from it was a game of runner roulette. And so I moved with as much urgency and economy as I dared and that the awkward, free-hanging situation would permit. Sweating bullets with every step, I gingerly crept up in my aiders. At last, with the RURP sling pressing like a grenade against my crotch, I found myself staring into a pocket large enough

Not even an ounce of prevention: a RURP—this one features a robust wire attachment loop

to accept pro. I was like a driver fumbling for his seatbelt with the car already out of control—every thought sharpened to razor clarity, every action mired in slow motion—as I struggled to release a nut from my rack, plug it into the constriction, and with a glorious snap, clip myself to it.

Royal Robbins may have placed the gear, but I earned that A4 crux, fair and square.

By the time I finished the pitch, I was so mentally frayed I could have given the RURP's sling a run for its money. I didn't even have the energy to be pissed when X finally arrived at my belay carrying little more than when he set out—to say he cleaned the pitch would be a stretch, since he'd left every one of my pitons fixed in the overhangs. Instead, I rationalized that leaving gear behind to fuel anxiety in subsequent parties was very much in the spirit and style of the first ascent. And besides, despite this transgression, *The Window's* fearsome reputation and A4 rating were still solidly (or, more correctly, precariously) intact.

Of course, nothing lasts forever. That old shoelace may have miraculously held my weight, but I doubt there was much life left in it (which may explain why, according to park records, *The Window* has only had about a dozen successful ascents). X also seems to have vanished like rotted cord. Meanwhile, free climbers are making serious inroads in the quest to open *The Window*—a blow to morons everywhere.

Originally published in CLIMBING, *No. 226, 2003.*

All that most maddens and torments: the brooding, mythic wall of the Eiger North Face

LEVIATHAN

A Whale of a Time on the Eiger North Face

TO TRAVEL HALFWAY around the world to see or do something is considered a pilgrimage, and falls well within the range of normal behavior. To make such a journey twice is still acceptable; after all, who among us has not nostalgically yearned to revisit the site of some memorable experience from our youth? To go a third time begins to arouse suspicions—it hints at obsession. As I stared up at the North Face of the Eiger, it was through the eyes of a modern-day Ahab; for the third time in my life I stood shivering in the shadow of my whale. Yet I considered myself lucky, I have a friend who has been here eight times and has yet to tie into the rope. If ever a mountain had the power to influence lives and empty bank accounts, this was it.

As I gazed once more upon the infamous rock bands and icefields, my brain, which houses neurons that are normally hard pressed to retrieve the memory of my last meal, amazed me by graphically recalling all the gory details of every Eiger horror story I had ever encountered. Images of iced ropes, hurtling bodies, and fatal stonefall assailed me, threatening to buckle my knees and pitch me headlong into the edelweiss.

Yet my most vivid impression was not from one of the classic "Wall of Death" disasters that are commemorated with tiny crosses on Eigerwand bath towels and other macabre souvenirs found in gift shops throughout the Swiss town of Grindelwald at the mountain's foot. Instead, my thoughts focused on a smoky tavern in Zermatt and an encounter with a glowering Frankenstein monster who muttered in a heavy Scottish dialect. The man's head suggested a shattered pumpkin that had been clumsily reassembled. From the extent of his injuries, I grimly deduced that he had either been crushed by a truck or struck with a maul.

In fact, he had been struck with the Eiger, repeatedly. His tale was of a routine bivouac gone dreadfully wrong: a sudden lightning storm bursting from the clouds with the explosive violence of an airliner ramming the face. The turbulent energy literally picked him up and hurled him from his ledge, leaving him suspended in space, dangling like a broken puppet from a single anchor peg. Even before he could react, the electricity had grasped him again and savagely slammed him back into the mountain. Then the process was repeated. Like a monstrous paddle-toy the Eiger storm bounced the unfortunate Scotsman against the stony surface again and again. Miraculously, he escaped with his life, but the deep scars etched like the tracks of a switching yard across his face made it plain that he would never be truly free of the Eigerwand.

Now, as I cowered beneath the hulking, familiar outline of the very culprit, the memory of this cruel attack had a profound effect upon me. I felt like throwing up.

WHAT I DID have going for me was the perfect Eiger partner. A physical description of Roger can be taken directly from the pages of Mary Shelley: "A being which had the shape of a man, but apparently of gigantic stature." He also possesses two of the most crucial mental attributes of a successful mountaineer: He is as stubborn and tenacious as a rusted bolt. As a result, Roger is a bold, gifted climber—and a weather-god to boot. Sunshine follows him around like a puppy. This had first come to my attention when he departed for the *Cassin Ridge*. In the weeks prior to his trip, the Alaska Range had been pummeled by storms. Even as I bid him farewell and wished him success, I privately doubted whether he would get an opportunity even to touch the mountain. Roger arrived in Talkeetna with the sunshine licking at his heels. His is probably the only expedition to Denali never to encounter a single cloud. And after two weathered-out trips to the Eiger, I resolved that the next time I went to the Alps, this guy was coming along.

It was beginning to look as though Roger's puppy had run off, however. We had been lured from the sunny south of France to the Bernese Oberland by an overly optimistic weather forecast. We arrived in Grindelwald to find the face in good, dry condition, the sky clear, and the barometer steady. In defense of the *Bureau de Météorologie* in Chamonix and in keeping with Eiger legend, the prolonged storms that arrived the next day really did seem to come out of nowhere.

Like so many Eiger hopefuls before us, we killed time any way we could: movies in Interlaken, reading, sightseeing. Roger took a day trip to Zermatt. He drove out of Grindelwald at 3 a.m. in the pouring rain. After hiking up the lower flanks of the Matterhorn in fog and steady drizzle, he proceeded to the summit in an icy whiteout. He bought a postcard on the way back so he could see what the mountain actually looked like. Anyone like myself who has been to the top of the Matterhorn will understand my skepticism upon his return; this is an immense and devious mountain, and any claim to have simply wandered up it in a storm

Eiger watching: assessing conditions on the North Face

must be regarded as suspect. But Roger described the huge iron cross that marks the summit with perfect accuracy. Personally, I could not imagine a more hideous outing.

And as fate seems to dictate in the valley of the Eiger, the storms dragged on until the time that remained before the return dates stamped on our airline tickets could be measured in days rather than weeks. I was resolving myself to yet another trip to Europe when suddenly the clouds lifted and the whale showed itself. Naturally, it was white.

There was snow—too much snow—on every ledge that could hold it, and where the face couldn't hold it, the snow was coming off. The wall was alive with avalanches, pouring like rivers of granulated sugar down the tentacled gullies and arcing off the icefields. If the Second Icefield was indeed a thousand feet across, then the continuous plume of snow now streaming directly down the first half of our route was at least a hundred feet wide. The only part of the Eiger that wasn't plastered with fresh snow was the lower third of the wall which lay below the freezing level. This section was stained a ghastly black by a deluge of running water.

In all my storm-plagued trips to Europe, I had never seen the Eiger so hopelessly out of condition. Any attempts at climbing the face would obviously have to wait at least several more days, and the morning weather bulletin prophesied only one more day of clear weather, and then the storms were predicted to return.

After the storm: "There was snow—too much snow—on every ledge that could hold it..."

Once again, it appeared as though the great whale had eluded me. Climbing the Eiger simply wasn't in the cards, and to my surprise, Roger was actually the first to voice it: "Let's go," he murmured. With some reluctance I nodded agreement, but I also admit to feeling relieved that, at least for this trip, there would be no opportunity for me to end up as yet another cross on an Eiger ashtray. Imagine then, my horror when I realized the true meaning of my companion's words: I turned to find the man readying his climbing pack!

"Look here," I stammered. "You can't possibly be thinking about going up there. It's madness...suicide...and I won't go!"

He looked at me with a penetrating gunfighter squint and said just about the last thing I expected to hear: "You are a chicken."

I think it's a safe bet that no matter how fiercely Lachenal and Terray disagreed over the prospects of a particular route, the one never resorted to calling the other "chicken." It seems unimaginable that Hillary could have goaded Tenzing to the top of Everest with scornful cries of "wimp." And although Whymper is reputed to have tumbled rocks from the summit of the Matterhorn to attract the attention of his rivals, he almost certainly did not stick out his tongue. I was genuinely wounded. Gentlemanly behavior is a code that is fundamentally rooted in mountaineering and gentlemen do not open a dialogue by hurling insults.

Roger, however, is not a mountaineer. He is an alpinist. Worse yet, he is an extreme alpinist. The difference is that to an extreme alpinist, the only acceptable ends to an expedition are the summit or the grave, and any means necessary to achieve these ends is fair game, including aggressive coercion. This he now pursued.

He bullied, I protested. He threatened, I stood my ground. He questioned my manhood, and I pronounced him a menace. We held little back—although he refrained from calling me "tubby" or making similar references to my robust Whillans-like morphology, or I think it might have come to blows.

Eventually we ran out of things to call each other, and we arbitrated the only possible compromise I would agree upon: We would return to the weather bureau in the evening, and if the forecast extended the period of settled weather by even a single day, I would attempt the climb. We brooded through the long afternoon, each of us anticipating our respective definitions of bad news.

So when at last the evening forecast went up, we were both surprised, to say the least. At first we wondered if there had been some mistake; surely, the bureau must have swapped forecasts with the Bahamas or some other tropical locale. But there was the map of central Europe and, beside it, perhaps the best Eiger area weather forecast ever seen—something to this effect: "Perfect sunshine and no precipitation for as long as it is possible to see into the future. Perhaps a week. No kidding." Roger's puppy had finally come home.

We were actually going to get a crack at the Eiger. I didn't know whether to laugh or cry. It was with mixed feelings of excitement and foreboding that I packed my gear and sharpened my harpoons.

MORNING FOUND US trudging up to the base of the wall from the tiny rail station at Alpiglen. With little difficulty we made our way around the initial snowfields and stepped into the mouth of the whale.

It is an unnerving fact that before you have climbed more than a few hundred feet up the dreaded North Face of the Eiger, you are suddenly confronted by metal plaques commemorating the demise of many of those who have preceded you. It made me want to turn tail and run, and perhaps that's the point: to weed out the sissies. But I hoped these markers had not been placed everywhere on the face where some luckless soul had perished. The place was going to be spooky enough without headstones.

After third-classing the hair-raising wet slabs and terraces of the lower wall, we finally roped up below the Difficult Crack, which was not really a crack at all but a flaky corner filled with a waterfall, old fixed lines, and, astonishingly, four other climbers. We were surprised to see these other people, since we had neither seen nor heard anyone in front of us on our long scramble up the lower section of the wall.

"Howdy!" I shouted. Roger frowned at me and I couldn't tell if he was bothered by the unexpected company or by my lack of sophistication—this was the Eigerwand, after all. The other climbers voiced or gurgled some reply, depending upon where they happened to be positioned relative to the torrents that were cascading down the route, but there was no mistaking the fact that everybody seemed to be speaking the same language—although an admittedly more cosmopolitan version than myself.

Some hours later, we all bottlenecked at the start of the Hinterstoisser Traverse. The pair engaged in negotiating the snow-plastered slabs were fellow Americans—Coloradans to be precise—and the other two were Scots, who graciously allowed us to pass in front of them. They were moving more slowly than expected. Being Scots, they had anticipated an ice climb; unfortunately for them, it had become apparent that underneath all the fresh snow the exceptionally dry year hadn't produced enough ice to chill a tumbler of Glenfiddich.

Across the traverse we discovered our compatriots bedding down in the Swallow's Nest bivouac. The Scots were also intending to sleep on this tiny perch, and so, with no room left in the inn, Roger and I climbed a long pitch up the First Icefield and hacked an ice ledge under a rock overhang. We brewed a liquid meal and snuggled into our bags.

THE NEXT DAY dawned bright and clear, just as predicted. What a joy to awaken on the Eiger to a sky that would not be out of place framing a placid Caribbean lagoon. I was actually beginning to relax. I was totally unprepared then, when the very first obstacle of the day almost killed me. The Ice Hose is a problematic runnel that links the First and Second icefields. The warm summer had reduced the hose to a slabby, verglased rock groove, and the recent storms had packed the chute with a two-foot icing of vertical corn snow. Ten feet up the situation was already critical: The dry snow crumbled away wherever I touched it and threatened to send me tobogganing into the abyss. Imagine a watermelon hurtling down a gigantic, near-vertical bobsled run that empties out over the edge of a 2000-foot cliff. I did.

A hundred feet out I finally gave up trying to get protection; tunneling through the snow in desperate hopes of finding one of the 10 billion fixed pins that everybody says are on the Eiger had repeatedly revealed only blank slabs of limestone. As I flailed up an increasingly precarious house of cards, my mind began to work it all out. If I came off, I would crash like a wrecking ball onto the First Icefield; the impact would undoubtedly break a lot of bones but the steep angle and the cushion of fresh snow would probably keep me from being killed. To my mind, the important thing was that Roger was still anchored to a rock-solid belay, so no matter how you cut it I was not going to become one of those detached bodies that tourists glimpse through the telescopes. Believe it or not, this thought calmed me, and just as I was starting to get a handle on things again, I risked a glance downward in order to judge my progress.

What I saw sent my breakfast dashing for the exits—the rope had long since run out between us and instead of alerting me to this fact, Roger, to my absolute horror, had simply unclipped from the anchors and was climbing up behind me. If either of us slid off now we would both be flying home in a body bag. Perhaps the thought of sharing a sack with chunks of Roger is what I needed to propel me up those last few feet. I do remember that as I finally gripped the knot of tattered slings at the base of the Second Icefield, I seriously considered tying my end of the rope to a loose block and trundling it off. Since I couldn't bring myself to actually murder the father of two children—especially since there was no way we really could have done the pitch any differently—I sought some small revenge the only way I knew how: I belayed him with a lot of slack. I doubt if he even noticed.

After such an ordeal, the thought of front-pointing sideways for a thousand feet across the face of the Second Icefield seemed a cruel joke, so I cramponed to the top of the slope in hopes of finding a bergschrund or a level crest that might allow us to dash across in comfort. No such luck. The 'schrund, if it ever existed, had been smoothly caulked with ice and neatly feathered into the vertical rock face. Worse yet, an enticing line of fixed pins (the first I remember seeing) shot horizontally across the rock band in a long chain of absolutely inaccessible protection—the shriveled icefield now placed the old pitons at least 20 feet over our heads. When I pointed this out to Roger, he shrugged. "Screw it," he said.

And so screw it we did, making sure at least one ice screw protected us at all times during the interminable shuffle across the face of the Second Icefield. I insisted upon it.

My calves were veal by the time we reached the foot of the projecting rock buttress known as the Flatiron. We had also arrived at ground zero with respect to the Eiger's notorious stonefall hazard, but so far the only projectiles we had witnessed were a few minor chunks of ice rattling down gullies. It was an eerie and disconcerting silence that we observed in the heart of such a notorious battlefield, but it was vastly preferable to being under siege.

We could see where we needed to go. The Death Bivouac was plainly visible several hundred feet above, but the best way to get there was not obvious. Some weathered fixed ropes dangled suggestively back to our right, but a complex little rock band in front of us seemed to offer a shorter and

Approaching the Death Bivouac; Second Icefield visible below

more direct route. Roger scrutinized both options and then, as I knew he would, chose the road less traveled. The two Coloradans came around the corner just in time to see him take a 30-foot fall. They made a beeline for the fixed ropes.

Remarkably, Roger was unhurt. His huge pack probably cushioned the fall and kept his spine in one piece. Undaunted, he brushed himself off and moved up the rock again. It was an amazing spectacle, the picture of futility—like watching a mountain sheep that has just rammed one of his compatriots shakily pick himself up and head back for more. This time, however, after Roger regained his high point, he moved slightly left and began poking about beneath a grim little overhang. "Ah-ha!" he announced triumphantly. He had uncovered an old piton at the lip of the roof that apparently gave the line just the legitimacy he had been looking for. My amazement turned to disbelief as I watched him clip a sling into the ancient peg and then reach over the roof, pull himself up on tiny downsloping edges and put one cramponed foot into the loop. Scabs of rust flaked from the flexing pin as he committed his full weight to the makeshift aider. His hands scrabbled for purchase on the snowy ledges above the overhang, and finally he stepped up, trusting his front points to the same beveled edges that had miraculously supported his fingertips. Teetering in his bulky pack, Roger manteled onto the snow-packed ledges.

I suddenly noticed one of the Scottish climbers standing beside me. He was staring up at the empty loop of webbing that beckoned like a hangman's noose from the lip of the overhang. "There is *noo* God," I heard him whisper. They also elected to go with the fixed ropes.

Roger's variation got us on top of the Flatiron several hours in front of the other climbers. The Death Bivouac was a weird place, full of strange vibes. No matter where you sleep on the Eiger you share a ledge with a ghost or two, but I was particularly glad we weren't going to be spending the night here. We wasted no time traversing left across the Third Icefield and into the long diagonal cleft of the Ramp.

I had been looking forward to the Ramp. Almost all the Eiger accounts describe it with friendly adjectives like "sheltered," and "protected." We hadn't seen a falling rock, but just the same, it felt good to be climbing somewhere where a lot of people hadn't died. We managed to tick off three long pitches, just over half the Ramp, before the setting sun dictated that we find a good place to set up camp. Those glowing descriptions of the Ramp had not included "loaded with excellent bivouac possibilities"—for good reason. Everything sloped. Luckily, a few short-lived rays of late afternoon sun had softened the thick layer of snow into moldable clay from which we were able to fashion elaborate terraces for sleeping and cooking. We were quite proud of our accommodations, glued to the angled walls of the Ramp like a miniature Machu Picchu.

As we settled in for the night, I heard a puzzling rumble in the distance. A jet, I thought, optimistically. The noise, however, pulsed and reverberated intermittently at an octave lower than any turbine, and soon became recognizable as the menacing growl of thunder. Sure enough, a cloud as black as a cave was moving up the valley from the direction of Interlaken. I couldn't believe it. The forecasters had blown it! A killer storm was poised to engulf us. The whale was sounding with us locked in its belly—we were going to die.

I peered from beneath my bivouac tarp at Roger, who was making mashed potatoes. He glanced up at me and smiled knowingly. "Don't sweat it," he said coolly.

The storm cruised right up the valley, Kleine Scheidegg got nailed, Alpiglen was blasted, and the folks in Grindelwald must have thought that all hell had broken loose. But the stars never went out over the Eiger. Something very strange was going on here. This relationship between Roger and the elements was starting to unnerve me. His uncanny ability to repel storms struck me as being almost…supernatural. I spent the rest of the night with one wary eye on the sky and the other trained on Roger.

THE FIRST OBSTACLE of the new day was the infamous "Waterfall Pitch." The late September weather had transformed it into a steep wall of spotty ice smears. Oh, man, I thought as I watched Roger scratch away with his front points, the Scottish guys are going to love this.

The next pitch would suit the highlanders even better: the "Ice Bulge." This 20-foot blue-green mushroom blocks the final chimney leading out of the Ramp. It was trivial in modern ice gear, but in deference to the pioneers, it must have been a horror in golf shoes.

The Ramp lay behind us, and we now began the long horizontal traverse back into the heart of the face. But after only a short distance we were confronted by a truly ugly looking vertical step that our route description called the "Rotten Crack." A number of fixed pins were visible in the snowy fissure, and this gave me the confidence I needed to move up it. But the next time someone scornfully tells me that the technical climbing on the Eiger is only 5.7, I'm going to hand them a set of mountain boots, crampons, gloves, strap a full rucksack to their back, and, after loosening a few key holds, point them toward Eldorado Canyon's *Bastille Crack*. That was the Rotten Crack.

The Traverse of the Gods was next, and it did not meet with our expectations. We had anticipated casual sidestepping across highly exposed ledges festooned with old pitons. There was exposure alright—5000 feet of it—but any fixed pins were buried treasure and the climbing was positively gripping. Everything was downsloping and booby-trapped with thick snow. A slip here meant dangling over a mile above the ground with no way to regain the traverse. I finally reached the lower appendages of the Spider, and should have gotten a cigar for the hammer blow with which I drove a screw into the firm ice.

The nefarious White Spider: Legend holds that this multi-tentacled icefield is perched like a fat arachnid on the upper reaches of the Eigerwand, patiently waiting for tiny insects to blunder into its lair. Two Spaniards had once been trapped in its clutches—their bodies had to be chopped from icy cocoons. We moved tentatively onto the gleaming web; the ice conditions were perfect. The Spider slept, its malice suspended. Like tiny spiders ourselves, we tiptoed furtively up the creature's broad spine. We were nearing its top and congratulating ourselves on such a stealthy escape, when the Spider suddenly moved. Our tiny vibrations triggered a small powder avalanche. Fresh snow streamed around our legs and down the icy gullies. Although we were not in any real danger of being swept from the face, we knew we had been detected.

For the first time in the course of our climb, we encountered objective danger. Ice chunks were breaking away from the upper edges of the face and being funneled down on top of us. A thick cloud also materialized and shrouded us in grey mist. The whole situation was taking on a decidedly more Eiger-like atmosphere. I supposed it had been asking too much for the whale to just roll over and submit to us, but I had hoped.

We doggedly threaded our way up the gullies of the Exit Cracks and past various minor Eiger landmarks. The "Quartz Crack" was a revelation— for some reason, I had always imagined a horizontal vein. Instead, we found a vertical offwidth crack lined with a smooth frosting of the mineral. Eventually we arrived at a cul-de-sac, and the point where all the route descriptions disagree. Some describe a pendulum to the left from this point, others an abseil. Roger found his own alternative. He simply clipped into a horizontal fixed rope that was so rotted not a thread of sheath was left on it—and slid off into space. A muffled shout through the fog confirmed that he had actually ended up alive and in some desirable location. I attached myself to the remains of what had once been a rope, took a deep breath, and stepped into the void. A terrifying slide down and around a projecting corner deposited me alongside my companion on the top of an airy pulpit. I almost gagged when I saw the bent piton that anchored the other end of the fixed line.

Roger led off up a shallow box-like chimney. The flak was getting serious—looking up the chimney was like trying to stare down a snowblower that is chewing up a frozen pond—and the fog was bordering on drizzle. These were the monster's last gasps, however, our hooks were in deep. We still couldn't relax. Better men than us had gotten the chop above this point, and the ice bombardment was relentless. But even I had to admit that the thing was almost in the net.

On the White Spider

The chimney lasted several pitches, until we found ourselves at the top of an abrupt shoulder. Around the corner we discovered an ice slope angling up through small rock outcrops. Then, just ice. And finally, as the last bit of daylight faded out of the cloud, there was only cloud.

Roger and I spent the night on the summit of the Eiger, and the great cetacean of my dreams was the finest bed I have ever known.

THE DAY AFTER our climb dawned fine and clear. The two Coloradans reached the summit just as we were preparing to descend the western flank, and we all went down together. The Scottish team had mysteriously disappeared. After spending a second night with them in the Death Bivouac, the other Americans had rapidly outdistanced them in the steep rock of the Ramp. It was the last any of us ever saw of them. We scanned the face at Scheidegg with telescopes so powerful that we could easily discern our own footprints in the Exit Cracks, but the Scots had vanished without a trace. Perhaps the sustained rock climbing in the Ramp had finally discouraged them to the point of retreat. Perhaps they were still climbing, hidden from our scrutiny in some dark corner or gully. This was our fervent hope.

Roger missed his plane. While he was battling across the thin ledges of the Traverse of the Gods, it left for home without him. It's the first bit of bad luck I think he has ever run into, but he took it well, forking over hundreds of dollars for a new ticket with typical grim determination.

I've got plans for that boy. I've never considered myself much of an extremist, but with a genuine weather-god lashed to the other end of the rope, who can say? The possibilities are tantalizing: Gasherbrum IV without a storm, Cerro Torre in shirt sleeves…

There are, after all, other fish in the sea.

Originally published in CLIMBING, *No. 131, 1992.*

Author's note: What else can I say about the Eiger? Plenty! There are at least three other pieces in this collection in which the North Face is featured or figures prominently. This was, after all, my dream climb. And I'll admit that succeeding on the Eiger left me a little rudderless. What's next, once you've achieved your greatest ambition at a relatively young age? I could have fixated on other substantial goals: an impressive career, starting a family, etc. Instead, I did what came naturally: rested on my laurels. I kept climbing and writing (a lot about the Eiger, apparently) and relied upon the joy and satisfaction taken from these experiences as my compass and my reward.

And yet…my buddy Rick—my Matterhorn partner—still aspires to climb the Eigerwand and trains for it incessantly. Now well into his fifties, he is the owner of a lucrative business, more fit than I've ever been, and climbing stronger than I ever did.

There is value, I now see, in measuring a dream over the course of a lifetime.

Near Windy Corner (13,500 ft.) on Denali's West Buttress; *Mt. Foraker in background*

THE WEAKEST LINK
A Denali Epiphany

BELMORE BROWNE has always been a hero of mine, if for no other reason than I know his pain. We share an unfortunate mountaineering trait: a tendency to snatch defeat from the hands of almost certain victory.

In June of 1912, on his third attempt to reach the summit of Denali (aka Mount McKinley), Browne thought he had it in the bag. From a high camp at 16,800 feet, he and his companions climbed to a point just beneath the final summit slope. "It rose as innocently as a tilted snow-covered tennis court," he wrote, "and as we looked it over we grinned with relief— we *knew* the peak was ours!"

Minutes later, however, a vicious storm developed that transformed his tennis match into a marathon. Browne's intended stroll to victory became a desperate struggle for every inch, until the blinding snow and numbing cold finally forced an epic, storm-battered retreat. Browne's high point is generally accepted as having been within a few hundred yards of the summit; Hudson Stuck is credited with making the first complete ascent of Denali the following year.

A list of my attempted climbs requires a very long sheet of paper, but my successes could be carved along the side of the pencil. Yet as I look over the résumé of my entire climbing career—part of the National Park Service mail-in application to climb Denali—I am heartened by what I see. As with Belmore Browne, the only thing that has truly eluded me on the climbs I did not summit is peace of mind; despite my many failures, in nearly 20 years of trying, I have amassed a respectable degree of mountaineering experience.

The same cannot be said of my two companions for this trip, and this has me worried. The pages listing their "previous mountaineering experience" contain a lot of white space, something that could cause the Park Service to view our expedition as weak, unbalanced, or unprepared. I feel this would be a mistake. My friends will make good partners on Denali for reasons not found on any climbing résumé, but trying to write between the lines leaves our form messy and confused. The fact that we all have the same name does not help matters.

Dave S. is young and stubbornly hard-willed—a great advantage in an alpine environment. The veteran of several summers working in Alaska, Dave has become obsessed with climbing Denali. Although his mountaineering experience is limited, his rock and ice skills are strong and, like the rest of us, Dave is a native Minnesotan, which means he can eat the cold for breakfast.

If Dave S. is the thoroughbred, then Dave O. (who thankfully prefers to be called Davo) is the draft horse. Huge, self-reliant, and good-natured, Davo has dragged a pack to every corner of the globe—including Antarctica—in search of a good time. While climbing may not be his strongest suit, Davo is the best skier in our group and has probably spent more nights winter camping than Belmore Browne ever did. His optimism is such that his glass is always half full; his penchant for strong drink is such that his glass is always half empty.

Together, we make a good team, probably better than most who try the *West Buttress,* since we have taken our training and gear preparation seriously. Perhaps too seriously: When I call a doctor friend who has climbed Denali and ask him to prescribe the extensive drug kit recommended by Jonathan Waterman in his book *Surviving Denali,* he laughs at me. "You've got to be kidding!" he remarks. "What are you going to do with all that shit, perform open-heart surgery? Forget it. Aspirin, that's all you need." Nevertheless, when we arrive in Talkeetna, our first-aid kit contains enough Demerol to OD an elephant.

I AM STILL FRETTING about that application when we make our mandatory check-in with the Park Service. It has been a deadly season for climbing on Denali, the worst on record, and I would not be surprised to discover that some new restriction has closed the mountain to all but the most seasoned parties. In fact, the rangers don't seem too worried about us, but it is clear my mountain experience has helped. One of them even pulls me aside and advises, "You're obviously going to be the one calling the shots up there. Be smart, keep an eye on your friends. Never forget, a chain is only as strong as its weakest link."

This chain, however, is in real danger of staying anchored to civilization. The weather is bad, too bad for flying to the mountain, and our pilots inform us that the forecast for the rest of the week is more rain and fog. We spend our days holed up in the Fairview Inn, the notorious Talkeetna tavern where, we are told, Warren Harding was poisoned to death. We hoist mug after mug to the big-wall pioneer's memory—until we learn that we're toasting some scandal-plagued Republican president. Around mid-week we

Ominous headlines while awaiting a break in the weather

discover that the TV in the front office at our flying service has a VCR attached. Davo returns from the video store with an armload of soft-core pornography, and suddenly, flying us to the mountain takes on a new sense of urgency.

"I don't care if there's a hurricane up there," I overhear the owner's wife hiss at him. "Get these guys out of here!" When at last the skies begin to clear, we are on the first flight out.

Basecamp at 7200 feet on the Southeast Fork of the Kahiltna Glacier strikes me as a peculiar place. The icy landing strip is marked out with wands, sandbags, and hordes of wildly waving climbers who rush forward as soon as our plane touches down. I feel a bit like MacArthur returning to the Philippines. These people, however, don't want to shake my hand—they want my airplane. The bad weather has stranded a number of returning expeditions, many of whom are running desperately low on food. As countless emaciated arms eagerly pull our equipment from the plane, I speculate that this may be the only place on Earth where you could trade a cheeseburger for a Rolex. One of the first things Davo does is to cache beer, whiskey, and a ham to safeguard our own return.

The Southeast Fork drops nearly 500 feet from the landing strip before joining the main body of the Kahiltna Glacier. There's irony in the fact that the 13,100-foot climb up the *West Buttress* of Denali begins as a downhill ski run. The Kahiltna itself is quite a spectacle. Nearly two miles across, this massive river of ice is the major thoroughfare for climbers headed "up the Butt." We have elected to traverse it at night, hoping the snow blanketing the Kahiltna's myriad crevasses will be more firm then. In June near the

The awe-inspiring mass of Denali dominates the view during the flight to basecamp

Arctic Circle, however, it is a fine line between night and day, and we find the going pretty mushy, even in the dusky twilight at 2 a.m.

The *West Buttress* is famous for the novel and dubiously equipped characters it attracts, and we are not disappointed. In the middle of a heavily crevassed minefield, a lone Japanese woman materializes from around a corner. She is poked through the middle of a 20-foot aluminum ladder like the bolt on a propeller, the theory being that if the trapdoor over a hidden crack suddenly opens beneath her, the ladder will bridge the gap. I shudder—some of the crevasses out here are over a hundred feet wide. Even with a smaller crevasse, if one end of the ladder comes up short, down in the narrows this bus-length metal skirt will fold around her like scissors. I want to ask her if the contraption has actually worked, but I'm afraid to say anything lest she turn and wipe us all out.

ONE OF OUR initial camps is near the mouth of the Northeast Fork of the Kahiltna—the entrance to the so-called "Valley of Death." We can see footprints entering the gorge, left by parties headed for the *West Rib* and *Cassin Ridge* routes. We can also hear the grumble of avalanches emanating from this corridor like the gurgle of a giant's stomach. Or could it be one of us? We have made a horrendous miscalculation concerning our food supply. To save money, we bought all our freeze-dried rations from the same manufacturer, and have discovered that no matter what the labels say, every meal tastes the same. To make matters worse, we were seduced into overstocking one particular entree that read like something off the menu at the Ritz: "A delicious pasta dish featuring a delicate blend of white-meat turkey and garden-fresh herbs in a rich sour-cream alfredo sauce." In fact, the stuff is turkey mac and cheese, and we're doomed to eat it almost every other night. Although we don't admit it to one another, we are all already dreaming about that ham buried at basecamp.

Despite our culinary crisis all the links seem to be holding together. By this time, we've seen at least one expedition turn tail and run away. Whether it was group disharmony or the sheer magnitude of the mountain itself that defeated them I cannot say, but we're doing OK on both counts. Maybe Davo seems a little overwhelmed by the surroundings, and perhaps Dave is a little slow to rise in the mornings, but we're moving forward, and we're still a long way from throwing any punches.

Four more days of hauling loads and sitting out storms brings us to the uppermost reaches of the Kahiltna and the steep headwall known as Motorcycle Hill. A number of expeditions are camped in the protected bowl beneath this slope, and it is here that we encounter another serious threat to our morale. Reading material is a valuable commodity on Denali; during prolonged storms, a book can mean the difference between staring at a tent label or escaping into another world. Beneath Motorcycle Hill someone trades us a seemingly innocuous detective novel. We soon discover, however, that this is the most evil book since Hitler's family album. The plot itself is benign—a typical potboiler—but the protagonist is a New York City Chief of Detectives whose sole purpose in life other than solving crimes seems to be inventing big, sloppy, mouthwatering sandwiches and eating them over the sink. Being condemned to freeze-dried gruel was bad enough; now we must endure the details of "cold roast beef, pickle relish, sliced onions, with a little pink horseradish, slices of canned Argentine corned beef with a layer of sauerkraut, slathered with Dijon mustard, all jammed into an onion roll the size of a Frisbee."

A few more days of toiling up snowslopes takes us around Windy Corner and beneath the walls of the West Buttress itself. At the head of this basin, we crest a rise and are confronted with the unique spectacle of the 14,300-foot camp—Denali's capital city. Dozens of tents and igloos are congregated around the box-shaped ranger Quonset like medieval hovels surrounding a cathedral. We set up home in a cozy suburb on the edge of town. Major tourist attractions include getting your blood-oxygen level tested, visiting the throne-like latrine, watching ant-like climbers ferry loads up the mighty Headwall, and of course the mountain itself. Before this, Denali's upper peak had been hidden from view, but at 14,300 feet it dominates. It is clear by the way he keeps trying to stare the summit down that Davo—normally a dominating presence in his own right—is feeling intimidated. Like any large, cornered animal, he appears to be trying to make up his mind whether to charge or bolt.

A STORM keeps us pinned in camp for nearly a week, making us all anxious and irritable, and allowing ample time for any uncertainties to fully incubate. And when it finally clears we find an entirely new stress to yank our chain. The first inkling comes when Dave wakes us up wondering, "Do you guys think it seems darker than before?"

"Probably clouds," one of us mumbles.

"I don't think so," Dave persists. "There's something weird going on." He crawls outside to investigate, and quickly summons us all on deck with the urgent suggestion, "You guys better get out here and look at this."

Denali is bathed in a subdued, yellowish light and the snowy mass of Mount Foraker—normally a gleaming pyramid—is mantled with what appears to be a layer of gray dirt.

As we ponder this surreal scenery, another climber, radio in hand, wanders over with an explanation. "There's been a volcanic eruption near Anchorage," he informs us. "The wind is carrying the ash this way, and there's talk about evacuating the mountain."

Everyone in camp gathers at the Quonset, and a ranger explains, "Ash on the glaciers means the planes can't land. So far, we've been lucky, the Southwest Fork and everything east of the Kahiltna is pretty clean. But we don't know what the volcano or the winds are going to do next. To play it safe we're pulling out the basecamp as well as our camp here. You have the option of descending now and flying out in the next day or so, or continuing and taking your chances."

This is a serious development; no basecamp means no daily weather reports, no flight out, and, with all reference points for locating our cache removed, no ham. It is also the capstone for Davo's mounting anxieties. "Tell you what, guys, this is high enough for me," he declares. "I'm satisfied just to have made it here. If you two want to try for the summit, I'll wait for you here."

I fear we may have found our weak link.

Dave and I are pretty clear we want this expedition to continue (the concept of possibly having to walk back to civilization is so incomprehensible that we simply ignore it), but leaving Davo behind is a bad idea for logistical reasons—food, fuel, etc. Mostly, however, it is a bad idea because Davo is well within his abilities on this climb, only his inexperience is nurturing failure. I have been in Davo's shoes—every climber has. In the mountains misgivings can quickly turn to dread and a fundamental part of the struggle is not to surrender a climb to these feelings. Davo is healthy, well equipped, and has the skills to meet this challenge—if he turns back now he will always regret it. But to convince Davo, I need to communicate in his terms. So I remind him of a favorite quotation, a pearl of wisdom from a former vice-president that has become our expedition motto: "If we do not succeed, we run the risk of failure."

Gray dawn at 14,300 feet; volcanic ash blankets the slopes of Mt. Foraker

Davo squints as he mulls this over, and finally grins. "OK, you can't really argue with that, now can you?"

The Headwall above the 14,300-foot camp is supposed to be the technical crux of the route, but fixed ropes have reduced the difficulties to a long, steep stair climb. The altitude, however, is beginning to take a toll. On the day Davo and I make a carry up the Headwall, Dave is confined to his tent with headache and nausea. Several days later we all climb the Headwall, and then push on up the spectacular rocky ridge leading to the 17,200-foot camp. Three thousand feet of altitude gain leaves us all wasted. Dave stumbles around trying to set up a tent, Davo is back to mumbling his "high enough for me" mantra, and I am puking up green bile. That evening, while the Chief of Detectives dines on an international sandwich of Norwegian brisling sardines in Italian olive oil heaped on German swarzbrot with a layer of thinly sliced Spanish onion and a dollop of French dressing, we choke down turkey mac for the third week in a row.

OUR SECOND DAY at 17,200 feet is the day we should go for the top. The weather is fine, but after moving around a little, I'm still feeling the altitude and want to wait a day. Davo also likes the idea of more time to acclimatize, but Dave is restless. He wanders off to visit some other climbers, and returns with a proposition. "I'll wait until tomorrow if you guys want me to, but there's another group going up today that will let me rope with them."

It isn't fair to make him wait. Although the weather seems settled at the moment, storms can spring up on Denali at any time. If this happens, it is

Climbers ascending fixed ropes up the Headwall, the steepest terrain on the West Buttress

doubtful we have enough food to linger here until the next fine spell. After coming so far together, I'm saddened at the prospect of separating the links, but waiting for us—even a day—could cost Dave his only opportunity to go to the top. We wish him good luck and soon he is tied in with four teenagers from California and heading up.

Davo and I spend the day reading, rehydrating, wondering about Dave and watching for his return. Some welcome news reaches us via the radio: The volcano seems to have shot its wad and Denali basecamp is back in business. That evening, even better news arrives as Dave stumbles safely back into camp. He is exhausted, but elated: He has summited Denali. As we brew him hot drinks he fills us in on every detail, including the news from back home in Minnesota—one of the California kids had a radio-phone, and Dave called his parents from the summit.

EARLY THE NEXT MORNING, Davo and I set off in hot pursuit of Dave's trail and his euphoria. The primary obstacle is the steep slope leading from the 17,200-foot camp to Denali Pass. This has been the scene of numerous falls and fatalities, and it could hardly be engineered to better facilitate disaster. The angle varies between 30 and 45 degrees, the surface alternates from soft snow to glare ice, and the runout terminates in giant crevasses. Davo and I are pleased to see that a guided party has tackled the face before us—pleased because they have installed pickets at intervals across the entire quarter-mile traverse that will greatly ease and safeguard our passage. I resolve to try to get in front of this group before they can return to reclaim their equipment so we might also enjoy this luxury on the way down.

Despite the fixed anchors, the climb to Denali Pass is long, exposed and taxing, and by the time I get there a biting wind is smacking me around like a playground bully. I am not surprised when Davo announces he is ready to throw in the towel. "You know," he shouts over the gale, "this is high enough for me. I never thought I'd get this far."

"What's the problem, Davo?"

"My feet are freezing—can't feel my toes. I think I should go down."

I'm certain the motivation to retreat is mostly in his head, but if his toes are numb, we need to do something about it. The first step is to get him out of the wind and moving around a little to restore some circulation. The quickest way to do that is to climb up a little farther.

"Here's the deal," I shout at him, "I think we'll be out of the wind higher up." I point towards a granite outcropping. "Let's try to get to those rocks. If you still can't feel your toes by then, we'll go down. OK?"

To his credit, even when his bags are packed, he's paid for his ticket, and he's seated on the bus, Davo is still willing to negotiate. "OK," he agrees, "let's give it a shot."

Plowing forward, we thread our way up the ridge above the pass. Remarkably, the wind does ease off and the climbing is a straightforward plod, although at one point we have to pull on some fixed ropes to get past an icy, exposed section. Finally we reach the outcrop.

"How are your feet?" I ask, bracing myself for disappointment.

I think the answer surprises us both. "Not bad," he admits. "I got a little scared going up those ropes back there, and it seems to have warmed me up!" Despite enough drugs in our med kit to raise the dead, good old-fashioned adrenaline has saved the day. With a renewed sense of purpose and hope, we return to the grind.

Several hours later we finally catch up with the guided party at the Football Field, the broad plateau at 19,500 feet. We are all in the homestretch, the summit lies only 800 feet above us. Davo and I grin at each other with relief—we *know* the peak is ours.

And then, without warning, the chain snaps.

I actually feel the warmth and vitality draining from my body; it is as if my feet are anchored to some massive conductor that is sucking the heat and energy out through my legs. Waves of nausea pound me. I go down for the count, crumpling into the snow, gasping for breath.

Davo is stunned. Seeing me suddenly sprawled out on the ground is a completely unexpected development. "What are you doing?" he demands, and then the concern in his voice becomes palpable. "What's the matter with you?"

"Sick…" I gasp.

"Are you sure?" he asks, still trying to comprehend the situation. "What does that mean? Can you climb?!"

It is like asking a man who has just been run over by a train if he can walk—there's really no point in even considering another answer: "No."

Davo contemplates our situation. We have sleeping bags and a stove. He could try to warm me up and get some liquids into me with hopes that I might perk up and be able to continue. On the other hand, any kind of delay means that the guided group is likely to pass us going down, stripping their gear from the Denali Pass headwall as they go. Crossing that precipitous slope without the security of the fixed anchors is not something Davo is eager to attempt; doing it while dragging a crippled partner isn't even an option.

The words are familiar, but infused with decisive finality. "You know," he says, "this is high enough for me—I'm really happy to have gone this far."

My eyes roll toward the summit ridge. A sinister-looking cloud is boiling around up there, obscuring the final peak. The hardest part, of course, is the realization that due to my incapacity, Davo will not summit. Even in my sickened state, I am conscious of the final cruel irony of this expedition:

Despite all my experience, and my partners' relative lack of it, on the day that mattered, at the critical point in the climb, the weak link, the piece that failed, the part that broke—was me. Failure, it seems, is born of both inexperience and bad luck.

THE RETURN to civilization is made awkward by the question of what exactly was accomplished by our expedition, and how to answer the inevitable: "So, did you make it?"

I find I need to qualify the question. Do I know what it's like to have climbed Denali? Without a doubt. Do I know what it's like to stand upon the ultimate pinnacle of that lofty peak? Sadly, I do not—and like Belmore Browne, this is the experience that will forever haunt me and set me apart from, and slightly beneath, the others who have trod those few remaining steps.

But Dave made it there, and so our expedition was a success. Sometimes a chain is stronger than its weakest link.

Don't shed any tears for me, however. I didn't know it as I disconsolately picked my way back down the slopes of Denali, but my moment in the sun was coming. Shortly after returning from Alaska I attended a party where I inadvertently took a shot from a paintball pistol point-blank in the testicles. In that life-changing moment, I achieved more lasting celebrity among my peers than if I had hopped the final distance to the summit of Denali on one hand. In an age when "brave" and "ballsy" are synonymous, I became a true hero, lifted onto the shoulders of my comrades and paraded about in triumph—on top of the world at last. I am unsure whether the roaring in my ears was the result of my own screaming, my cheering admirers, or the sound of Belmore Browne turning in his grave.

Originally published in CLIMBING, *No. 179, 1998.*

Beneath the exquisite headwall of the Lotus Flower Tower (V, 5.10c)

TRIAL BY FIRE

Human Devolution Below the Lotus Flower Tower

*C*ANADA IS BURNING, threatening to send us up in flames with it. If we somehow escape being roasted alive, we run a fair risk of being torn apart by bears or dying of starvation or killing each other over the remaining food scraps. Needless to say, there's a lot of uncertainty at the moment, but the one thing I'm sure of is that despite having just completed what is likely the best climb of its grade in the world, our trip is unraveling at the seams.

What has brought me and my climbing partner Dave to this remote corner of the Northwest Territories is the flawless, sweeping shaft of the Lotus Flower Tower. Like something out of Tolkien's Middle Earth, this gray monolith looms at the head of the Cirque of the Unclimbables with a form so striking it seems impossible that it's merely a product of random geology. For climbers, the main attraction is a single, legendary fissure that runs the length of the 2000-foot tower, varying in size from a chimney on the lower section to a perfect hand and finger crack splitting the 10-pitch headwall. In addition, darker inclusions in the snowy granite have weathered into weird blobs of texture—like bolted-on artificial holds—allowing this amazing line to be free climbed at 5.10. As an aficionado of moderate cracks, I have lusted after the Lotus Flower Tower ever since seeing the photos in *Fifty Classic Climbs of North America* from the 1968 first ascent by Bill McCarthy, Tom Frost, and Sandy Bill. Now, after finally realizing the dream, I should be in a state of euphoria. Instead, I am in what we from the Midwest call "a pickle."

Our current situation is not directly related to the Lotus Flower Tower. The route was everything I imagined it would be and, by electing to do it in late August, at the end of the climbing season, Dave and I had this world-class attraction practically to ourselves. But now we are the only party left in the Cirque, which means that there is no one else to share our predicament, resources, or even just some conversation to take our minds off the fact that we are engulfed in smoke.

"...the haze filtering into the Cirque grew progressively thicker."

During the long flight into the Cirque, we'd had ample opportunity to survey the massive fires raging unchecked across the Canadian wilderness. For over a hundred miles we'd flown with noses pressed to the windows of our chartered floatplane, gaping in awe at the charred, ashy swaths and flickering walls of orange flames unfolding beneath us. After looking down on so much blackened devastation, it had been a relief to swoop in for a landing amidst pristine green hillsides surrounding the small glacial lake beneath the Cirque of the Unclimbables. In the days that followed, however, as we made our approach hike, climb, and descent, the haze filtering into the Cirque grew progressively thicker. But we never imagined that by our floatplane pick-up date, visibility would have dropped to less than a few hundred feet. A boomerang couldn't find its way back to us in this murk, never mind an airplane.

Considering the fact that we are now essentially marooned in a distant and inaccessible corner of the planet, Dave seems remarkably unconcerned. Squinting into the acrid haze he declares, "This stuff will move out once the wind picks up." I'm not sure we've got that kind of time. We haven't seen more than a breath of wind in two weeks. I'm also worried that where there's smoke, there's fire. But the most pressing concern is starvation. Not wanting to hump a lot of excess provisions around the Cirque, nor stash any surplus food at the lake where it would be a bear magnet, our supplies for this trip were calculated down to the minute. Now that the game has gone into overtime, Dave and I find that we have exactly 10 one-cup packets of instant oatmeal between us.

It would be a shame to be mauled by a grizzly over such meager rations, so I set about rigging a (tiny) hanging bag in a distant pine. In doing so, I burn more calories than I've cached. And I find there is more than hunger gnawing at my stomach. Panic is also a bear; lurking, ready to roar in without a moment's warning and rip everything to shreds. At the moment, I'm not sure which is the bigger threat: the bears in these woods, or the one in my belly.

We've placed our camp on a gravel bar where a stream empties into the lake. The surrounding forest is so choked with deadfall, alder, and wild rose that we practically need dynamite to go take a crap, and so we are pretty much confined to this 30-foot strip of open beach. The lines are quickly drawn. Dave, who is by nature a solitary person, retreats into the tent, where he spends long hours—which soon stretch into days—reading, napping, and conserving his energy. I, on the other hand, spend my days relentlessly pacing the beach. Thick clouds of mosquitoes are my only companions as I endlessly troll a bit of second-hand fishing line through the cold, still waters of the lake. This activity is less a pathetic attempt to catch food as it is a way to keep my mind occupied.

As time grinds slowly by, I'm having a harder and harder time keeping the internal bear at bay. I am convinced that our pilot has either crashed in the smoke or been forced to abandon us to find our own way out of the wilderness. But that's not an option—we don't even have a map. And even if there was a paved trail leading out of here, the entire region is ringed in flames. In fact, squinting in any direction, I'm almost certain I can detect a flickering orange glow behind the dark veil of ash.

Suddenly, the line jerks tight in my hands. After 10,000 fruitless casts, nobody could be more astonished than I am that I've actually hooked a fish—unless it's the fat arctic grayling that I tug onto the rocks. All my wimpish panic suddenly dissolves, as the caveman buried deep in my collective unconscious bubbles to the surface: I can survive here, I have a fish. With the energy I will take from this animal, I will hunt others. I will make snares from fishing line to throttle the fat geese feeding in the reeds across the bay. I will hide in wait for the bull moose that occasionally swims the inlet, leap upon its back, and ride it into deep water where I will finish it off with a homemade spear. I may even kill a bear, not because I have to, but because—dammit—*I* am king of this forest!

"What's going on out there?" I hear Dave call from the tent. His curiosity has been roused by the sound of the flopping fish. *My* fish. My eyes narrow. Dave is as hungry as I am, yet he hasn't lifted a finger to try to find food—he's barely left the tent in days. *What's he been plotting in there?* My mind fixes on visions of rugby-team-in-the-Andes-type cannibalistic horrors. I feel an urgent need to start sharpening my spear. But primal drums aren't the only things banging around between my ears. I also hear a curious buzzing sound. I swat at the bugs, but the noise only gets louder. And then, like Tarzan getting his first glimpse of New York City, I watch dumb-founded as a floatplane emerges from the gloom and skims up onto the gravel next to our tent.

As the pontoons leave the surface of the lake, so does the bear clawing in my gut. The primitive urges and instincts have retreated back into the Neanderthal recesses of my brain. Soon enough I'll be steaming in a hot shower, and then sinking my teeth into some anonymous meat that I will have happily played no part in stalking, killing, or cooking. Just before the plane is swallowed up inside the thick currents of smoke, I catch one final glimpse into the Cirque of the Unclimbables, where the natural order has been restored. Once again, the grizzly bear is king of the forest, and the mosquito is lord of the flies.

Originally published in CLIMBING, *No. 215, 2002.*

Author's note: For readers who are disappointed that this story didn't include a pitch-by-pitch account of climbing the Lotus Flower Tower, I can only say that writing such a thing is beyond me. I've never encountered another route like it: a climb so unvarying in character that it utterly confounds colorful narrative. The granite cracks and surreal knobs define uniformity—and perfection. Climbing the headwall on the LFT is like eating your favorite dessert until you're sick. It is one enormously transcendent and euphoric feast. See what I mean? My thesaurus only has so many synonyms for "glorious."

The view from midway up pitch 15 on the Lotus Flower Tower

Something rotten in the state of Utah: the moldering edifice of the Titan

THE BIG NASTY
Dirty Tricks on the Titan

*A*CT 1 - *NO JOY IN MUDVILLE*

It is Halloween, and the Titan is wearing the scariest costume I've seen. Robed in flowing red curtains of sandstone, and topped with a solid helmet of brown caprock, the 900-foot formation presents a magnificent edifice—perhaps the tallest and certainly the proudest free-standing desert spire on Earth. Upon closer inspection, however, it is clear that both it and the surrounding Fisher Towers are only masquerading as pieces of substantial geology. In fact, the region's sweeping folds and fantastic contours are an artful disguise: muddy cloaks with less resistance to weathering than a sand castle to an ocean wave.

The most frightening aspect of this imposture is my belay one pitch up the Titan's *Finger of Fate*. Among the half-dozen fixed anchors that have been knit together to create this hanging stance, there is not a single one with greater holding power than Velcro. The assemblage includes three ancient bolts half-weathered from their holes, several cocked and down-angling pitons buried in mud, and something that looks like a tied-off nail. Only the sheer quantity of the bad protection keeps me from wetting my pants.

And then it starts to rain.

I HAVE BEEN drawn to the Fisher Towers to experience the unique. I have climbed rock, I have climbed ice, and I have climbed mountains. But I have never climbed mud.

In the spring of 1962, the legendary Layton Kor teamed with Huntley Ingalls, who had struck a deal with *National Geographic* to document the conquest, and George Hurley, who so "enjoyed" the route he returned four years later to bag the second ascent. Doubtlessly, Kor was attracted by the tower's awesome size, although—if the stories are true—he relished the crappy rock as well.

Over the course of two consecutive weekends, Kor's team nailed and clawed at the Titan's dirt-filled cracks and bulging mud formations. Kor placed over 50 bolts, most of them during the final two days, a testimony to the tower's pitiful rock: Hand drilling that many bolts in granite would have occupied a week. Finally, with eyes inflamed from wind-blown grit, with nerves and gear nearly worn to the breaking point, the climbers topped out. Their route, dubbed the *Finger of Fate* after a prominent gendarme at half height, was a milestone in American desert climbing. But, despite the booming popularity of tower-bagging after this ascent, the Titan was only repeated an average of once a year for the next decade. The horrendous rock and the fact that the climb had given up only 200 feet a day to the likes of Layton Kor, had forged a fearsome reputation. Put simply, the Titan was, and to a large extent still is, a dirty word to most climbers.

I admit that this was part of the attraction. I had grown weary of the hordes infesting the "classic" rock climbs, and was seeking something less mainstream. I also reasoned that 35 years of subsequent ascents and an arsenal of modern climbing widgets would make the route as straightforward as it would be uncrowded.

But, the effects of three-and-a-half decades of weathering on bolts placed in rock the consistency of a Pop Tart never entered my thinking. Now, as I hightail it down ropes anchored to these eroding artifacts, this thought dominates.

The storm quickly develops into a deluge; sheets of rain fall so hard that once we finally make it back to the parking lot and start the van, the windshield wipers are so completely overwhelmed that they give up. I know how they feel.

ACT 2 - MUTT AND JEFF

The following spring I discover that the real crux of climbing the Titan may be finding a partner. My previous partner is unavailable, and the seasoned climbers I approach all behave as if they owe me money: ducking out when they see me coming, refusing to return my phone calls, and spewing excuses when I finally pin them down. One cites business commitments—but promptly leaves on a kayak trip. Another has family concerns: His wife let him climb the Eiger but doesn't want him going anywhere near the Titan.

I finally decide I'm going about this all wrong. Experience be damned; what I need is someone strong and fit, but with only a dim concept of what's to come. I need someone who thinks the Fisher Towers are the corporate headquarters of a nut company and the Titan is a boat that hit an iceberg. I need a young gym climber.

Jeff is 24 years old, works at the climbing gym in my hometown of Duluth, and is honed. He is yin to my yang, and I am delighted to discover that his enthusiastic mantra to almost any climbing proposition—including the Titan—is "Right on!"

The sum of its parts; a typical Titan belay anchor

Jeff is not totally clueless, however. He spends nearly the entire drive from Minnesota to Utah studying a book on self-rescue techniques.

ACT 3 - THE FISHER KING

I learned some things about the Titan during my aborted climb the previous year. For example, I know that the trail sign in the parking lot that reads "Titan: 1 mile" is as misleading as a government statistic. True, a mile of contouring along the various canyons and lesser Fisher Towers brings Jeff and me to a marvelous overlook beneath the west face of the monolith, but at this point the real approach has only just begun. To reach the start of Kor's route we must hike entirely around the Titan in an enormous, circuitous loop. The consolation is that while circumnavigating the spire we get a glimpse into the half-brilliant, half-whacked minds of the Fisher Tower pioneers. Tottering under our heavy packs, we pause to scope one of the most impressive lines, the *Sundevil Chimney*.

Like a split log, the *Sundevil* cleaves the south face of the Titan as a single, tapering fracture. The route was spearheaded by the prolific desert climber Harvey T. Carter, who had hoped to make the first ascent of the Titan, but was astounded to discover that Kor's team had beaten him to the prize. In 1969 Carter returned to drill the vainglorious direct-start bolt ladder to the *Finger,* but it wasn't until 1971, when he established the *Sundevil Chimney* that he got his just compensation.

Jeff and I also contemplate the nebulous line of *World's End,* Jim Beyer's solo A5 effort to the right of the *Sundevil.* The topo for this climb is covered with so many asterisks you'd swear it's the most recommended route in the world—until you realize the stars mark bad bolts. The gear list from the first ascent indicates that Beyer placed 20 RURPs in this fudge; it's no wonder he had to do the thing alone. We shudder and move on.

The final scramble to the base of our route crosses a steep and insecure dirt slope above a seemingly bottomless pit. I remember this spot from the previous year, when I named it the "Traverse of Death." I wobble across in my big pack, pawing at the soil with both hands and feet. Jeff seems barely conscious of the exposure or the insecurity, and traipses across like a goat. He even pauses midway to take my picture. I try to play it cool, but I wouldn't stop here for the last beer on Earth.

Finally, we're at the start of the climb, where we discover that we've brought enough cams, pins, and other hardware to outfit half a dozen parties. It's hard to know what to leave behind since the crack here is packed with mud. About the only thing I can toss aside with any confidence is an antique set of giant Hexes.

From the first second that I touch the rock, I am engaged in a grim and grimy struggle. Every surface is coated with a sticky layer of red soil, and my slightest movement releases a cascade of grit. The bulging crack that starts the route seems relatively solid, but is so troweled and spattered with mud that it could grow carrots. Each time I reach to a hold I feel as if I'm clawing my way out of a grave. Naturally, the only good pro placements I encounter are wide constrictions that would have swallowed big Hexes.

After 20 feet I flop onto a rounded ledge, where I can catch my breath and let the dust settle. It is on this precarious stance that I decide that free climbing this stuff is like asking for a punch in the face. I whip out the aiders and start mining for placements.

By the time I reach the belay I've endured a full rope length of unpleasantries. My nose is clogged, my knees are shredded, and I've weathered a particularly tense moment when the nut supporting me suddenly skittered six inches through the crack, only to hang up on a button of mud the size of a Hershey Kiss.

Jeff has been eager to lead, but I detect a quiver in his enthusiasm when he confronts the next pitch. The crack for this next section has sealed up, and all he has to work with are a couple of circular pin scars that look as though they were drilled with an ice screw. Normally, I'd take perverse pleasure in watching a younger, fitter partner squirm, but if Jeff falls, he'll drop like a sack of bricks right onto the motley collection of belay anchors.

Jeff fiddles around with the pins until he finally manages to plug one of the holes. I grimace as he tests the piece. Whatever he's done, however, seems to be working. I'm impressed—you don't learn something like that climbing indoors. As he continues a steady stream of sand rains on my head, where my helmet amplifies it into a hissing buzz like mindless radio static.

I am jolted out of my stupor by the rope reeling through my belay plate. For a moment I am certain Jeff has come off, but then realize that the line is being pulled out in steady tugs. Evidently, Jeff has reached a section where the crack has opened up and, a true child of the gym, has decided to go free climbing.

Confused, I check our topo. Nothing free is indicated on this pitch. I look up at Jeff—he is 20 feet beyond his last piece of gear. Hmm…maybe I should join a gym.

Later, as I clean the pitch, I marvel at the lad's courage. Clutching and jamming up this crumbling crack took a pretty cool cat, but he appears to have used up a few lives on some of the aid. I clean a ladder of down-sloping pins with my bare hands.

Though it's still relatively early in the afternoon, our plan is to rappel and call it quits for the day. We've combined four of Kor's original pitches into two long leads and are just under the fateful Finger itself, nearly halfway to the summit, but there are some weird looking traverses ahead. We'll want a full day to deal with the complexities of the Titan's upper ridge. Our spirits are high as we start down the fixed lines. It's hard to imagine anything, short of rain and lightning, that can keep us from standing on top of the Titan tomorrow.

ACT 4 - RAIN AND LIGHTNING

In my dreams, the sand pouring onto my helmet sounds like water drumming on sheet metal. It's an oddly comforting rhythm—until I realize I'm not asleep. A steady rain is beating the roof of the van like a timpani.

At this time of year, the desert is normally dominated by unrelenting sunshine. But there is nothing normal about the Fisher Towers. In fact, they owe their creation—or more properly, their destruction—to a relatively wet climate. The culprits are the La Sal mountains, a compact range of 12,000-foot peaks situated just to the south. The snow-capped La Sals are an incongruous sight, juxtaposed above the parched desert sands of the Canyonlands. But they are a moisture magnet, concentrating and draining precious precipitation from the lofty currents of the atmosphere. Much of the year, this precipitation develops as massive thunderstorms, centered on the mountains, but enough nasty, wet stuff lingers on the fringes and gives the Fisher Towers regular beatings—lightning licks at the ice-cream formations, while the rain bonds with silt grains to create the thick muds that ooze and drip like dark frosting down the dissolving towers. No time to be climbing the Titan.

By evening all hell has broken loose. Thunder is cannoning, there's enough rain to drown Noah, and the Titan is looking more and more like a soft, wet dog turd.

ACT 5 - PAY DIRT

The following morning dawns damp and dreary, but, for the moment, the rain has stopped. Low, heavy clouds have banked up against the entire Colorado Plateau and a ragged drizzle is visible to the south. Neither Jeff nor I are excited about climbing in these conditions, but this weather is clearly part of a prolonged system that is packing a lot of moisture. If we don't polish off the Titan soon, we may not get another chance. Not long after first light, we begin the approach.

Beneath the west face of the Titan we pause to consider our route, now visible as the upper left skyline. Even silhouetted against such a dismal sky, it is easy to trace our intended path, a ragged warbonnet of lumps and pinnacles that gradually rise to meet the awesome summit ridge, a dorsal fin of sandstone crowned by overhanging caprock. This straightforward line stands in marked contrast to the other routes on the face. *Scheherazade*, a

Jeff ascending the fixed ropes

product of Lou Dawson and Harvey Carter's disturbed imaginations, incorporates 11 pitches of hard free and aid up a rib that was so eroded the team had to wrap the bolts with tape to hold them in place. The truly imaginary *Naked Lunch,* a wild Duane Raleigh/Pete Takeda creation, links fragile features on the Titan's steep southern keel. Its first ascent introduced a new bag of tricks to the Fisher Towers: ice tools and lariats.

When we finally reach our fixed lines we are amazed to find that the rock is almost completely dry. Kor, in his wisdom, couldn't have chosen a more user-friendly line, sheltered from both the hot sun and prevailing rains.

I, on the other hand, have not made a wise choice by electing to jumar behind Jeff. He's kicking down a lot of loose debris. Just below the belay I find that all our bouncing has gnawed a disconcerting white patch into the lead rope. I can't help feeling like the *Finger of Fate* has just flipped me off.

The route description refers to the next pitch as the "Scary Traverse," but at a glance it seems to hold little terror. I shuffle horizontally across airy footholds and then onto a sloping shelf, where I reach out and clip a bolt at the very lip of an overhang. With a renewed sense of security I lean back and face my protection. The bolt is positively prehistoric and a fair portion

115

of the rock underneath its hanger has eroded away. The scare-o-meter is pegged in the red—there's only one way to surmount the overhang, I must dangle from the bolt.

Whimpering like a slapped hound I clip an aider to the bolt and ease into position. It holds. I move up a step. It holds. I clip a fifi-hook just beneath the stud and sit on it. It holds! This is such a miracle that I half expect to see the Virgin Mary in the oxidation patterns of the rusted hanger.

My problems, however, are far from over. The hairline crack above sports two pin scars the size of gopher holes, and the largest pins we've brought are barely field mice. I manage to bypass the first cavity by getting the tip of a baby angle into the crack and tying it off, but I now consider the crappy bolt to be my good piece.

I'm not so lucky with the second scar. Into it I desperately stuff my biggest angle. It rattles around like a nail in a tin can. I shove a second pin beside it. Then a third. And a fourth. A few hammer taps on this last pin cause the whole arrangement to shim up tightly. I regard the cluster with dread: This would be an excellent grouping for darts, but is not something I want to stand on. I tie off the entire lot and commit my weight. I can almost feel the angels supporting me.

The stack gets me to a good hand jam, and a short squeeze chimney later I am straddling a mud formation behind the upturned Finger of Fate. We have unlocked the door to the upper ridge of the Titan.

Jeff's pitch is a short but nasty offwidth. Watching him thrash inside the grungy flare, tennis shoes scraping on the flaking mud, I'm afraid the route is beating the hell out of him. But the minute he reaches the belay he grins and shouts, "Man, what a great pitch!" I'm thinking this kid wouldn't mind falling down a well because it would give him the chance to climb back out again.

Jeff's belay is situated at the base of a gigantic duck-shaped mud ball perched atop the ridge and held in place by a fragile nest of rock chips and clay. Gingerly, I make an exposed traverse around the massive mud hen— I don't dare disturb its tenuous roost by trying to place protection. A squalid chimney choked with filth is the final obstacle before the belay ledge. About the time I finish worming through this foul crevice, the first growls of thunder begin.

Peering anxiously to the south I see that the sky around the La Sals is black. With any luck, the really bad weather will hang close to the mountains, but I vow that if lightning comes anywhere near the Titan, I'm going to send our pin rack screaming into the void. My spacious ledge is the site where the first-ascent party endured a blustery bivouac. We never considered spending the night up here, mostly because of horror stories we've heard about climbers being feasted upon by blood-sucking beetles and poisonous spiders.

The "Mud Duck" formation, roosted high on the Titan

Jeff doesn't waste time taking over the lead. Just around the corner he's discovered a crack filled with fixed gear, and is moving so rapidly that, for a moment, I wonder if he is practicing those gym moves again. Soon he's on a bolt ladder below the belay, having led the entire pitch with just a rack of biners and draws. His stance is a tiny triangular crow's nest high on the boney spine of Mudasaurus Rex.

The anchors suck, but we've grown remarkably indifferent to bad gear, and I'm more concerned about the weather. Thunder is banging through the canyons like a funeral drum, and there is moisture in the air.

I launch up the final pitch aiming for the first in a long series of antique bolts. It's a good thing most of my carabiners are also museum pieces because Jeff's fancy new sport biners are too fat to slip through the old hangers. The bolts themselves protrude from the rock as if the Titan is trying to spit them out. But these bolts haven't been extruded; they have been exposed. Three-and-a-half decades after Kor banged them home, the Titan has shed about a half-inch of its skin. At this rate, 35 years from now these bolts will be gone.

Right now I'm wishing I was gone. Layton Kor was a tall man—but my dimensions extend along a different axis, and I am having to make dicey free moves between each of his anchors. After each hair-raising move, there is only the hollow reward of another weathered stud.

At last, however, I am confronting the overhanging bulge of the cap-rock. A wide crack breaches this obstacle and in my zeal to finally get solid protection I plug in enough cams for a belay. Dangling and spinning from the lip of the skyscraper, I strain to clip one final, agonizingly distant bolt in the vertical face of the caprock. My feeble abs scream as time and again my groping biner fumbles against the spinning bolt hanger. And then I have it. I practically yank the thing from its hole in my enthusiastic scramble to the final belay.

Jeff arrives just as thunder detonates near our heads, but we both agree that we have come too far to be denied the summit. We make a mad dash up a short blocky slope and tag the high point. For the first time since leaving the ground we have a view toward the advancing weather, and it takes only a glance to know we are screwed. An angry curtain of thick rain has already engulfed nearby Castle Valley and is steadily swallowing all the other landmarks to the west. Even before we can get back to our ropes, it swallows us as well.

LATER, LONG AFTER the gritty ropes have been cleaned and coiled, and the sticky red clays have dried and crumbled from our shoes, our descent from the Titan—despite all the wind-snarled ropes and muddy, rain-soaked rappels—seems wholly unremarkable. In the context of the constant drama that climbers are destined to experience on this amazing tower, with all its utterly unique challenges and perils, anything other than an epic descent would have been an anticlimax.

What I do find remarkable is that we climbed this thing at all. And not just because of our unlikely teaming of a paunchy traditionalist and a young disciple of plastic. I've always shied away from the notion of climbing as Russian roulette, and everything about this route—from the filthy rock to the nauseating protection—has the feel of cold steel pressed to the temple. It is no wonder that so many climbers regard the classic outline of the Titan as the sail of a plague ship—something to be avoided at all costs.

Originally published in CLIMBING, *No. 170, 1997.*

Author's note: In truth, this climb was not my idea. If memory serves, it was Duane Raleigh on the phone from Climbing *magazine: "Dave, we'd like you to write a feature about climbing the Titan."*

"Um...one problem Duane, I've never climbed the Titan."

"I see. How long will it take you to do it?"

As it turned out—after one unsuccessful attempt, two partners, three cross-country drives (one aborted after a vehicle break-down), and with storms nipping at my heels throughout—about six months. And during the three days I spent climbing on the Titan, I probably aged another year.

But even if the magazine had pulled the plug early on, I think I would have pursued the climb. Once the seed is planted, the Titan is the kind of perversely compelling objective that gets under your skin...and under your fingernails, and in your eyes, and down your shorts.

The twin summits of Mount Kenya: Batian (left) and Nelion

ZERO LATITUDE
The Equatorial Challenges of Africa's Mount Kenya

AS AN AMERICAN, I have been conditioned by innumerable KOAs, Jellystone Parks, and their like—sanitized campgrounds, turfed and pruned with cemetery-like fastidiousness—to view sod as a safe haven. On the forested slopes of East Africa's Central Highlands, however, the exact opposite is true. The occasional patch of grass is a bad place to lie down, an even worse place to camp. This is because as predisposed as I may be to bedding down on this lush green blanket, other things—things with the size, ferocity, and killing power of Panzer tanks—are equally intent upon devouring it. I am finding this out the hard way.

The deep, snuffling grunts and guttural chomping noises outside the tent are nightmarish, like foraging dinosaurs rooting for a midnight snack. Gingerly raising my head to peer out the mosquito netting, I find the reality no less terrifying. Scant inches beyond the tent door the moonlight is reflecting off masses of dark, rippling muscles and distinctive, mustachio-shaped horns. Our tent is completely surrounded by Cape buffalo, notoriously aggressive and ill-tempered beasts that my guidebook describes as "perhaps the most dangerous animals on the mountain." The sliver of green lawn where my climbing partner and I have parked for the night is ground zero in a buffalo buffet.

We have come to climb a mountain that the world pretty much ignores. At 17,058 feet, Mount Kenya reigns supreme over its own considerable plateau, over the east-central equatorial nation of Kenya, and over the entire continent of Africa—with one notable exception: It is several thousand feet lower than Kilimanjaro. Thus, although it dwarfs such celebrated peaks as the Matterhorn or Grand Teton, Mount Kenya is doomed to being perpetually overshadowed by Africa's highpoint. As such, most people, including an astonishingly high percentage of mountain climbers, know little to nothing about it. The irony is that in terms of aesthetics, substance, and technical climbing potential, Mount Kenya is the superior mountain on the continent.

The hardy remnant of a once colossal volcano (geologists speculate that the prehistoric mountain may have soared to nearly 25,000 feet above sea level), Mount Kenya juts like a rhino's horn from the African savanna. Today's mountain is, in fact, a crystalline cast of the ancient cone's molten interior. Over the millennia, the lavas and other ejected debris have eroded away, and glaciers have worked the mountain's stony core into a stupendous fortress of soaring buttresses, dogtooth spires, and serrated ridges. As a result, every aspect of the peak presents a sheer facade of excellent, rough-textured stone. Unlike its famous, snow-domed counterpart in neighboring Tanzania, there are no trekking or scrambling routes to the top of Mount Kenya. This is, to borrow a well-worn phrase, a mountaineer's mountain.

For us, just getting to the peak has been a battle. We have endured extended periods of excruciating confinement on multiple airlines as well as the death-defying liberation of Kenya's notorious roadways (local climbers have been known to wear their helmets during the three-hour demolition derby linking Nairobi with the Central Highlands). And now, on foot at last on the approach through Mount Kenya's sub-tropical forest zone, where deer the size of jackrabbits bark like guard dogs and troops of black-and-white colobus monkeys caper among the treetops, we have unwittingly placed ourselves in serious jeopardy simply by pitching our tent on flat, open ground.

Strait-jacketed inside my mummy bag, I am acutely aware that a few millimeters of nylon are all that separate me from monstrous, skull-crushing hooves. I'm afraid to move, afraid to even breathe, lest the beasts start stampeding and I die like a slug on the streets of Pamplona. Every gibbering twitter from nocturnal critters in the surrounding forest canopy causes me to wince, but the buffalo don't seem the least bit affected. In fact, it isn't until everything suddenly falls deathly quiet that all hell breaks loose. At first I'm not sure whether the ground is actually shaking, or whether my blood pressure—which by this time could peg a tire gauge—is hammering my arteries with such force that it just feels that way. And then a new sound rumbles through the African night: whole bamboo trees snapping like kindling, footfalls with the weight of toppling oil drums approaching steadily, purposefully, and with impunity through the thick forest, like a bulldozer with the throttle jammed open. The buffalo amble into the trees to give the elephant wide berth. It plows past the clearing only a stone's throw from our tent. Remarkably, my partner has slept through it all.

It is a frustrating, but inevitable fact of life that my roster of prospective climbing partners has thinned along with my hair. A shift in priorities as once dependable companions have pursued careers, started families—to use their term, "gotten lives"—has drained the pool of my contemporaries willing or able to take extended climbing vacations. For this trip, I've had to

"Um…what are you focusing on?" (black rhino below Mount Kenya)

recruit fresh talent: Dean is 15 years my junior. Thankfully, his advanced maturity meshes with my stalled adolescence making us well suited to one another. I'm also impressed (and a little envious) that he is able to doze to the point of coma in an environment teeming with oversized, marauding mammals. I may have been reduced to robbing the cradle, but this is no place for babies.

In fact, when I relate the night's harrowing details to him the next morning, Dean is dubious. But the proof is littered all over the ground, and if there's one thing a lad from Wisconsin knows when he sees it, it's a cow pie. When our porters emerge from their barracks in the nearby meteorological station they assure us that as long as we stay inside our tents at night, the forest animals are "no problem." Of course, the porters slumber inside a stone building.

DEAN AND I are developing a bit of a reputation on the mountain: the two Americans who can't seem to get out of basecamp. After our first day of walking I stalled here beside the Met Station (elevation 10,000 feet), felled by a bout of altitude sickness. Today it is Dean's turn. After hiking just a few hundred yards up the trail he begins to exhibit the same telltale signs of nausea and headache that plagued me the day before. Altitude is the bane of climbers on Mount Kenya. The mountain literally straddles the equator, where the relatively temperate conditions make it easy to forget that the summit is only a few thousand feet lower than Denali. In addition, the ready and affordable services of the local porters facilitates a rapid advance up the mountain—indeed hikers commonly attempt to ascend from the trailhead to the minor summit of 16,355-foot Point Lenana (an elevation gain of 8000 feet) over the course of a weekend. The result is that this single African mountain claims a lion's share of the world's annual cases of high-altitude pulmonary and cerebral edema, serious, life-threatening afflictions. The solution, according to sound Swahili wisdom, is to ascend Mount Kenya *pole pole* (slow-slow).

Dean and I couldn't be more *pole*. Once again we are back camping in the cow dip beside the Met Station; Dean is groaning inside the tent while I chase down and wrestle our food bag back from a large Syke's monkey who has burgled our vestibule. To the other hikers and porters in camp, our unique acclimatization program (i.e. a complete lack of upward movement) is the subject of great curiosity. Waiting out the afternoon thunderstorm under the eaves of the Met Station, I find myself trotting out our pat explanation for what seems like the thousandth go around, this time with a pair of swarthy-looking types who, despite monster packs, practically run into camp:

"You have to understand," I tell them, "that we live on the Great Plains, almost at sea level. For us, a measured pace is not only normal, it's a necessity—keeps us from charging off before our bodies are properly adjusted. But never fear, we lowlanders eventually bring home the bacon. Little bites, that's the way to eat an elephant."

I'm not sure if it's the mixed metaphors or the defensive posturing that is giving them trouble, but they look baffled. Nevertheless, I am eager to move the conversation forward, "And where are you two from then?"

"Israel," one of them informs me, "Near the Dead Sea. One-thousand-three-hundred feet below sea level."

"Lowest place on Earth," his companion volunteers.

WE ARE FINALLY on the move again. After a few hours of steep hiking we leave the forests and all their alien weirdness behind and emerge onto Mount Kenya's vast moorlands—with all their alien weirdness. The landscape seems a cross between the Scottish Highlands and the planet Mongo. The broad, U-shaped glen of the Teleki valley is a rocky moonscape softened with a scrubby veneer of coarse grasses and heather. The rest of the flora is strictly sci-fi: Lobelias (mutant artichokes the size of beach balls) and groundsels (surreal plants that appear to be half Joshua tree, half giant pineapple) poke like sentries from the expansive heath. The objects most riveting our attentions, however, are mineral rather than vegetable. Towering at the head of the valley are the craggy battlements of the upper mountain itself, the great, twin-summited mass of Mount Kenya and its satellite towers, Midget Peak and Point John. This view, one that we've circumscribed half the globe to realize, is like helium in our veins: Despite already having gained nearly four-and-a-half thousand vertical feet over the course of the day, we float the remaining miles to Mackinder's Camp at the foot of the alpine zone.

Halford Mackinder is one of the unsung heroes in the annals of mountaineering. Outside Africa, it is the rare mountaineer who will recognize his name. Yet Mackinder conceived of, organized, and—against all odds—managed to pull off a climb that was arguably decades ahead of its time. At the end of the 19th century, he was employed as a geographical scholar at Oxford University. In those days, many blanks on the map remained to be filled, and there was an expectation that a serious geographer would play an active role in remedying the situation. To realize his professional ambitions, Mackinder needed to add the title of "Accomplished Explorer" to his résumé.

In terms of where to make his mark, the recently partitioned beachhead of British East Africa contained a convenient and compelling objective. Despite all the European energy that had gone into illuminating the Dark Continent over the past 50 years, Mount Kenya was still unclimbed. Mackinder seized the opportunity, made the necessary preparations (including spending several seasons in the Alps learning how to climb), and finally, with only six months leave from the university, he departed on an audacious campaign.

Setting sail for Mombasa in June of 1899, traveling by train to the swampy railhead known as Nairobi, and finally on foot across 120 miles of famine- and disease-plagued countryside, Mackinder and his expedition arrived at Mount Kenya in mid-August. Here they were beset with difficulties ranging from a native ambush in which two of their porters were killed, to nearly incinerating themselves after accidentally setting fire to the moorlands. To make matters worse, the climbing was a bitch. After reconnoitering the mountain and finding no easy ice or snow routes, Mackinder and two seasoned guides he had imported from the Mont Blanc region concentrated their efforts on the sheer rock walls of the 1000-foot southeast face. After climbing to a ridge-crest cul-de-sac on one attempt and nearly being killed by a snowstorm on another, they ultimately had to abandon their quest when the expedition ran desperately low on food. Virtually simultaneous with their complete evacuation of the mountain was the arrival of a re-supply caravan with enough provisions for one last attempt.

Again, Mackinder and his stalwart guides retraced their tenuous line up the cracks and chimneys of the southeast face. This time, however, after cresting the ridge, they traversed to a prominent hanging glacier on the mountain's southernmost aspect. Chopping holds into the surface of this steep and treacherous slope was so difficult (requiring 30 blows per step) that Mackinder gave it the name Diamond Glacier. After three hours of hard and precarious labor at nearly 17,000 feet, the trio reached an easy rock gully on the other side. A few hundred feet of steep scrambling brought them at last to the pinnacle of Mount Kenya. It was a stunning achievement; at an altitude higher than the summit of Mont Blanc, the objective hazards and technical difficulties of both the rock climbing and the ice work were of a standard shared by few, if any, alpine climbs done anywhere else in the world. To this day, the traverse across the Diamond Glacier is considered so dodgy that it is rarely undertaken.

Mackinder called the highpoint Batian, in honor of a prominent Masaii leader. Three hundred feet away is a slightly lower (by 36 feet), more inaccessible summit that was left unclimbed, but which he nevertheless named Nelion after another native chieftain. The icy gap separating the two peaks he poetically christened the "Gate of the Mists." These, along with many other names Mackinder applied to major features of the mountain are still used today. The site of Mackinder's basecamp in the Teleki valley—where a spacious alpine hut now stands—bears the name of the man himself.

A CACHE of supplies and gear is waiting for us at Mackinder's Camp. Our three porters are energetic and enterprising. While we've been wrestling altitude and other primates down at the Met Station, they've managed to complete their services to us and are already hard at work again doing the same thing for another party. Most of the porters on Mount Kenya are farmers who eagerly supplement this livelihood by farming themselves out to haul loads for trekkers and climbers. Our original intention had been to move everything under our own power, but after being bombarded with everything from sly solicitations to sales tactics that would put Amway to shame, we caved. At the time, we rationalized this sloth as an opportunity for cross-cultural interaction, and in fact, time spent with our porters in camp and on the trail has turned out to be an unexpected highlight of the trip. So much so that on his next lap up the mountain, we re-employ a porter named Charles to accompany us higher and guard our camp while we climb.

Charles. He makes us laugh; he makes us cry. Case in point: When he gets wind of the fact that we are considering treating ourselves to a night in the hut, Charles takes the initiative and in place of the hut arranges bargain-basement lodging for us in a nearby outbuilding. He is so proud of this negotiation that we simply cannot refuse. As a result, instead of slumbering in relative luxury, we are condemned to sleepless misery in a dank,

Rock hyrax outside Mackinder's Camp

hantavirus hellhole, where a plague of mice burrow under my sleeping bag and crawl freely through my hair and across my face. The bright side, of course, is that Charles has saved us two dollars.

Rodents aren't the only pests with which we have to contend. During our acclimatization period at Mackinder's Camp, our food supplies are under constant siege by rock hyrax: furry, marmot-like critters whose close genetic relatives are, bizarrely, elephants. Dean and the two Israeli hikers enjoy endless fun pelting the hyrax with stones. To me, however, this activity seems the epitome of bad karma, and I vow that I will keep some distance between Dean and myself when we re-enter pachyderm territory.

After a few days of easy living, we're eager to press on. The next upward leg is a grueling 1500-vertical-foot slog to the Austrian Hut, a windswept structure perched on a desolate boulderfield beneath the southeast face of Nelion. Arriving one step ahead of a furious hailstorm, we quickly erect our tent and establish the high camp for our climb. The line that Dean and I are tackling is the *Normal Route* on Nelion, a route that in terms of its quality and history is not normal at all. It's extraordinary.

IT IS FURTHER testament to the skill and fortitude of Mackinder's party that after their remarkable ascent no one managed to climb Mount Kenya again for 30 years. In 1928, however, one of the legendary figures of 20th-century mountain exploration took up residence in the newly formed colony of Kenya. Eric Shipton came to Africa to grow coffee. He probably also drank a lot of it, because in terms of climbing the mountains it seems he never slept. All of equatorial Africa's snow- and ice-covered massifs, including Kilimanjaro and the Ruwenzori range (the fabled Mountains of the Moon), were on his hit list, but first Shipton zeroed in on the closest and, in many ways, most tantalizing objective of all: the virgin summit of Nelion.

For Mount Kenya, Shipton partnered with fellow British settler Percy Wyn Harris, another talented mountaineer (it was Wyn Harris who, in 1933, discovered the enigmatic Mallory-Irvine ice axe high on the North Ridge of Mount Everest). The pair initially approached the mountain with the intention of repeating Mackinder's route, but once they got a look at the soaring face of Nelion, with its fine rock and numerous incut holds, they were eager to give it a whack. For the first 500 feet the pair zigzagged up a line that eventually intersected Mackinder's path. Above the southeast ridge, however, Shipton and Wyn Harris tackled the summit block directly, where, with great effort, they managed to overcome the difficult terrain that had confounded the earlier party. The steep and intimidating headwall yielded to some persistent and clever route-finding, and by noon the pair were the first to stand upon Mount Kenya's penultimate summit. In an apt finish to this tour de force, Shipton and Wyn Harris descended into the Gate of the Mists, crossed over, and bagged the second ascent of Batian. A few days later, they repeated the entire adventure with a novice companion in tow.

OUR OWN novice companions, our two Israeli friends, are turning blue. Like so many of the non-climbers who attempt to circumnavigate the peak or scramble up Point Lenana, they have come too high too fast. They've also made the classic mistake of underestimating the weather on the upper mountain, which is more polar than solar. As a result, they are nursing killer headaches, shivering in their thin jackets, and gradually acquiring the color of windshield-wiper fluid. After only a day at the Austrian Hut, they turn tail and flee the mountain. We're sorry to see them go, but at least they have a novel tale to take back to their home below the sea—not many people can say they nearly froze to death on the equator.

Ours is a different story. Those few extra days of acclimatization at the Met station and our tortoise-like progress up the mountain are paying off in spades. We've also got the weather dialed. In fact, I've never seen a mountain with a more predictable pattern. Each day dawns clear, but around mid-morning clouds begin to build against the western facets of the peak. By noon, the entire mountain is shrouded, and within an hour or two rain or snow lashes the highlands until late in the afternoon. By early evening the clouds are on the wane and the final pockets of mist dissipate as alpenglow plays out on the high cirques and ridges. What all this means is that we don't have to give a second thought to whether we can climb the next day. What we do have to be concerned with is making sure we have things wrapped up by noon.

It is with this thought in mind that we creep out of camp in the wee hours and begin the traverse over to the bottom of the face. Nine-tenths of this approach is strolling across the gently angled ice sheet of the Lewis Glacier, the largest snow and ice formation on the mountain—for now. Photographs from the 1920s show the glacier overrunning the top of Point Lenana, the 16,355-foot lava hill looming above the Austrian Hut. Today, Point Lenana is an isolated rock outcropping and the Lewis Glacier has shriveled like a piece of dried fruit into the basin between Nelion and the hut. Sadly, all of Africa's glaciers are in mad retreat, and some of the world's premier ice and snow routes along with them. Although climbing guidebooks continue to list, describe, and rate these climbs as though all that is needed to restore them to proper condition is a good snow year, classics like Kilimanjaro's *Breach Icicle* and Mount Kenya's *Diamond Couloir* have essentially vanished until the next Ice Age. At this rate, all the continent's ice and snow will disappear just about the time scientists finally agree that global warming just might, in fact, be happening.

For me, striding purposefully in my instep crampons, the glacier crossing provides a welcome opportunity to study the moonlit face looming overhead, and to pick out the major features that define our route. For Dean, the Lewis Glacier is where our Midwestern roots come back to haunt him. Dean is wearing ice-fishing cleats, and he's discovering that the difference between walking across a frozen lake and an inclined glacier is a whopper. Watching him scrabble for traction as he slowly works his way down to where the ice levels out, I can't help but wonder at his tenacity—I'm also wondering what other kind of budget tackle he's got in that pack of his.

We rope up under a waning moon and unfamiliar constellations, but by the time we've finished the first pitch, the sun is up. It's not that we're dogging it; on the equator the sun practically vaults over the horizon and morning breaks faster than dropped crockery. The initial pitches follow a series of easy ramps and gullies. Soon enough, however, the route wanders onto steeper ground, and as each line of weakness peters out, we must traverse to link with another climbable feature. As one apparent dead end after another yields to unseen possibilities, we are amazed at the cunning and persistence of Shipton and Wyn Harris. And theirs are not the only ghosts whose presence is felt here. Midway up the lower wall, we pass beneath an ugly looking chimney scaled by Mackinder and his guides. Thankfully, modern gear and methods make it easier for us to climb an exposed rib off to one side, but again, we spare a thought of admiration for the pioneers, shinnying desperately with their hobnails and wool pressed to the sides of the dank fissure.

On the Southeast Face of Nelion

We find that past efforts on this route range from mighty to mighty strange. Just below the crest of the southeast ridge, we are confronted with a sheet-metal shed rigged to the cliff face. This is "Baillie's Bivy"—an emergency shelter constructed in the 1960s by the Rhodesian climber Rusty Baillie. Although the structure is largely in ruins (choked with ice and missing its door) we marvel at the ingenuity and fortitude it must have taken to put it here. It turns out we ain't seen nothing yet.

Soon we are straddling the crest of the knife-edged ridge, and able to contemplate the diverging paths of the first- and second-ascent parties. The Mackinder route drops over the ridge and contours left toward the Diamond Glacier; Shipton's descends a sharp cleft and then works up around the side of a huge gendarme. Our line goes somewhere else altogether. A modern variant, known as *De Graaf's Variation,* ascends a steep, square-cut trough. Although this is the crux of the climb, and despite snow and ice lingering in the cracks and on ledges, we find the holds and protection are so bomber we don't even need to haul packs. Above, a ledge leads us around another corner where we reconnect with the original ascent line and follow it up more perfect cracks, across more airy traverses, and finally up a broad gully to the summit of Nelion.

We've put in a full day: climbed 20 pitches, navigated a devious route, carted packs to over 17,000 feet, and managed to stay one step ahead of the weather. We check our watches. It's 11:30 in the morning. As if on cue, towering cumulous are detonating like atomic tests over the west face. The fallout is headed our way, but we're not worried—thanks to Ian Howell and his remarkable hut.

Howell is the modern bearer of the torch ignited by Mackinder, and carried by the likes of Shipton, Wyn Harris, and the other Mount Kenya climbers who have pushed the standards over the past century. Of the 33 major alpine routes on the mountain, Ian Howell, often partnered with Iain Allan, has pioneered one-third. Yet it was during Howell's very first ascent, a long traverse encompassing every major summit in the massif, that he decided what this mountain really needed was a bivouac shelter—on top. Howell designed, fabricated, and built the structure in his garden. He then disassembled it and packaged it into bundles that he arranged to have air-dropped onto the Lewis Glacier. Finally, he carried it, piece by piece, on his back, solo, to the summit of Nelion. It took him 13 round-trips on the *Normal Route* to cart everything to the top, and he down-climbed the route after every load.

As the first waves of hail pelt the summit of Nelion, Dean and I pull off our rock shoes, spread out our sleeping bags, and seal the hatch. Our first brew is a toast to Ian Howell: a true visionary, a man of action, and one who takes his comforts very seriously. We have no doubt that if he wanted to, Ian Howell could put a hot tub on Everest.

THE NEXT MORNING we are up early, perched on ledges beside the Howell Hut to witness the African dawn from 17,000 feet. A sea of broken clouds dots the ochre plains. As color floods the horizon, the outline of Kilimanjaro is revealed. It squats like a compressed Mayan temple, its form and dimensions markedly unimpressive, until we consider that it is over 200 miles away. Far below, camera strobes flash on top of Point Lenana as sunrise trekkers try to capture the spectacle, but to us, their grand summit is just another piece of texture on the shadowed landscape. Save for that flattened hump on the horizon, we are the highest point in all of Africa.

Well, not quite. From the top of Nelion, we gaze longingly across to Batian, less than a football field away and only 12 yards higher. Our hope had been to follow in the footsteps of Shipton and traverse the Gate of the Mists. Peering down into the icy cleft, right into the dizzying maw of the *Diamond Couloir* (or what's left of it anyway), we can see that managing this in instep crampons and ice-fishing clogs will be tough—especially if we hope to get there, back here, and down the mountain before the weather breaks. Regretfully, we come to the realization that to tag the highest point of this mountain, it would be easier to stack 36 feet of rocks.

There is nothing *pole pole* about our descent from Mount Kenya. A thousand feet of rappelling lands us back on terra firma just ahead of the storms. Charles shouts his congratulations as we approach the hut and suggests that we break camp immediately despite the weather (we're tired and hungry, but he's bored and cold and wise to the fact that we are total pushovers). By evening, we are all the way back down to Mackinder's Camp in the Teleki Valley. Early the next morning, we re-enter the jungle and book the remaining miles to the Met Station.

Originally, Dean and I contracted to have a sturdy Land Rover meet us at the trailhead, but Charles has taken it upon himself to arrange alternative, cut-rate transport. We depart Mount Kenya rattling like loose change in the back of a dilapidated Toyota pick-up that coasts for over a mile down the rutted track before what must be the single remaining tooth on the flywheel manages to start the engine. Later, sitting on the grass beside the road watching as our driver struggles to replace one threadbare tire with another, a familiar, throaty rumble causes me to stiffen. A herd of Cape buffalo—all flaring nostrils and menacing eyes—has emerged from the trees and is advancing slowly toward the truck.

On Mount Kenya, the equator is not the only thing that comes full circle.

Originally published in CLIMBING, *No. 207, 2001.*

Author's notes: After climbing Mount Kenya, Dean and I spent a few days rock climbing near Nairobi in the company of the great pioneers of modern African alpinism, Ian Howell and Iain Allen. The day we climbed with Howell he took us to a lovely crag in the Rift Valley, where belaying was as thrilling as the climbing as we contemplated giraffes grazing in the Cradle of Mankind. At day's end, we got a firsthand glimpse of the taste for amenity that has resulted in a cozy summit hut atop Mount Kenya (photo, p. 258) when Howell, rummaging in the rear of his car, suddenly produced lawn chairs, a crate of snacks—including homemade pies!—and cold beer. Ian Howell (below, center) is indeed a man who takes his comforts seriously.

For a more detailed profile on the climbing history of Mount Kenya, see "Shipton Select: Mount Kenya," page 253.

The CIC Hut at the foot of Ben Nevis

BIG BAD BEN

Mining Winter Misery on Scotland's Ben Nevis

FOLLOWING A ROUTINE physical exam, a Scotsman is stunned to discover that he has only a short time left to live. "Is there nothin' Ay can doo?" the man begs his physician.

The doctor thinks a moment, then tells him, "Take a mud bath three times a day."

"That'll cure me then?" the Highlander asks hopefully.

"Nah," the doctor says, "but it'll get you used to the dirt."

I am telling—no, *screaming*—this joke into the teeth of a howling gale because, at the moment, Ben Nevis seems the physical embodiment of that morbid jest. Dark and heartless, it is, to me anyway, a mountain that defines mean-spiritedness. Squatting on the northwest coast of Scotland, where it is raked by some of the cruelest weather on earth, this truncated troll of a peak has dashed my hopes during two previous winter climbing trips, and now seems intent upon delivering yet another pitiless punch line.

My three companions and I are huddled behind a pile of stones, trying to catch our breath amidst the kind of wind and rain that would send us scurrying into our storm cellars back home in Minnesota. If the irony of my grim humor has reached any of them, I can't tell. In the quaking beam of my headlamp, all I can see within the sodden layers of polypro caps and parka hoods are their eyes, wherein is written a weary frustration. Being exhausted, benighted, and besieged by weather during a winter climb on Ben Nevis is not unusual, in fact it's something for which my friends and I are steeled. But the four of us are still on the fricking *approach* to the peak. One by one, we rise from our makeshift bunker, grit our teeth, and stumble forward again, backs bent into the tempest. Within a hundred yards, however, the mountain springs a new trap and we find ourselves mired to the knees in the sucking black mud of a bog. Ben Nevis is getting us used to the dirt.

ON THE SURFACE, Ben Nevis (4406 feet) seems a perfect destination for winter climbing. The mountain's modest elevation means that acclimatization is not an issue and bargain airfares make journeying to Scotland during the off-season very cheap. Most significantly, this peak is arguably the Eden of ice climbing, the place where mankind first stood erect on waterfall ice (although a lot of time was spent bent-over, chopping steps), and home to some of the most important routes in the history of winter mountaineering. Climbs like *Zero Gully* and *Point Five Gully* are world-class objectives, timeless classics possessing nearly Eiger-like magnetism and prestige. There is, however, one factor that makes traveling all the way to Ben Nevis in winter an epic gamble: weather that could drive a polar bear insane.

"The Ben," as it is referred to locally, is rounded over by the shearing forces of ancient glaciers, and drops away on all sides into lush glens and rocky corries (curved, bite-like hollows in the hillsides). The mountain is a jutting bulwark sitting directly in the path of vast cyclonic weather systems that whirl off the North Atlantic. Slamming into Ben Nevis, these storms regularly produce in excess of three meters of annual precipitation and winds that can pluck cars and trucks from roadways in the nearby town of Fort William.

It is only natural that a place of such extremes should inspire a range of emotions. Ben Nevis may have the distinction of being the highest point in all the British Isles, but it is a mountain that only a Scottish heart can truly admire. When Bruce and Dean the Elder, two of my three companions, flew directly into Glasgow, they were met with quite a positive reaction. "Ahh, the Ben!" the Scottish customs agent smiled reverently, as if our friends had named some hallowed and beloved cathedral to which foreigners would dutifully pilgrimage. In Scotland, where stamina and perseverance are a way of life, there could be no prouder or more appropriate monument to the local mettle than Ben Nevis.

On the other hand, when Young Dean and I entered the UK through London, the mere mention of our ultimate destination caused the English customs agent to eye us up as if we were escaped mental patients. "That'll be a misery," he finally muttered, waving us by with a kind of all-knowing pity reserved for anyone loony enough to travel "north of the border" in February.

The four of us finally met up at the youth hostel in Glen Nevis, located in the very shadow of the Ben. We greeted each other with much backslapping and cries of "Och laddies, you're a sight for sore eyes!" (It is a simple fact that when in Scotland, it's impossible not to adopt a thick Scottish brogue.) And in fact, the pair who'd come through Glasgow were a fine sight indeed—Dean the Elder sporting a handsome tweed coat, and Bruce bonneted beneath a woolen driving cap. They seemed the picture of native Highland gentility. And so they might have been but for the cruel fate of having been born in the wrong place and time.

Even back home in Minnesota, these lads, both well into their 40s, carry themselves more like citizens of the Great Glen than the Great Plains. Bruce can recite long passages of Robert Burns from memory (in a perfect brogue), is an aficionado of single-malt whiskeys, and named his son Ian. Dean the Elder has Old World genius in his hands: Whether playing his antique concertina or plying his trade as prop-master for the state opera company, his fingers are equally capable of accompanying the Highland Fling or furnishing a Highland castle. Both men are quick wits, born romantics, and gentlemen to the core. And they each have another inherently Scottish skill: Both know their way around a set of ice tools.

In contrast, these grizzled veterans (among whom I must also be counted) have sampled whiskey older than Young Dean. While he has brought the energy and enthusiasm of youth to our party, we have brought him perhaps to the end of his momentum. On the heels of a remarkable climbing year that has seen him topping some of the finest summits on three continents, Young Dean has cast his lot with us, gambling that our experience and shared fixation with the crucible of Scottish ice might be the pathway to yet another climbing coup. Instead, he—along with the rest of us—is sunk up to his knees in muck on the path on Ben Nevis.

"HERE BOYS, over here," I call out hopefully, having momentarily clambered onto a narrow strip of gravel. Two steps later, however, my footing cuts out from beneath me and I'm back in the goop. Bruce is employing a different strategy, leaping between hummocks slightly up slope. "Up here, lads!" we hear him shout. "It's a wee bit spongy, but I think it'll go." But in the next instant—*sploosh!*—and then, "Scratch that, it's shite!" The Deans are faring no better, judging from all their splashing and muffled curses.

By the time we've finished wrestling the bog, we're wetter than if we'd swum Loch Ness, but now we're getting our first taste of the real beastie. Despite the driving rain and darkness, we can sense the massive, black crag rising above us: the 1800-foot northeast face of Ben Nevis, the largest alpine wall in Britain. As we contour beneath the brooding rocks of the Carn Dearg, a sub-peak of the Ben, the atmosphere is positively Gothic. We glimpse dark, mist-shrouded buttresses and deep, menacing gullies veined the color of bone. Between squalls, the clouds are torn back just long enough to reveal heavy accumulations of wet snow clinging to the uppermost ramparts. Squinting up into the gloom, Dean the Elder voices what we're all thinking. "This," he shudders, "is a *baaad* place."

Basically, there are two options for climbing on the Ben: tacking an arduous, two-hour hike onto either end of a route, or basing oneself for several days beneath the face. Bunking in the luxurious stone CIC hut at the toe of the wall—a memorial to Charles Inglis Clarke, a pioneering Nevis climber killed during the First World War—is the dream, and for the vast majority of climbers it will remain such. The hut is overseen by the Scottish Mountaineering Club (SMC) and was officially opened to visitors in 1929. In those days, parties climbing on the Ben in winter were so few and far between that even during rare spells of settled weather it was rarer still to fill the eight teak bunks in the hut. Today, in order to keep the hut from being overrun by the great unwashed, the SMC must administer it as selectively as the gates of heaven. Entry into the latter, even for a climber, is doubtlessly easier. Popping into the hut for a momentary respite from the cold or just to sneak a peek at the fabled sanctuary is forbidden without "The Key," and though the accommodations have been expanded to sleep 18, these spaces are reserved many months in advance. Except for a lucky few (or the diehards willing to endure the inevitable misery of tenting), Ben Nevis must be considered a day climb.

Crouched in the lee of the hut, dawn is breaking but the weather is not. Anticipating warm temperatures, we've kitted ourselves out for one of the Ben's classic ridges, now unthinkable in the present conditions. A few other climbers have disappeared into the murk, intent upon wallowing up one of the easier gullies. But, to me, the threat of avalanche and our lack of snow protection dictates a more measured course: retreat. Young Dean is with me; despite the rain, the battle of the bog has left him looking as though he's waded through roofing tar, and in the absence of serious climbing, he's ready for a hot shower and the high stool. With less vacation to spend here in Scotland, however, our friends are determined to make the most of every second.

"A baaad place!" The forbidding gullies and ridges of Ben Nevis in winter

"Perhaps we'll just have a look?" Bruce suggests, and Dean the Elder concurs. "Why not?" he says, "No harm in checking things out." And then the Elder says to us, "Don't worry about us lads, just a little reconnaissance. I'm sure we'll be along shortly. Cheerio." Jet-lagged, half-blinded by rain and mist, and with no guidebook by which to steer, the pair toddle off into a cloud.

That evening, just as we're dialing up the Lochaber Mountain Rescue Team to see if they've stumbled across any middle-aged corpses, Bruce and Dean the Elder stagger in. They're all smiles, but absolutely knackered. They've managed to climb Ben Nevis by plowing up a snowy gully, but the crux of the day was the descent. Disoriented in the whiteout on top, they were unable to locate the tourist track—up which cars have been driven—and so elected to go "off-road."

The summit plateau of Ben Nevis is rimmed with immense cornices overhanging deadly chasms. Negotiating a way off in a storm requires deft work with the compass, and epics and fatalities occur regularly as climbers stray off course. Thankfully, Bruce and Dean the Elder have run the gauntlet unscathed, despite going terribly wrong. The guidebook describes their descent route this way: "The slopes descending northeast into Glen Nevis comprise the biggest and steepest hillside in Britain. It is a dangerous place, rent by deep gullies." When pressed for details, the Elder can only shake his head and hearken back to his earlier assessment, "It's a *baaad* place."

WE SPEND the next week bashing our heads against the Ben, to little avail; it's just too warm for decent ice to form in the gullies, and too sloppy for the big ridges. Instead, we content ourselves with immersion in the local culture: single-malt whiskey, steaming plates of haggis, and the writings of Tom Patey. Patey was a pioneering climber during the 1950s and 1960s—watershed years for winter climbing on the Ben—who wrote hilariously about the Scottish climbing scene and its characters. A driving force among these was Hamish MacInnes, who, along with Patey and Graham Nicol, made the first winter ascent of *Zero Gully* in 1957. Patey died in 1970 while rappelling off a seastack, but MacInnes, also known as "the Fox of Glencoe," still lives in that quaint mountain village, less than a half hour from Fort William. Fortified by the whiskey (or is it the haggis?), we've found the courage to phone up MacInnes in the hopes of a living history lesson, and he's graciously invited us for a visit.

"I have to say, I think you've managed to arrive during quite the worst season in memory," declares MacInnes as we are seated round his living room in Glencoe. "It's too bad, really." The man may be the final word when it comes to assessing Scottish climbing conditions, but he isn't telling us anything of which we aren't already painfully aware.

Like the remarkable house he's built in a cleared corner of the glen, MacInnes is a blending of Highland tradition and modern styling. He isn't nearly as big as we've imagined, but then living legends rarely are. His hands and face have the ruddy, weathered look of a man who has spent most of his life living and working in the outdoors, while his neatly trimmed gray hair and beard mirror the sophisticated and cosmopolitan decor inside his home (which includes everything from a five-foot Chinese vase to a wall-mounted machete).

"I think you've got to be prepared to accept Scottish winter climbing in the long term," he continues (unaware that with my previous trips I practically qualify for residency). "You can get out and do something here maybe 80 percent of the time. But you can't just come and get guaranteed conditions for the hard routes unless you're very, very lucky."

MacInnes knows something about rolling the dice. During the decades when he made his mark, the techniques for climbing ice on Ben Nevis were basically the same as those employed by Harold Raeburn and other turn-of-the-century pioneers. Step-cutting with a single, wooden, thigh-length axe was the principal method of upward progress, and there were no such things as front points. In many cases, climbers used no crampons at all! What about ice protection? "There really wasn't any," MacInnes muses. It's astounding to contemplate what the Nevis pioneers pulled off using these methods, dumbfounding when you consider that *Zero Gully,* perhaps MacInnes' finest moment on the Ben, is still a much sought-after, 1000-foot Grade IV testpiece.

The lads, (left to right) Bruce Walker, Dean Einerson and Dean Hawthorne, with Hamish MacInnes

And what of "The Zero Gully Affair," as Patey titled his classic report of the first ascent in the *SMC Journal*? Patey's side-splitting narrative is filled with cinematic moments, such as the appearance of MacInnes, who, according to Patey, got wind of a rival team's intentions to have a crack at the climb (turf MacInnes practically held deed to after six previous attempts) and arrived at the CIC hut in the nick of time.

"The door crashed open," Patey wrote, "and the self-appointed guardian of *Zero Gully* stood before us in a state of wild disorder...It was impossible to remain indifferent towards such a man: His appearance alone invited controversy. A great rent extending the whole length of one trouser leg had been repaired unsuccessfully with string.

"Cunningham challenged him gruffly, 'Just where do you think you're going?'

'*Zero Gully,* of course.'

'Solo?'

'I suppose I might allow you two to come along as well.'"

In fact, it was Patey and Nicol—self-confessed second-stringers—who were recruited from the hoi polloi in the hut to join with MacInnes for the epic first ascent of *Zero Gully,* completed in just five hours.

"That was quite fast, wasn't it?" MacInnes remarks to us. "Not many people today do it faster—and, of course, modern parties have crampons. Tom and Graham relied on nailed Tricouni boots—good for mixed climbing, but a bit of a handicap on pure ice."

And does Hamish MacInnes still climb, the gallery wonders?

"I've slowed down," he admits. "Too busy in the summer for climbing. In winter I try to get out. I do a fair bit of soloing still, you know. Grade IVs and the like."

"Jesus." I mumble. *Zero Gully* is a Grade IV.

On our way out the door, I feel I must ask MacInnes about Patey's writing. Like all Patey's stories, the *Zero Gully* account seems almost too perfectly scripted. It's hard to believe that the author didn't stretch things for effect.

"Tom had a sense of humor," MacInnes tells me, "but he was also quite accurate."

"So you did crash in the door of the hut?"

The old Fox smiles. "I'm sure it must have been the wind."

LIKE A JOB we've come to loath, the Ben is wearing us down. The cheerless cycle of the 4 a.m. start, the brutal hike, the inevitable bog, the discouraging assessment, the ignominious retreat, and the consoling whiskey have taken a toll, especially on Young Dean. For months he has dreamed of whacking his way up frozen Scottish classics. But this year is a freak, the ice a bust, and the lad has taken to his bunk for long hours with the volume on his Walkman dialed to the limit. In an attempt to rouse him from the depths, I play the "experience" card.

"Let's face it," I tell him, "you may have had an unbroken string of success up till now, but climbing is a hard game, and believe me, there's plenty of defeat in your future." To push the point, I offer up my own tender underbelly, "Look at me, third trip over and still nothing to show for it, but you won't find me lolling about in bed. In fact, I'm just off to the pub. Enjoy your time here, boy, that's my advice."

In the end, however, all I've roused is a new addition to our company: Dean the Cruel.

"Enjoy my time here?!" An apparition of Black Donald—the devil himself—couldn't fill a room with more dread than the sight of Dean rising from his bunk, eyes bulging with pent-up emotion, his headphones dangling loosely about his neck, popped from his ears like champagne corks by the veins swelling on his temples.

"This," his hand sweeps our dank and cramped lodgings, festooned with wet ropes, dripping polypro, and other soggy mountaineering paraphernalia, "*this*," he repeats, finding his octave and his stride, "is my time here! Drying out! And going into town and drinking liquor that I can't afford, and shopping for souvenirs that I can't afford, to bring back so other people will get pleasure from a trip I hate! The weather sucks, getting up in the middle of the night sucks, the hike sucks, and in the end, the conditions suck, so after going through it all, I turn around and come back down here again, soaked to the bone, where all there is to do is dry out and drink. And that's my day, day after day!"

"I see," I tell him. "Here, have some whiskey."

But his depression is beyond even this pat therapy. The rage, however, has been spent, the pressure released, and the poor boy flops back into his pillow and sobs, "People at home are doing more climbing."

In this poignant (if somewhat pathetic) finale, I realize that the lad has hit upon a kernel. Climbing, after all, is why we are here, and the beauty of climbing is that it can be enjoyed irrespective of whether the route is worth mounting on the wall. The words of Hamish MacInnes float back to me, "You can get out and do something here maybe 80 percent of the time..." Perhaps this is the key to Scottish winter climbing: ratchet back the expectations. Bugger saving ourselves for classics that'll never form, let's take a lesson from Bruce and Dean the Elder, and just climb something... anything on this mountain.

THE NEXT MORNING finds us once more upon the hated treadmill, but this time we have new life, new hope, and a new guidebook. No sooner have we staggered onto the terrace of the CIC hut, when four petite French women emerge from the doorway, dressed in full climbing kit. Suddenly the almighty "Key" seems a trinket; rules or no rules, I can't imagine any hut warden turning away such a group. Sidling up to the nearest of their party, I attempt an urbane pose, guidebook in hand. I'm here to garner information that will help us narrow the field for the day's work. "Bon *jour*," I manage, and then pointing up the hill, "And where do you go today?"

She bats her lashes and smiles. "Tooday, we climb zee Lej root."

"Right. *Ledge Route,* Dean, that's the one for us."

Happily, the guidebook confirms this as a worthy objective: "Probably the best route of its grade on the mountain, with sustained interest and magnificent situations." We won't be carrying this one home on a spear— the climb is only Grade II and was first climbed in the winter of 1897—but given the current climate, we'll most likely enjoy ourselves.

Bruce and Dean the Elder won't be joining us for this ridge romp up the Carn Dearg. Even though their previous prospecting in the Ben's chutes has turned up little more than wet snow, they're off to *Green Gully,* the scene of Raeburn's greatest triumph, and a drainage high enough (they hope) to have some real ice in it. They walk with us as far as the throat of *Number Five Gully,* where the path made by the Gallic lassies forks sharply right. The tiny, child-like bootprints in the snow give our friends a moment's pause.

"Will you look at that," Bruce sighs. "Like tiny goats."

"Aye," the Elder comments, "so small, and so dear." But then, pulled like trout by the powerful lure of Scottish ice, they push on toward

On the move in full Scottish conditions

the upper reaches of the great basin of Coire na Ciste where *Green Gully* is located.

In fact, all Young Dean and I are destined to see again of the French Quartet are their footprints. Despite our epic hikes up and down the mountain, the past two weeks in the fleshpots of Fort William have left us dragging—at least relative to these gazelles. By the time we reach the start of the route, they have scampered out of sight.

It feels good to finally uncoil our rope and tie in, even though we could undoubtedly move faster and more efficiently without it. I know Dean could. From the moment we start climbing, he is like a hound unkenneled, exuberantly straining at the leash, practically towing me up the steep snow and rocky steps.

At a broad ledge midway up the route we pause to survey our surroundings. The cloud cover, nearly even with the great Nevis cornice, has quit spitting and suddenly parts to let morning sunshine stream over the mountain. All over the Highlands, winter-hardened Scottish citizens are probably bursting into flames, while we bask in the rays, relishing every golden photon.

As we look across the mountain, nearly the entire face is laid out before us, offering up a bird's-eye view of all the features we'd hoped to climb this trip and won't: the impressive stair-step crest of *Tower Ridge;* the steep, slabby mass of *Observatory Ridge* bounded by the striking clefts of *Zero* and *Point Five* gullies; the distinctive, diagonaling geometry of the Minus Face couloirs; and finally, the awesome profile of the *Northeast Buttress,* where lurks the legendary crux known as the Mantrap. But we won't be fooled into squandering the moment on regrets or false hopes, because if Ben Nevis has taught us anything, it is that soon enough the clouds will slam shut again, the horizontal rain will return, and we will be up to our necks in the dirt. Right now we've done more than seemed possible, and we savor it like a fine dram that spends a few seconds on the tongue and a lifetime in memory. Life itself is a death sentence, and whether heaven exists or not, Ben Nevis in winter has given us a taste of what's to come.

Originally published in CLIMBING, *No. 216, 2002.*

Author's notes: Cry not for Young Dean. He and I tempered this trip by traveling on to southern Spain for a week of sunny rock climbing on the Costa Blanca. Shortly thereafter, he aced Denali's Cassin Ridge, *proving that his alpine momentum was (is) still on a roll. Perhaps most tellingly, Dean's dram of choice whenever he plants himself in front of my hearth on damp or wintry nights is single-malt whiskey, where he talks now and then of a return to Scottish ice. Time heals all wounds.*

More detailed suggestions for drowning one's sorrows during a Scottish winter expedition are offered up in "The Whiskey Song," page 358.

Among Legendary Mountaineers

The King and I; the Author with Anderl Heckmair

MY DINNER WITH ANDERL
Hanging with the Hero of the Eiger

SECRETLY, I HAVE ALWAYS BELIEVED that lurking within me, waiting for an opportunity to manifest itself, is the ability to socialize with important people without making an ass of myself. My chosen path, largely a straight line between mountains—or bar stools—rarely affords me the opportunity to mingle with celebrities. Nevertheless, I have remained confident that if a situation should ever require it, I could muster at least some degree of grace and charm. Until now, that is, because as I pass the ornate brass mailbox proclaiming the name "Heckmair" in bold relief, I am seized with the realization that I am hopelessly out of my element. No point in kidding myself: My social skills are pretty much defined by rough manners and asinine conversation. And not a bar stool in sight.

I have traveled to this address in the picturesque Bavarian postcard-village of Oberstdorf to meet my guru—the man whose life has most influenced my own. With my girlfriend, Dina, I have come seeking a connection with the celebrated German mountain guide whose life winds like a strong thread through an extended tapestry encompassing the most famous—and infamous—of mountains and men. Anderl Heckmair is best known as the person who, in the summer of 1938, led a team of two Germans and two Austrians on the dramatic first ascent of the Eigerwand, the much-feared North Face of Switzerland's Eiger. This success, so hard fought against a deadly wall, has inspired respect and sparked obsession among countless mountaineers of every subsequent generation, myself included. But for Heckmair, the Eiger climb was only the prelude to a lifetime of extreme journeys among mountains, deserts, jungles—as well as to the poles of humanity: Over the course of nine decades he has crossed paths with personalities ranging from Hitler to the Dalai Lama.

And now, perhaps as a result of my own improbable success on the Eigerwand, Anderl Heckmair has agreed to meet me. But I am afraid I will barely see the man through the thick condensation clouding my glasses. And it is not the humidity causing me to steam up like a green-

house window. This is a perspiration of nerves, and it progresses from a damp anxiety as Dina and I contemplate the Heckmairs' mailbox to a persistent fog as I finally summon the courage to ring the bell. By the time the door opens I'm almost completely blind, and I prove this by impulsively groping for Herr Heckmair's hand, only to be rewarded with a mitt-full of air. Dina is having better luck. Peering over my blinders, I perceive that the members of this household observe strict social protocol, and it is only after Dina has been shown all the proper courtesies that I am ushered inside.

I gape about in an attempt to get a fix on our hosts, and my first impression is that we have entered a time warp. It is inconceivable that the square-shouldered gentleman standing before me is more than ninety years old. His small but well-proportioned frame is neither paunchy nor stooped, and the famous profile, featuring a round face and prominent nose, is crowned with a thatch of dark hair that shows no sign of thinning or graying. By all outward appearances Anderl Heckmair appears to have found a way to stop the clock sometime in his mid-fifties. There are signs of an inner youth here as well: He greets me with a handshake and a wink that cannot conceal a mischievous sparkle.

His wife, Trudl, is similarly tiny, trim, and good natured, but in her case the youthful appearance is less of a disguise; she is decades younger than her husband, and so they seem a perfectly matched couple. Frau Heckmair's most singular feature, however, is her broad smile, which beams out warmly—a defroster on my clouded spectacles.

"Welcome," she says, taking our jackets, "it is so nice you have come to visit us." As I stammer some sort of reply about what an honor it is for us to meet such a great man, the humor in Heckmair can no longer be restrained. He beats his chest importantly and utters a solemn declaration before breaking into a fit of laughter. "Yes, yes," his wife translates, "Anderl says he is very proud!"

Clearly, Anderl Heckmair is a bit of a character.

Communicating Anderl's thoughts to visitors is second nature for Frau Heckmair. Like me, Anderl speaks only his native tongue and in a thick Bavarian dialect that even Dina, whose mother grew up near Frankfurt, is hard pressed to understand. Trudl, however, knows five languages, all self-taught, and—if her English is any indication—all quite fluently. Even now she is translating effortlessly and almost simultaneously as her husband invites us "into the sitting room, where we will be more comfortable."

The Heckmairs' parlor, a dimly lit, cozy room overlooking the garden, is furnished with a sofa and three chairs arranged in close proximity around a little table. Cake has been set out, cordial bottles are nearby, and, as we settle into place, Frau Heckmair goes in search of a vase for the fresh flowers Dina has brought. I also have a gift, something I suspect will greatly surprise Heckmair. In a letter I wrote to arrange this visit I asked about the book written by Fritz Kasparek, one of Heckmair's companions on the Eigerwand's first ascent. Kasparek's autobiography, printed shortly after the war and only a few years before his fatal plunge through a Peruvian cornice, is among the rarest of published Eiger-related materials. In my letter I asked the Heckmairs if they could offer any suggestions as to where I might acquire a copy of this volume. Anderl wrote back, "It is indeed very difficult to find; I, too, have no copy." I was excited then, when only a few weeks before our trip, I received a catalog listing this title for sale. I knew I had found the perfect gift.

Now, however, I'm worried I may have mistakenly wrapped up a copy of *Mein Kampf.* Anderl is thumbing through the book, frowning and shaking his head in a decidedly negative manner. His disapproval finally extends to the point of mumbling something under his breath that even I don't need a translator to understand. Dina is giving me one of those what-have-you-done looks, but I am shielded by my glasses, which are, once again, utterly opaque.

Thankfully, Frau Heckmair returns, and, after a short conversation with her husband, she explains: "Anderl has always climbed for his own reasons and has never been interested in doing climbs for the purpose of generating publicity. Fritz was the opposite. He was always saying to Anderl, 'We must make some important new route, or they will forget about us!' Anderl and Fritz were not close friends."

This is something of a revelation. With a personal understanding of the bond that often forms between climbing partners, I have always assumed that the four members of the successful Eiger party, united by such an epic experience, must have enjoyed a special camaraderie. It had never occurred to me that the fact that Kasparek's autobiography never made it onto Heckmair's shelf might have been intentional. And now, thanks to me, Fritz and his philosophies are back from the grave. All I can think of to say is: "I didn't know," which I suspect Dina translates to Anderl as, "He is very stupid."

It is not long, however, before the whiskey and schnapps are flowing, and Anderl is in a good humor again, happily puffing a cigar and explaining to us that the relationships between the members of the Eiger team were complicated, right from the start. The two Austrians, Kasparek and Heinrich Harrer, were initially a separate party, and had never met the Germans before encountering one another on the mountain. And the two Germans had only recently met; Heckmair originally hoped to attempt the Eiger with Hans Rebitsch, a friendly rival with whom he proposed joining forces. Rebitsch, however, had been invited to join the 1938 German expedition to Nanga Parbat, and reluctantly informed Anderl, "I leave the Eiger to you." But he also left Heckmair his partner, Ludwig Vorg, known to his friends as "Wiggerl." The previous year, Rebitsch and Vorg had retreated from the Eigerwand after climbing nearly halfway to the summit, and in doing so became the only men to return alive from a serious attempt on the face. Vorg's first-hand knowledge of the face, along with a strong recommendation from Rebitsch, made him the natural choice to accompany Heckmair.

"In many ways," explains Frau Heckmair, pouring us another whiskey, "Wiggerl was probably a better partner for Anderl than Rebitsch. In those days, it was common for one man to lead and the other to follow an entire climb. Both Anderl and Rebitsch were born leaders and would have competed with one another, but Vorg was ideally suited to the role of the second man; he was perfectly content to belay Anderl and remove the pitons."

The Austrians, I recalled, had a similar arrangement, with the lead falling naturally to Kasparek. I can only imagine how these dynamics must have complicated things once the two parties joined—it's no wonder Fritz and Anderl didn't get along. The memory of this encounter gives Anderl a chuckle. His wife explains, "Anderl did not want to combine the teams. When he and Wiggerl met the others on the Second Icefield, he immediately told them, 'You must go down now, because if you continue, you will surely be killed.'"

While this must have raised Kasparek's hackles, it was a valid observation, because although the Austrians were prepared to tackle any

Anderl and Trudl Heckmair

rock pitches the Eiger might throw at them, they were poorly equipped for ice and snow. The reason the Germans caught up with them so quickly on the traverse of the Second Icefield is because without an ice axe or even adequate crampons, Kasparek was forced to chop steps for hundreds of feet using only a small hammer. Heckmair and Vorg, outfitted with the most sophisticated ice gear of the day, including twelve-point crampons, literally ran across the same ground.

"Anderl is convinced," his wife informs us, "that the reason he was successful where so many others failed is because the others prepared for the Eiger as a rock climb with just a little ice and snow. But Anderl saw that the Eiger was mainly an ice and snow climb, with only a little rock. This is what made the difference."

"Why, then," I ask, "did Herr Heckmair decide to join forces with the Austrians?" Though she has doubtlessly heard the answer a thousand times, Frau Heckmair waits patiently for her husband to finish, and then explains: "The Austrians were quite determined to continue, and Anderl was inclined to leave them to their fate. But it was Wiggerl, with his big heart, who said, 'Well, if you insist upon going on, then perhaps we should all go together.'"

Even Kasparek must have felt some relief at this proposal, since their inferior equipment meant he and Harrer could never out-pace the Germans—and if you can't beat 'em…

Anderl's glass is empty again, but his wife, ignoring his good-natured pout, has cut him off. "And one more thing," Frau Heckmair smiles warmly, "Anderl would like me to tell you that he is not 'Herr Heckmair'; he is Anderl and I am Trudl. And now he must go play cards."

Every afternoon at precisely five o'clock Heckmair plays cards with his neighbor for exactly one hour. While outsiders may view this as a curious ritual—particularly since no words are ever spoken during the game—it is, in fact, a cathartic method of relaxation for the neighbor, one that Anderl is happy to oblige. I suspect whiskey is also involved.

While he is gone, Trudl takes Dina and me for a walk to see the place in Oberstdorf where three major rivers merge into one—a unique geographical landmark. Dina borrows a pair of Anderl's boots for the hike; needless to say, I am proud to have a girlfriend who can fill Anderl Heckmair's shoes.

I ask Trudl if they are often pestered by climbers like us. "Oh yes," she grins, "every now and then someone will climb the Eiger and then phone up to ask if it is possible to stop by and meet Anderl. And sometimes we are invited to visit them. Recently we went to see one young man here in Germany who went to the Eiger fifteen times before finally succeeding. His town threw him a big party with Anderl as guest of honor."

I envy this persistent and celebrated German alpinist. The Eiger took me three trips—and the only thing my town has ever given me is a parking ticket.

WHEN WE GET back to the house, Anderl has returned and it is time for dinner. Dina and I insist upon taking the Heckmairs out, so we all pile into their car and Trudl drives us to a quiet little restaurant that doesn't cater to tourists (no lederhosened accordion players or dirndl-dressed barmaids). The beer, however, is classic Bavarian lager and we lift our glasses to our new friends.

Speaking of friends, I feel I must ask the Heckmairs about Heinrich Harrer. Harrer's well-publicized adventures—particularly his wartime escape from a British POW camp and subsequent journey over the Himalayas into Tibet—have made him an international celebrity. I ask Anderl and Trudl what they think about the upcoming Hollywood adaptation of Harrer's Tibetan experiences.

"Heini has just rushed off to America to help with some changes to his movie," Trudl informs us. In fact, this is a polite way of saying that he has been summoned by the film's producers to help with damage control. "He is a man who likes attention," she continues, "but now I think it has brought him serious problems." She is referring, of course, to the recent sensational disclosure that in the years surrounding the Eiger climb, Harrer was an active, card-carrying member of Hitler's SS. Although Harrer initially denied these charges, journalists, catalyzed by the publicity surrounding the film, unearthed incontrovertible proof: papers and records, some in Harrer's own handwriting, positively identifying him as an SS man.

Controversy has always surrounded the relationship between the four Eiger climbers and the Nazis. There is no doubt that after the climb the men were used to fan the flames of the nationalistic fervor that gripped Germany prior to the outbreak of World War II. Almost immediately upon their descent they were whisked away by the SS, publicly congratulated by Hitler, and held up to the nation and the world as symbols of Aryan accomplishment and pride. For this, it would be difficult to fault them, since history-making mountaineers of every time and nationality have been similarly feted by their proud governments. But it has been suggested that the motivation to climb the Eiger might have been linked to some promised compensation—or for the specific purpose of advancing a political agenda. Some have gone so far as to accuse the team of climbing under orders from the Reich. Both Heckmair and Harrer have written at length on this subject and have dismissed these theories and accusations as so much bunk. In *The White Spider*, Harrer's famous history of the Eiger, he writes, "To ascribe material motives and similar external rewards of success to our climb would be a lie and a slander. Not one of us improved his social position one whit thanks to a mountaineering feat which excited such general admiration."

Unfortunately for Harrer, history now records that it is he who lied with regard to his "social position." Membership in Nazi organizations was illegal in his native Austria until March 1938, and he had joined the SA, Hitler's paramilitary stormtroopers, many years earlier. He apparently joined the SS even before the Eiger climb. Such affiliations cannot avoid casting dark shadows across Harrer's reputation—and his character.

Despite these revelations, the Heckmairs have great respect for Heinrich Harrer—he has, after all, spent most of his life attempting to focus public attention upon the plights of oppressed peoples, particularly the Tibetans. The Heckmairs feel that his greatest blunder is in not having come clean about his youthful mistakes. As with Kasparek, however, they have clearly been uneasy with Harrer's penchant for self-promotion over the years, and they cannot hide their bemusement at his current predicament. "Now, I think he finally has more attention than he wants," Trudl says. For the Heckmairs, there is a lesson here: A person who persists in dancing close to the bright flame is asking to get burned.

I wonder, however, if the mutual respect between Harrer and Heckmair would have developed if these two men hadn't survived to such ripe old ages. In fact, in the turbulent months following the Eiger climb, politics and personal vanities conspired to drive a wedge between them. It is clear from nearly all accounts of the Eiger's first ascent that it was Anderl who cracked this nut, always out in front finding the route, coming to terms with extreme technical difficulties, and drawing upon all his resources during the summit push to keep the team moving upward despite an intense blizzard. But soon after the Eiger ascent the four men were separated, with Harrer and Kasparek sent on tour through Austria, while Heckmair and Vorg were paraded around Germany. Considering the egos involved, it is hardly surprising that in Austria a somewhat different version of the Eiger conquest emerged, a version more generous to Kasparek and Harrer.

Tonight Anderl laughs at the memory; after all, history records a fair version of the events. Kasparek is long gone, and even Harrer, not known for minimizing his own role in anything, recently introduced Anderl to the Dalai Lama as "my life-saver."

Anderl is also determined to give credit where it is due by making the point that the Eiger ascent was a team effort, and, despite his initial misgivings, he feels the Austrians played a crucial role. "Heini and Kasparek knew the way down," he says. "They had already climbed the Mittellegi Ridge and gone down the west flank as part of their preparations for the North Face." And so, when Heckmair and his exhausted companions finally crawled onto the Eiger's summit—at night and in a raging blizzard— it was the Austrians who led them all to safety.

"It was a lucky thing when Wiggerl suggested they should all climb together," Trudl remarks, and Anderl chuckles his agreement.

And what of Vorg? I had read that he was a casualty of the war, killed on the Eastern Front on the very first day of fighting. But the Heckmairs reveal a chilling detail that elevates this tragedy to a new level. "He was killed by Germans," Trudl tells us, and her voice is a sad whisper. "He was posted as a sentry to watch a building until a demolition team arrived. But when the flame-throwers finally came, they didn't know he was there."

Our dinners arrive, a fabulous spread featuring curried chicken, buttered pasta, fish, and shrimp salad. The entrees that the two Eiger veterans have chosen are easily deduced from our physical appearances: Anderl is enjoying a lean portion of fish, while I wolf down the buttered pasta *and* the curried chicken. It was almost a decade ago that I climbed the Eiger, and the years have not been kind. It has been nearly six decades since Anderl climbed it and he looks like he could do it again tomorrow. This reminds me of a story.

I ask Anderl if he knows of the American climber Paul Petzoldt. As the venerable Wyoming mountain guide who pioneered the north face route on the Grand Teton—perhaps the closest American equivalent of the Eigerwand—he could be described as sort of a wild-west version of Anderl.

"Yes, Anderl has heard this name," Trudl says. Petzoldt also came close to making the first ascent of K2 the same year Anderl climbed the Eiger, and the Heckmairs remember this expedition.

I tell them of a dinner I had with Petzoldt several years before. At some point during the meal the topic of the Eiger came up. Petzoldt had never climbed it but always wished that he had. Puffing out my chest and sucking in my gut, I seized the opportunity to mention that I had climbed the Eiger just a few years earlier. No, no, he said, he was talking about the North Face. Yes, I insisted, I had climbed the North Face. Petzoldt looked me up and down, slumped back into his seat, shook his head sadly, and asked, "So, does everybody climb the Eiger these days?"

Anderl and Trudl get a big kick out of this. Dina, hard-pressed to see the humor in any story that hinges upon my indolent lifestyle, rolls her eyes. I have a point, however: Clearly, the Eiger is no longer a climb for just the "cream of the crop." I suggest to the Heckmairs that modern equipment is a principal reason why these days, a few curds like me are able to float to the top.

"When Anderl climbed the Eiger," Trudl tells us, "there was not even such a thing as a safety helmet. He kept a folded handkerchief under his cap to protect against falling stones."

This reminds Anderl of a story.

"Anderl once thought of adapting an Italian army helmet for climbing," his wife translates, "but first he wanted to make sure that it was strong enough. So he had his brother hit him over the head with an iron bar." To emphasize the point, Anderl grins and spreads his arms wide. Clearly, we aren't talking about some dinky little tire-iron here. "His head was okay," Trudl smiles, "but his neck was sore for weeks!" Now it is Dina and I who are cracking up, and it is Trudl's turn to roll her eyes a little.

AFTER THE MEAL the Heckmairs invite us back to their home again for a nightcap. Once I have been liquored up a bit, I feel I have an excuse to ask about something I'm not sure is an acceptable topic of conversation among Germans who lived through the war: Adolf Hitler. I am fascinated by the fact that Anderl actually met the man.

"Oh, yes," Trudl nods—and I am relieved that I haven't offended anyone. "It is quite amazing, really. Many important Party members never met Hitler, and then there is Anderl, a simple mountaineer with no interest in politics, so poor he didn't even maintain an address, and he met Hitler on more than one occasion."

In fact, the huge public rally that Hitler used to exploit the Eiger climb as a tremendous accomplishment for the Fatherland was not the first time Anderl came face to face with *der Führer*, nor, incredibly, was it the most surreal.

Among Anderl's clients during his early years as a guide was the well-known moviemaker and actress Leni Riefenstahl. As the star of a string of popular mountain-themed motion pictures, Leni possessed both a compelling beauty and a natural athleticism that captivated German audiences. But even these extraordinary outward qualities were eclipsed by an inner measure of ambition: She courted the rich and the powerful with the intensity of a shark prowling a kiddie pool. Eventually, Leni charmed herself into the graces of Hitler himself and was selected by him to make the infamous Nazi propaganda films of the 1934 Nuremberg Rally (*Triumph of the Will*) and the 1936 Berlin Olympic Games (*Olympia*).

After hiring Anderl for an outing in the Wolkenstein Alps and bonding with him during the epic climb and forced bivouac that followed, Leni managed to convince her resolutely apolitical guide to accompany her to a Party meeting in Nuremberg by promising him free access to the Olympic training facilities in Berlin. With the Eiger fixed firmly in his sights, it was an offer that even Anderl, despite his reservations about Nazi politics, could not refuse. While in Nuremberg, Leni was summoned to a late-afternoon tea with Party officials at a local hotel. With Anderl in tow, she was given the seat of honor at Hitler's table, and Anderl passed the time as anyone suddenly seated near his country's head of state might: trying to keep a low profile while studying the man. "I could see absolutely nothing so extraordinary about him," Anderl has said. Eventually, the conversation turned to Leni's recent mountain adventure. At this point Hitler became agitated and scolded her for risking her life so freely, especially in light of the great "mission" with which he had entrusted her. Leni answered that by hiring an experienced mountain guide—this man Heckmair sitting right here—she had never been in any danger. Anderl froze in mid-bite as every eye in the room suddenly drew a bead on him. Hitler then insisted upon posing to Anderl the most vexing question in mountaineering: "So, why do you do it?"

The reasons that compel a person to climb mountains are such a personal mixture of sensation, emotion and experience that attempting to communicate them satisfactorily to others is a challenge akin to proving the existence of God. And while a flip and meaningless answer like "because it is there" or "it keeps me out of real trouble" might be enough to pacify a casual friend or relative, it's not something I would want to try on a room full of Nazis. If I've never been able to explain the value of climbing to my own mother, I can't imagine having to convince Hitler.

Choosing his words carefully, Anderl did his best to explain to the *Führer* what is gained from a hard climb that cannot be found in a casual walk in the hills. Hitler was intrigued—not about climbing, but by the motivations behind it—and persisted in questioning Anderl throughout the course of the meal. Even when, at last, an aide informed the Leader that his presence was required elsewhere, Anderl was forced to tag along and continue the conversation. The two men moved out onto an outdoor balcony, where, to Anderl's astonishment, they beheld a massive throng of humanity that cheered and saluted their appearance. Hitler returned the gesture, as did the other Party leaders on the platform. And so it was that

Anderl, Dina Post, and the Author getting well oiled in the Heckmairs' parlor

for the first time in his life, Anderl Heckmair was reluctantly obliged to raise his arm in the infamous *Heil Hitler* salute.

"But Anderl still managed to express his disapproval," Trudl tells us, "and it was a lucky thing for him that no one else noticed. He raised the wrong arm—his left one, which is something of an insult. And then he put his right hand behind his back." Anderl chuckles while Trudl explains the significance: "In Germany, when you do this, it means you are not being truthful." In other words, standing at Hitler's elbow and before a crowd of thousands, Anderl Heckmair did the German equivalent of sticking out his tongue and crossing his fingers.

For the two hours Anderl was forced to stand on the balcony, watching the torchlit mob parade past beneath him, he yearned for the loneliness of the mountains. And the next day, at the political rally, he was gripped with a deep foreboding. Anderl has written, "I felt a kind of shudder in my soul. I understood that something was in motion that was going to sweep everything away with it, but where to I could not tell."

As Trudl finishes relating this bizarre and extraordinary tale, we all sit silently for a moment. Dina and I are so lost in thought that we barely notice when Trudl gets up to go in search of some photographs. It is Anderl who finally breaks the silence. Nudging his empty glass toward the whiskey bottle he winks, *"Schnell! Jetzt ist sie weg!"* ("Quick, while she's gone!")

Anderl survived World War II by serving as a mountaineering instructor for the army troops. His skills and experience were so valuable that his commanders defied the regulations by refusing to rotate him into the fighting.

After the war he made his way back to Oberstdorf and returned to the things he loved most: the mountains and guiding. With the good fortune to have had one of Germany's richest industrialists as a regular client, Anderl has explored every corner of the globe, leading climbs and treks from the Andes to the Himalaya well into his eighties. And he shows little sign of slowing down.

"At Anderl's age it is important to keep moving," Trudl remarks with a grin. "Who knows? If he stops, he may never start up again!" I tell him that I think there is little danger of this any time soon. Anderl laughs and tells another story.

"When he was young, a fortune teller told him he would die an unnatural death," Trudl explains. "To Anderl, this means he will probably die in bed." He also wants us to know that the town of Oberstdorf honored him on his ninetieth birthday by making him an Honorary Citizen. "Because of this, he gets two things," Trudl says. "First, he doesn't have to pay any city taxes. This is very nice, except his age already exempts him from these taxes."

"And the second?" I ask. Trudl smiles. "They gave him a cemetery plot." As his laughter fills the room, I can't decide which of these honors is more useless to Anderl Heckmair. With time growing short and the whiskey running low, I feel that the moment has come when I must say to Anderl Heckmair the thing I have come all this way to tell him. Taking a deep breath, I blurt out, "I want Anderl to understand what an important man he has been in my life."

As when we first arrived upon his doorstep, Anderl's modesty forces him to instinctively try to get past this comment by waving me off and joking self-importantly, "Yes, I am very proud, very proud!"

But I persist. "The life Anderl has led, his climbs, and his philosophies—when a young man reads about these things and decides that these are the examples that he will follow, it can have a very profound and positive influence. It can lead a person on a very good path through life—and I really want to thank him for this."

Anderl fidgets and listens uncomfortably as Trudl translates. But when he finally responds, two things are clear: He appreciates my desire to express these feelings, and he really is proud.

"Anderl says that you are making him choked-up."

Before we say goodbye, Trudl smiles and hands me the dreaded copy of Kasparek's autobiography. "In Germany, when you give someone a book, you must write something in it and sign it."

I couldn't disagree more. The unique history these men shared, from the landmark climb that brought them together, to the differing ideologies that kept them apart, seems to dictate that the pages of this particular book remain free of sentiment—especially from the likes of me.

But the Heckmairs are insistent. And so I find myself—as obscure a mountaineer as ever put pen to paper—in the awkward and unsettling position of having to compose a line of presentation to the man who first led the Eiger, in a book written by the one member of the team who probably never came to terms with this fact. Before my glasses can fog again, I manage to scribble an inscription that not only expresses my admiration at such a lifetime of unsurrendered potential, but that Fritz himself, had he lived to gain the wisdom and perspective of old age, might also have written:

"To Anderl, who showed us the way."

Originally published in ASCENT, *1999.*

Author's notes: One of my favorite Anderl Heckmair stories occurred during his visit to Yosemite where he stayed at one of the Valley's sprawling, labyrinthine campgrounds. One night before bed Heckmair decided to wash up, but upon exiting the shower building he suddenly realized he had no inkling of the location or even the number of his campsite. Because he spoke no English, he couldn't ask for help. He wandered for hours until his companions finally tracked him down. The image of the great route-finder of the Eiger meandering aimlessly in his bathrobe through a dark maze of tents and RVs…it defines irony. It was a story Anderl loved to tell, I suspect, because he instinctively shied from any notion of superhuman status.

Anderl Heckmair passed away in the winter of 2005 at the venerable age of 98. He remains a hero and an inspiration to many—at every stage of life.

The historic Banff Springs Hotel, site of the Banff Mountain Summit

THE HIGH AND MIGHTY
Social Climbing and Higher Learning at the Banff Mountain Summit

I AM WEARING dirty underwear, spaghetti sauce, and a smile. I can't stop grinning because so many of the people eating lunch with me in the dining hall at the Banff Centre for Mountain Culture are mythic figures in the pantheon of mountaineering, people I have read about, admired, even worshiped throughout my life, but with whom I never imagined I would ever share a room, much less a meal. Across the table, Tom Hornbein, whose 1963 traverse of Everest via the West Ridge is one of the landmark feats in the history of that mountain, is chatting with Nick Clinch, leader of the 1958 expedition to Gasherbrum I, the only 8000-meter peak first ascended by Americans. Behind them, Yosemite icons Royal Robbins and Yvon Chouinard are trading war stories, while Anderl Heckmair, the architect of the Eiger North Face first ascent, is eyeing up the barman in the hopes of scoring something a little stronger than beer. Elsewhere in the room, Chris Bonington is exuberantly detailing his latest expedition, rock climbing aces Lynn Hill and Peter Croft are eating fast and light, and fabled storyteller Todd Skinner is shoveling more than pasta.

It's all so utterly thrilling that any frustration or discomfort over becoming "disconnected" from my luggage (the airline's term for routing it to Timbuktu, thus forcing me to wear the same clothes three days in a row) is momentarily forgotten. In fact, so awed am I to be among such distinguished company, I am blissfully unaware that each time I lean forward to take another bite, my dangling necklace of press credentials is alternately trolling across my plate and settling back against my only shirt like a wet paintbrush of marinara.

What has brought us all together—the movers and shakers, and the great unwashed—is the Banff Mountain Summit, a rendezvous without precedent in the history of mountain men and women. Over the past 25 years, the cream of climbing celebrity have walked the red carpet in this Canadian mountain town as guests of the world-renowned Banff Mountain Film Festival. As part of the festival's silver-anniversary celebration, the organizers have invited them en masse to participate in a millennial conference centered upon the future of mountain adventure.

To this end, each of these luminaries has written an essay upon an assigned aspect of mountain experience, applying his or her unique expertise and insight to peer into the crystal ball. Most have come here in person to share their visions with the greater mountaineering community. Other famous faces are here to show films or take part in panel discussions throughout the Mountain Book and Film Festivals later in the week. People like me have come to listen, learn, and, perhaps most importantly, gawk.

For my buddy Scott, however, Banff is more than a chance to ogle Catherine Destivelle in the flesh: It represents salvation. When I first heard about the Summit, I knew I would attend, but I also recognized that finding a companion to accompany me was going to be a challenge. When Minnesotans pull together enough time and money to hit the road for someplace where a contour map is more than a blank outline of the state, we climb like demons to make up for lost time. For this trip, however, I needed a partner willing to spend a week sitting on his ass. Scott was beginning to drift away from the climbing scene, gravitating toward an inexplicable interest in swing dancing. I figured that if the lineup slated to attend the Mountain Summit couldn't re-ignite his passion for more dignified pursuits, he was beyond saving. Thankfully, one look at the Banff guest list was enough to convince him to buy tickets a year in advance.

THE VENUE for the Mountain Summit is the historic Banff Springs Hotel. With its gabled turrets, intricate stonemasonry, and opulent interiors, it is the Canadian equivalent of Mad King Ludwig's Bavarian castle. All the bigwigs are lodged here. Scott and I, of course, taxi in from more modest accommodations on the outskirts of town.

One flaw in the organization of this event is immediately apparent. Between the seating in the main ballroom and the dais upon which the presenters will speak, a raised platform has been erected for the TV cameras. The result is a comical game of musical chairs as attendees snatch what appear to be prime seats, only to rapidly abandon them again moments later after discovering their view is completely obscured by cameramen. By the time the lights dim, a swath of empty chairs has fanned out like a formation of geese across the vast hall.

In terms of glimpsing true greatness, the day peaks early. The opening salvo in the Mountain Summit is appropriately fired by Sir Edmund Hillary. Perhaps no one has gained so much celebrity from the activity of mountaineering, and certainly no one has applied it more nobly. Throughout an adventurous life, Sir Edmund has traded on his notoriety, not for fame or personal wealth, but to build schools and clinics throughout the Nepal Himalaya. A kindly and compassionate gentleman, he nonetheless pulls no punches reproaching the trends of selfishness, commercialization, and media hype that are pervasive in modern adventuring. He particularly "despises" expeditions like the one that cashed in on George Mallory's corpse, for their "completely heartless approach." Although it may be unrealistic to expect that mountaineers will be immune to the moral ills that have infected Western society as a whole, I can't help but notice a fair number of big-name climbers shifting uncomfortably in their seats.

Throughout the morning, as the brightest stars in the mountain universe orbit the microphone, two styles emerge. Some read their essays verbatim. Others address the audience more directly, buttering their remarks with delicious layers of personality. It would be unfair to criticize those who read; after all, the oratory polish of Churchill is not one of the skills required to be an exceptional climber—but it may have something to do with being British.

Among the more fascinating off-the-cuff presentations is that of young Leo Houlding. Houlding is a 19-year-old Brit, enthused with the simplistic optimism and ego of youth, and prone to opinions that are hard to swallow coming from a teenaged authority. Things like: "Working a job isn't real; climbing is real." In short, Leo is a cocky punk. He is also a rock climbing prodigy who knows more about why he climbs than people three times his age. Leo's lust for "bold climbing," which he describes as traditional rock routes of extreme technical difficulty with marginal, if any, protection, is fueled by the feelings of extreme calm, satisfaction, and appreciation for living that he experiences after the fact. While it would be easy to dismiss Leo as a reckless adrenaline junkie and bold climbing as an aberrant tremor rather than earth-shaking, he applies such thought and discipline to this high-stakes game—and frankly, seems to have transcended to a mental plane well out of reach of most of us in the audience—that by the time he's finished we are convinced it is all quite sane. "What we are willing to climb and the style in which we are willing to climb it depend entirely on how we look at it," he says. "Perception and vision are our keys to evolution in rock climbing."

So much has been packed into the Mountain Summit that different presentations are being made simultaneously in different halls. In the afternoon, I jump venues in order to see the great Italian pioneer Riccardo Cassin, French superstar Catherine Destivelle, and my personal hero and friend Anderl Heckmair speculate on the future of European climbing. Because Anderl does not speak any English (in fact, his thick Bavarian dialect is nearly incomprehensible to those who speak German), a towering blond *bergfuhrer* interprets for him. At the age of 93, Anderl relies heavily upon his wife, and so Trudl Heckmair—who does speak English—also sits with him on stage, whispering translations and advice into his ear, until titters of amusement from the audience cause him to roll his eyes in a mock display of spousal acquiescence.

After his essay has been read, he entertains us with some choice anecdotes and sage wisdom. More than a few eyebrows are raised when he reveals that athletic doping is hardly a modern or Olympic phenomenon; indeed, performance-enhancing "heart drops" played an important role in the first ascent of the Eigerwand, and Anderl's most essential piece of equipment during the epic second ascent of the *Walker Spur*—second greatest north face in the Alps—was his flask of whiskey.

When it is Cassin's turn to speak, the language barrier really goes up. Perhaps best known to Americans for his brilliant ridge route on the South Face of Denali, Riccardo Cassin has also left his fingerprints on nearly every important handhold in the Alps. His lecture leaves absolutely nothing out— except the man himself. After making a very brief statement in Italian, Cassin retires to a chair while an interpreter reads his entire essay, a lengthy homage to the historic European routes in minutia. By the end, even Cassin is sacked out—a source of some bemusement to Catherine Destivelle, who keeps nudging Trudl Heckmair and motioning with her head toward the somnolent Italian. Since I am here to see the man, not his mouthpiece, I am less amused.

Despite the fact that fully half the presentation has been a literal snore, ducking out to see these legends of European climbing has been a rare privilege, yet no sooner have I rejoined Scott in the main hall than I begin to regret the decision. He has been listening to alpinist Jack Tackle, Royal Robbins, and Tom Hornbein speak on the topic of role models. Hornbein's musings in particular, delivered with modest, introspective eloquence, have moved Scott almost to tears. Besides being an amazing mountaineer, "Tom Hornbein," he tells me, "is a very good and decent man." It is clear that Scott has come away from this session with something far more substantial than voyeuristic pleasure—including a new hero of his own.

The day ends with a discussion centered on mountaineering's last frontiers. Chris Bonington's unbridled enthusiasm for exploring various god-forsaken blanks on the map, along with the Slovenian Silvo Karo's descriptions of the storm-wracked nightmares awaiting the next generation in Patagonia, inspire a request from Todd Skinner: "Please, the next time either of you is planning a trip, don't call me." Instead, what keeps Todd awake nights are the free-climbing prospects on exotic big walls—and getting to them ahead of anyone else. Skinner credits a Wyoming upbringing "outside the mainstream of opinion" for his maverick attitude that the actual summit and first ascent credit are of no consequence. While this may or may not be hyperbole (Skinner has clearly learned how to work an audience during his tenure as a corporate motivational speaker), he does deliver one of the most honest answers of the day. When an audience member asks him whether someone else claiming a first ascent of one of his unreported routes would bother him, he chooses his words carefully, "I *aspire* to be the type of person who wouldn't be bothered by that."

I, on the other hand, aspire to a pint of stout and a huge dinner. It has been a day so chockfull of food for thought that there has been precious little directed toward the belly. As the lights come up and the Big Guns retire to their private gatherings and conversations, the rabble streams out into the streets in search of local pubs or restaurants where we can satisfy our less cerebral appetites.

THE NEXT DAY is Halloween. My costume, courtesy of Northwest Airlines, is still "The Guy Who Never Changes His Clothes." Kitty Calhoun's getup is more in keeping with the spirit of the holiday. She kicks off the morning session sporting a black witch's hat and magic wand. Her goal is to put some of the enchantment back into Himalayan extreme climbing. Kitty notes some ominous trends: The ranks of the top-level Himalayan performers are being siphoned by the lucre of commercial guiding (which has also caused some peak fees to triple over the last 10 years), and by the quest to summit the "Big 14" 8000-meter peaks, endeavors that may bring fame and fortune to an individual, but do nothing to advance the sport. To Kitty, a proponent of lightweight, alpine-style assaults, it is a tragic waste of potential.

Mick Fowler is not one of the people Kitty is looking to smack with her wand. Mick is perhaps less well known outside his native England because he is not a "professional" climber. In fact, he is a professional tax man, who has credited such Himalayan plums as the *Golden Pillar* on Spantik and the North Face of Changabang to his account. In a delightfully well-structured and absorbing presentation (I'm beginning to think these British guys could read the phone book and make it sound interesting), Mick lays out the watershed events that have reshaped our concept of style in the Himalayas, and the relevance of different styles as we move forward. He urges those who may be tempted to apply outdated methods to first ascents to reconsider, "because we have only one set of objectives on this planet, and we must respect the potential of future generations." These words drive home how far and fast we've come. Fifty years ago only a handful of summits throughout the Himalayas had ever known the boots of men; today we are invoking the concept of Earth as a finite playground. It is no wonder people like Mick fear for the mountaineers of 50 or 100 years from now.

Other than the foibles of foreign language, the speakers at the Mountain Summit have, as a group, communicated their thoughts with impressive clarity. But, if there is a common thread that the participants have struggled to jam through the needle (at the risk of impaling themselves in the process), it is the underlying motivation for standing atop a particular lump of ice or rock. George Mallory's hackneyed "because it is there" has been trotted out, the vagaries of "risk and reward" alluded to on several occasions, but most have simply (wisely) chosen to duck the question altogether. That's not so easy for the next group of panelists.

"The Collectors" features Canadian Pat Morrow (one of the originators of the "Seven Summits" concept), 10-time Everest summiteer Babu Chiri Sherpa, and Polish mountaineer Krzysztof Wielicki, the fifth person to climb all 14 peaks over 8000 meters (and a name I'm going to remember the next time I play Scrabble). In the cases of Pat and Krzysztof, they became collectors almost by accident. Only after realizing they had already climbed the lion's share of a unique category of peaks did each make the conscious decision to pursue other summits for the singular reason of completing their "collections." At the risk of mangling Mallory, these men climbed these mountains "because they were left."

Babu Chiri is utterly unique to this conference. He is the only participant who knows exactly why he pursues a spectacular climbing record—indeed, why he climbs at all. It's his job. All of his climbs have occurred during the course of his employment as a guide, route-finder, and pack-mule for "tourists" like us. And by working hard and building his résumé—lapping Everest again and again, doing it faster (16 hours from basecamp to summit in May of 2000), and with unique twists (spending the night on top in May 1999)—he is better able to provide for his family and neighbors. Like Sir Edmund Hillary, Babu Chiri is cashing in on his fame in order to build a school in his native village. He is a humbling presence in this hall, and for the first time brings real perspective to the proceedings. After all, we're not gathered here to make peace or feed the masses. For all the pomp and circumstance, serious discussion, money and effort that has gone into the Mountain Summit, climbing is ultimately a self-indulgent game. And by the standards of many cultures, even the most penniless vagabond in our crowd (are you there Leo Houlding?) enjoys incredible luxury. Babu Chiri Sherpa, however, does not seem the least bit affected by these disparities; in fact, his livelihood depends on them. When asked his thoughts about the future of Himalayan climbing, he answers with the perspective and sincerity of a true sirdar: "I wish you all the best!"

It's a fitting segue into the next forum, an examination of adventure ethics. Among the presenters is the Canadian ethnobotonist Wade Davis, an intellectual smarty-pants who leaves both Scott and I feeling like we have yams for brains. He urges a sort of Hippocratic oath for adventurers, to go forth into delicate ecosystems and among native cultures armed with enough information and foresight to "do no harm." After listening to this (and with Babu Chiri still very much on my mind), I'm wondering if we shouldn't all just stay home and work on a cure for cancer.

When Yvon Chouinard takes the stage, however, things quickly lighten up. The projected image above the podium is of the famous smithy at his workbench, surrounded by the tools he used to forge a revolution in the design and manufacture of mountaineering gear. His opening line, "I hate equipment," brings down the house. He means it too. It quickly becomes clear that Chouinard hates anything that adds unnecessary complexity. He is a master of boiling things down, cutting through the crap, and expressing his opinion. To his way of thinking, ethics and style are two separate codes for conduct: "Ethics are so you don't screw it up for the next guy. Style is so you don't delude yourself into thinking you're so hot."

Ethically, he believes that anything goes, as long as it doesn't alter the environment or the next person's experience. In reality, of course, this means that a heck of a lot doesn't go: no chalk, bolts, fixed ropes, or garbage left on the mountain. Chouinard is convinced, however, that when we resort to these kinds of tools, aids, and laziness, we lose our way. Technology, specialization, and commercialization are all conspiring to needlessly clutter and dilute our experiences, and at the same time threaten the environment that is core to our activities. He urges adventurers to think, simplify, keep it real, and in the words of the late David Brower, "Turn around and take a step forward." I'm about to set fire to my Patagonia jacket when an imposing figure mounts the platform.

Even in this assembly of Titans, the closing speaker in the Banff Mountain Summit occupies a higher, Zeus-like position of authority. From Himalayan extreme climbing to exploring the last frontiers to ethical adventuring, he is the embodiment of nearly all the topics we have heard discussed throughout the last two days. And in terms of fame, he is the only individual who could bookend a conference opened by Sir Edmund Hillary. From the moment he walks on stage, Reinhold Messner grabs the spotlight like he owns it, which he clearly does. So what if he is prone to speaking in such absolutes ("We should not make rules for others!") that nearly everything else he says seems somewhat contradictory? So what if he takes a few sideways shots at what he clearly considers dubious style (i.e. climbers who "parasitically" use the fixed ropes of others, or who "solo" in groups)? This is the first man to "collect" all 14 8000-meter peaks, who with Peter Habeler shifted the entire paradigm in the Himalayas when they climbed fast, light, and unsupported to the top of Hidden Peak and without oxygen to the summit of Everest, the man who single-handedly proved there are no limits to what is possible with his solo ascents of Nanga Parbat and Everest. He's earned the right to speak in Klingon if he so pleases, and we will hang on every word.

Messner's message is an exuberant call to recognize the true values of the mountains, and to use adventuring as a way to collect experiences that will ultimately lead to a richer life. And life is the key. Over and over he exhorts us to recognize our limits so we can push them without going too far. "It is not so important how far or how high we go," he declares, "everything is a success if we come back safely. Coming back is like starting a new life—it is a deep, deep breath. To go, to risk, to search for our limits, and to come back." This is the decree from Mount Olympus.

AS THE FINAL thunderclaps from on high disappear into echoes, the mob filters out into the foyer, and for a brief while, Scott and I stand shoulder to shoulder with legends. A book launch is in progress. All the essays from the Mountain Summit, along with a series of specially commissioned portrait photographs, have been published in a volume titled *Voices from the Summit*. Some of the contributors are hobnobbing with appreciative and inquisitive admirers like Scott. Others are graciously signing copies of the book for pesky little autograph hounds like me. In addition to all the amazing people we have seen and heard, these pages also document the impressions and predictions of people that we didn't see, either because they spoke in the other theater, or because the authors were unable to attend: Jeff Lowe on the future of ice climbing, David Breashears on the power of an image, historical perspective from Dr. Charles Houston (the explorer of Nanda Devi and K2), the list goes on and on. Clearly, even as the chairs are being folded and the annoying camera platform finally comes down at the Banff Springs Hotel, there's more to be gleaned from this remarkable gathering.

So what's the bottom line? What, according to the high and mighty, does the future of mountaineering hold? Frankly, I think the real legacy of the Banff Mountain Summit lies not in predicting the future, but in inspiring it. I know one thing for sure: Scott's back on fire. Late into the evening he works scribbling numbers and diagrams on a pad. Finally he drops his pencil and announces with triumph that he has it all figured out.

At the sink, where I am washing out my shirt for the umpteenth time, I pause, "You have what figured out?"

"How I can partition my house. So I can rent out sections. So I won't have to work," and then he grins, "so I can get out there."

Originally published in CLIMBING, *No. 201, 2001.*

Author's notes: Many of the great alpine pioneers (Heckmair, Cassin, and Hillary, among others) have now passed on. Adventuring is still alive, but the new generation of climbers is more torn than ever between old-school minimalism vs. modern commercialism. Leo Houlding, for one, has managed to neatly straddle the divide by climbing Mount Everest dressed like George Mallory—as part of a book and movie deal.

The reason why my friend Scott originally drifted away from climbing may have had something to do with his experience on Eldorado Canyon's Naked Edge, *recounted in "Chew On This," page 201.*

A CONVERSATION WITH BABU CHIRI SHERPA
Schooling Everyone

FROM THE MOMENT that Babu Chiri walked on stage at the Banff Mountain Summit, a millennial conference featuring many of climbing's best and brightest, I knew I was looking at a very different sort of mountaineer. A squat linebacker of a man, Babu has tackled an incredible number of Himalayan expeditions during his 12-year tenure as a high-altitude guide. In the process, he has tagged the summit of Mount Everest 10 times, a record attained by only two other climbers (also Sherpas). He has also climbed Everest faster (just under 16 hours from Basecamp to summit in May of 2000) and stayed on top longer (21 hours in May 1999) than any other person to date. These achievements have put him in The Guinness Book of World Records, given him a marketable name in the climbing world (he is a sponsored consultant for Mountain Hardwear), and made him the Michael Jordan of mountaineering in his native Nepal.

What really set Babu apart from the other high achievers at the Mountain Summit, however, was his motivation for climbing. While Western mountaineers typically struggle to rationalize the time, money, and risk required to stand atop stratospheric patches of ice and rock, Babu's impetus is as simple as bread, butter, and books. For him, mountain climbing represents a means to provide for his family (he is the father of six daughters) and to better the lives of his neighbors. His record-breaking climbs have been undertaken with the express purpose of garnering international attention that he can parlay into support for his real passion: building schools in the remote villages of the Solo Khumbu region. To Babu Chiri, Everest is not the ultimate pinnacle of climbing ambition; it is a meal ticket and the medium by which he exercises a mighty social conscience.

I caught up with Babu one morning in Banff, while he and his friend Lhawang Dhondup attacked the Himalayan-sized breakfast buffet in the Banff Springs Hotel. Babu and Lhawang are partners in Nomad Expeditions, a trekking and climbing company, and Lhawang also serves as an interpreter for Babu—although Babu's grasp of English is good enough that he sometimes jumps in or corrects Lhawang, episodes that repeatedly brought down the house during their presentation at the Mountain Summit.

People know you because of Everest, but you have quite a record on other peaks as well.

I've been to the summit of Shishapangma two times. Cho Oyu, six times. Dhaulagiri, I've been one time. Kangchenjunga—I've been to the top there. I did Ama Dablam three times. I've been to other mountains but only in Nepal. I don't climb outside Nepal, except I've been to the Tibet side of Everest four times.

Tell me about the first time you climbed Mount Everest.

In 1990 I went with a French expedition. Marc Batard planned to spend 20 hours on the summit. He made the summit, but it was impossible for him to stay there. He went down to the South Col, and I met him there. The next day he was to climb Lhotse, and I was to be support for him, but he was very weak and couldn't go. So I went by myself to Everest, climbing from the South Col to the summit. I reached the summit at around 8:30 in the morning, but I didn't have a camera, I didn't have anything to make proof of the summit. But I was lucky because Marc left a sleeping bag, walkie-talkie radio, and some clothing at the summit, and I brought these things back down to Basecamp (broad smile) and then I had really good proof.

So they believed you.

(still smiling) They believed me. They said, "This guy's a really good mountaineer."

You've gone from having to prove yourself, to proving there are no limits when it comes to Everest. For example, spending the night on top—what was that like?

I reached the top around 11 o'clock in the morning, so during the day-time when there was light I wasn't worrying about anything. It was beautiful and I was enjoying the view. Once it started to get a little bit darker, then I was worrying about the wind. The wind up there gets really nasty…the whole tent and everything could take off, that was the worry.

Did you sleep?

No, because if I go to sleep, I might not wake up. It was really cold. Outside of my sleeping bag and inside of my tent, like two inches of frost.

You've done almost all your climbs without using supplemental oxygen. After the disaster in 1996, the guide Anatoli Boukreev was

criticized for climbing without oxygen. Some thought that he had put his own personal goals ahead of the safety of his clients. Boukreev stated that he felt better able to do his job climbing without oxygen. What do you think?

I think that not using oxygen is much more reliable in terms of saving other people's lives and doing a lot of things. For example, in 1995 I was with a British commercial expedition on the north side [of Everest]. At that time five people made it to the top and on the way back down they ran out of oxygen. If I were using oxygen [and it suddenly ran out], then my condition would be the same as the other people...But because I wasn't using oxygen I ran down, got the five bottles of oxygen, went up, met the other climbers, and saved their lives.

Is climbing Everest even hard for you now?

Everest is a big mountain. It changes every season. You never know what the weather's going to be, how the route's going to be, so it's always difficult in some ways. But because I've been so many times, I can understand the mountain maybe a little more than other people.

Do you feel fear up there anymore?

Of course, like anybody.

How did you accomplish your speed ascent of Everest?

I sent two Sherpas and Lhawang to the South Col, and they are waiting there at Camp 4 for me...in case they need to break trail on the upper part from the South Col to the summit. I start from Basecamp. All night: the icefall, from Camp 1 to Camp 2...At Camp 3 I need to make some food and change my clothes, so I take about a 40-minute break. I meet my friends at Camp 4 and we go to the summit.

(To Lhawang) You guys kept up with him?

Lhawang: No, his brother Dawa started with him, but Babu ran away!

You smashed the old record with your time of 15 hours, 56 minutes...

Babu: The reason wasn't to break all the different people's records. The main reason was to raise money for the school project.

Tell me about the school project.

Lhawang: Whatever money he got [from his record-breaking climbs] he put it toward the school, so it's almost finished. And then he wants to continue the same project, to build [other] schools in remote areas of the Solo Khumbu area, so he can give back something to his community.

Babu: The first reason is because there are so many poor people in the hilly area, and to help them. And also, I never had an education in my childhood and I know that education is so important here in the world, so that's why I wanted to do this.

If you had enough money to take care of your family and to build the schools, would you still climb?

If I have all the money, then I would put all my effort and energy towards the school project, and I wouldn't be climbing. I wouldn't have to climb.

Originally published in CLIMBING, *No. 201, 2001.*

Author's note: Sadly, on April 29, 2001—less than two months after this interview first appeared in print—Babu Chiri was killed in a crevasse fall near Camp 2 on Mount Everest. As of 2014, his record for the longest time spent on the summit of Everest still stands.

HOUSE ON FIRE

Steve House Is Pushing the Possibilities of Alpine Climbing to the Brink—
What Makes Him So Hot?

S TEVE HOUSE is determined to carry my pack.

Ordinarily, this might not be unusual—as someone who earns most of his living as a professional mountain guide, House is used to shouldering the burden for those in his charge. But House is not my guide and we aren't slogging up some snowy peak. Instead, we're about to traverse the corridor of a budget hotel in Canmore, Alberta, and we've known each other less than two minutes.

"Let me carry your pack," he offers, whipping it onto his shoulders.

"That's OK," I assure him, "I can take it."

"No really," he says, "I'll carry it."

"Steve, I don't have anything else to carry."

"I've got it," he replies, and he's off down the hallway.

All I can do is follow, conspicuously unencumbered, while one of the hottest players in North American alpine climbing ferries my gear outside. There are, I will come to realize, a couple of reasons why House is so insistent upon being my Sherpa.

First, Steve House is a nice guy. He knows I'm dogged after a sleepless night of travel. But House himself is also a little off his stride this morning. He's agreed to be profiled by a writer he's never met—to spend a few days climbing and talking with a stranger about ideas and events that make up the core of who he is. House is an intensely private and self-effacing person, and it goes against his grain to thrust himself into the media spotlight. Watching him tote my load across the hotel parking lot, I realize that he's thinking hard about how and what he's going to unload on me.

THE FIRST indication that House would orbit close to the nucleus in alpine circles came in 1995, when he and Eli Helmuth climbed *First Born* (Alaska Grade 5), the first ascent of Denali's Father and Sons Wall, a 6000-foot "Last Great Problem" on the mountain's northwest buttress. The wall had

175

been targeted by the legendary Mugs Stump, a torchbearer of cutting-edge North American alpine climbing throughout the 1980s and early '90s. When Stump perished in a crevasse collapse in 1992, the project was left to the next generation of big guns—a group mostly in their early to mid-30s at the time—that included the likes of Mark Twight, Scott Backes, and Alex Lowe. But they never got a crack at it either. Instead, the seasoned veterans had to content themselves with reading about the climb in magazines after House and Helmuth, a couple of virtually unknown youngsters, sprinted up the wall in a 33-hour push.

"I thought, 'Damn! Okay, who is this guy?'" Twight recalls. "And you know, [the name] didn't register, and I thought, 'Ahh, some kid from Bellingham just got lucky.' But the next year…"

The next year House's name was on everybody's lips when he established *Beauty Is a Rare Thing* (Alaska Grade 5, 5.8 AI 4+, 7000 feet) on the northwest face of Denali's West Buttress. And it wasn't just the route that had people talking—it was the style. Alone, and outfitted more appropriately for a session of ice bouldering than climbing in the Alaska Range (carrying just ice tools, a water bottle, and a few energy bars), House left camp intending merely to explore the lower face. Fourteen hours later when he returned to his tent, he had become the first person ever to achieve a solo, single-push, first ascent of a major route on Denali.

"He wasn't just following the old recipe," Twight observes. In fact, this ability to think outside the box, combined with obviously superb technical skills, so impressed Twight that in 1998 he invited House to join him and Johnny Blitz for an attempt on Mount Bradley in Alaska's Ruth Gorge. It was another watershed climb for House. Not only did the trio succeed in putting up a major new route—*The Gift (That Keeps on Giving)* (Alaska Grade 6, 5.9 A3 WI 6X, 2400 feet)—but House led the key pitch, an appalling, poorly protected stretch of thin mixed climbing that both deeply impressed, and deeply horrified his companions. The memory of House's lead still conjures up visions of doom for Twight: "That type of risk belongs within the reach of 9-1-1," he asserts. "So I was a little upset."

In the end, however, Twight came away from *The Gift* with a cemented respect for the younger man's formidable climbing skills, particularly the mental toughness that allowed House to keep it together on the bowel-churning crux pitch. Despite any perceived transgression, House was someone that Twight wanted to do business with again in the mountains. Thus, the real gift of the Mount Bradley trip was House's introduction to Twight, an important mentor, a fellow traveler in terms of style, and a key player in a fraternal order of alpinists—a group of talented and free-thinking climbers who have bonded together not only to create cutting-edge climbs, but as brothers.

Steve House with Catherine Mulvihill in the Canadian Rockies

HOUSE AND I are headed out to do a little ice climbing. Our companions for the day are Catherine Mulvihill—her husband is the well-known Canadian alpinist Barry Blanchard—and Catherine and Barry's fluffy lion-of-a-dog Finnegan. Mulvihill is entertaining House for a few days while Blanchard is away guiding. The fact that Mulvihill and Finnegan are coming with us is good for all concerned. For House, they offer a safe harbor in these uncharted waters of journalistic scrutiny—and because Mulvihill and House enjoy a boisterous friendship, their interaction gives me a chance to see more of the real Steve House. In other words, he lets Catherine carry her own pack.

House is an American Mountain Guide Association-certified alpine, rock, and ski-mountaineering guide who has risen to the highest levels of his profession (he is currently the coordinator for AMGA Alpine Guide courses and exams). He lives in the small mountain town of Mazama, Washington, in the North Cascades with his wife, Anne Keller, who is also a guide (and also protective of her privacy—she declined to be interviewed for this article). But this is the first time I've laid eyes on the man, and he's not exactly what I expected. House, age 31, has a clean-cut, almost military appearance—square-faced and strong-jawed with shortly trimmed, dark hair—but the thing I find most striking is that he's not as big as I'd imagined. People often say the same thing about movie stars and other larger-than-life personalities when they finally get a chance to experience them up close and in the flesh, but that's not exactly what's going on here. He's a man of average height and solid build, but he is in no way muscle-bound, and that's what surprises me. House's strength is legendary. His climbing partners marvel at how he can hang on, sometimes for hours, grappling with a steep, technical crux—so I have envisioned him with bison shoulders, action-figure biceps, and forearms like hams. He's a Superman all right, but the movie version, not the comic book.

Once we begin threading our way up toward the vertical blue streak that is our destination, another celebrated talent of House's becomes apparent, something that is doubtlessly the result of his decades of batting around in the complex wilderness of the Cascades: the ability to move comfortably and quickly across any form of mountainous terrain. Near the base of the climb, the trail traverses a slabby, snow-covered rock band. Mulvihill and I kick steps, placing our feet deliberately and using our hands to steady ourselves. House romps up with Finnegan straining at the leash. By all accounts, the late Alex Lowe (another of House's mentors) also had this same comfort level with the mountains, the same gift for negotiating ice, rock, and snow without breaking stride. "The typical North American alpine climber is really good walking on flat ground, and really good when it's steep and technical because of the background we have here: Yosemite, frozen waterfalls in Canada, etc.," explains Twight. "But we don't have really good moderate alpine terrain here—5.5 to 5.9 rock, Grade 4 ice, and big swaths of 60- to 65-degree mixed terrain—so most guys just can't move fast on it. Going out with Steve I realized this guy has all the skills."

Of course, steep and technical is what House eats for breakfast, and this climb is a Pop-Tart. Watching him lead the plumb-line, WI 5 pitch (a lead that I would rent billboard space to advertise if I'd done it) is like watching a champion prizefighter punch a bag: Impressive, but it's just practice. Later, after we've all lapped the column and are back on the ground, I ask him if ice that's merely vertical is even hard for him. He smiles sheepishly. "When the ice gets really, really thin, and I have to think hard and work just to get something to stick…that's difficult." And what about the risk? How does he justify pitches like the crux on Mount Bradley—pitches that can appear almost suicidal, even to a seasoned alpinist like Twight? "One of the things I learned from Alex is that as long as the opportunity for gear exists, why not have a look?" On Bradley, he contends, at the crux—a torso-sized free-hanging icicle off a chockstone overhang—there was reasonable gear.

Steve House goes for a stroll

"Above the crux..." he smiles. "Beyond the crux there was no gear for awhile. It was definitely out there. But there was no way of knowing that."

While House sorts the rack, Mulvihill puts the screws to the journalist. She kids about how she and House had imagined me: festooned with dangling Nikons and tape recorders, desperate to document his every breath, but beneath the good-natured ribbing there is a palpable concern that I have come to bury Caesar. She asks me point-blank what my angle for this story will be. Being the wily investigator that I am, I turn the tables by probing for what it is about House and the rest of his crew that she fears might be misrepresented. Her answer could apply to almost anyone who has ever shaken things up through innovation: "These guys are so evolved," she says. "That's why they're amazing."

Moments later, House, who is now wrestling the dog, suddenly announces that he has a friend who has discovered the perfect pet for climbers. "It's a kind of tortoise," he grins. "When you leave on a long trip, you just put it in a drawer and it hibernates for months. Isn't that awesome?"

NO TURTLE IN a cupboard ever felt more confined than Steve House does right now. We can't go climbing today, probably not tomorrow either. A dump truck of a snowstorm (the largest since 1967) has backed up against Canmore and is slowly raising its bed. Our cars are buried under two feet and counting, but it hardly matters since the roads are closed. To make things even worse for House, I have moved from the hotel into the Blanchard-Mulvihill flophouse for wayward alpinists. Out comes the dreaded tape recorder.

House is a measured, almost cautious speaker. He chooses his words carefully, often staring out the window for long seconds while he searches for just the right phrase or description. He appears to be a genuinely introspective and articulate person, and one who applies a great deal of thought to everything he does—especially climbing.

In his early years, House was raised amidst the mountains of the Pacific Northwest, and became a good all-around athlete; it was almost inevitable that the two would merge and he would start climbing at an early age. The clincher was that his parents, particularly his father, were also mountaineers and not only introduced him to rock climbing, they remained very supportive of his adventures as he grew older. "Once we got our driver's licenses we'd go to Smith Rock or the City of Rocks," says House. "I can't believe that my parents let a couple of 16-year-olds drive five hours to go rock climbing for the weekend. What were they thinking?"

Throughout high school he continued to rock climb, but he also participated in more traditional sports like track and Nordic skiing. After graduating in 1988, he spent a year abroad as part of a student exchange program, and this was the seminal experience that not only ignited his life-long dedication to alpine climbing, it probably had the greatest influence in shaping his current perspectives about risk and style. And yet it happened almost by accident.

"I wanted to go to Switzerland or France," House explains, "one of the Alpine countries." Instead, he was assigned to somewhere he knew nothing about: Yugoslavia. He didn't even bring climbing gear with him.

Few people there spoke any English, and House didn't know a word of the Slavic dialect. For him, the foreign classroom was a Tower of Babel. "They just put me in school and I'm sitting there and blah, blah, blah— I don't understand a thing." After a month he quit attending classes and focused on the language. "I tried to memorize 20 new words each day," he says, and within a few months he had mastered enough vocabulary to engage in basic communication, but was still frustrated. "I had nothing to do. I was just memorizing words every day." House's host family was sympathetic. When he told them that he liked climbing, they took him to a nearby city and hooked him up with an alpine club—and the entire experience was transformed.

Ironically, climbing was practically the national pastime in the part of Yugoslavia where House had been languishing. He quickly made up for lost time. "I'd go out with anybody, any day, anywhere, it didn't matter," he laughs. "For the next nine months, four to five days a week, it was awesome." And the way the general population got behind mountaineering also blew him away: "Every Monday morning the whole front of the sports page would be about climbing. What people had done, what routes were in. And you didn't have to be famous to have your name in there."

What House had stumbled into was one of the crucibles of world alpine climbing: Slovenia. Pinched between Austria and Croatia, Slovenia is a small region (now its own country) encompassing the relatively minor summits of the Julian Alps, but it is a powerhouse of mountaineering enthusiasm and talent. One out of every 13 people there is a member of the country's official alpine association. And Slovenian society, economically poorer than western European nations, not only embraces alpinism, it fosters an attitude of less is more, specifically less reliance on fancy or expensive equipment and more reliance on "can do" ways of thinking. As a result, Slovenian climbers (people like Silvo Karo and Tomaz Humar) and their achievements (new routes on Cerro Torre, Dhaulagiri, Everest, and many others) are among the most respected in the world. It was this culture, and these ideals into which House was immersed—and he soaked it up like a piece of dry bread.

"Just as an example of the kind of stuff we would do," says House, "Four of us went up in winter to climb the north face of Triglav (9396 feet), which is a 6000-foot limestone face. It has climbing up to 5.8, a lot of 4th class and low 5th class. But it's winter, and I'm like, 'What do I need?'

And they say, 'Just your lunch.' We got up early, climbed all day, and at dusk there we are at the top of the face. And all we had was our lunches and wind shells. So I started out thinking that was normal."

These were the first technical mountain routes that House had ever done, and he thrived in the alpine environment. In addition, the Slovenian attitudes of moving fast and light, keeping it simple, and the belief that the mind is the greatest tool in the climber's box of tricks also appealed to him.

THE BROTHERHOOD. Twight, Backes, Blanchard, and House, among others. It began, at least for House, with a Gathering.

For many people, the weeks leading up to Christmas are a pain in the ass. But for a select group of climbers, it is indeed the most wonderful time of the year. From every direction they converge upon the little town of Cody, Wyoming, for a weeklong bacchanal of hard partying and even harder climbing. The Gathering, as it has come to be known, was conceived by Alex Lowe in the early 1990s as a way to stay connected with good friends, and it quickly became an annual tradition. For an up-and-coming alpinist, an invitation to the Gathering is the ultimate backstage pass—a chance to mingle and hang out, and if you're lucky, pick up a guitar and jam with the band.

After returning from Slovenia, House went to college at Evergreen State in Olympia, Washington, met and married his wife, and ultimately committed himself to a career as a professional guide and to pursuing alpine climbing. In 1995, while guiding a client in the Ruth Gorge, he met Alex Lowe, who told him about "this thing we have in Cody. You really ought to come."

At the Gathering, House was introduced to a number of future partners and mentors—including the man whose photograph had been taped up inside House's high school locker—Barry Blanchard.

"A de-mentor," Blanchard smiles, clarifying his relationship to House. "I actually didn't get to go climbing with Steve in Cody," he explains. "But Steve Swenson said to me, kind of as an aside at breakfast one morning, 'You should take Steve on one of your routes up in Canada in the wintertime. He's a really good mixed climber.' And I believed that because he was repeating some of Alex's routes on-sight."

And so the next winter, when Blanchard and Joe Josephson were looking for a third person to join them for a whack at a new route on Mount Robson's Emperor Face, they gave House a call. The trip was the best and worst of times for House. He climbed strongly and formed instant and lasting friendships with both Blanchard and Josephson, but they were forced to retreat from high on the face when House dropped the plunger for their stove. "If there is any one minute that Steve House could relive in his life so far, that might be it," Blanchard laughs. Blanchard and House still meet nearly every winter, hoping to put the final nail in the Robson coffin.

Another important relationship for House that sprang from the Gathering was with Scott Backes. Like Twight, Backes was a kindred spirit in terms of bringing and applying new ways of thinking to the alpine arena. House's ascents of *First Born* and *Beauty Is a Rare Thing* on Denali were, at least in part, an answer to the call sounded by Backes and Twight in 1994 with their 72-hour round-trip first ascent of *Deprivation* (Alaska Grade 6) on the north buttress of Mount Hunter. In Cody, however, Backes' first impressions of House were affected more by what the young gun didn't do. "What caught my attention," Backes explains, "was when he asked me about this mixed route that I had led. Alex led it that same Gathering, and then I went up…and I thought it was dangerous. And I said, 'Don't do it. Wait.' He waited. And that's what impressed me." And then Backes laughs, "Because I know what I would have done."

In 1999, Backes, Blanchard, and House teamed up to climb a new route in winter on Howse Peak in the Canadian Rockies. Despite some team judgment that all involved agree was flawed (they pushed on despite a heavy storm and Blanchard was nearly whacked in an avalanche on the descent), *M16* (VI A2 WI 7+), done in traditional alpine style, was another tour de force for House. It included another of his infamous "make or break" crux leads. Blanchard does a slow exhale when recalling the difficulty and seriousness of this pitch, and the other "just extraordinary pieces of climbing" he has seen House commit to over the years, "No bolts, ground-up, first time being there. There's only a dozen guys in the world who can pull that sort of thing off."

Climbers outside the clique are no less impressed with House's talent and potential, but urge caution when applying titles. "It's difficult to tell, as these things are unfolding in front of you, how it's all going to fit in," says alpine veteran Michael Kennedy. "Time will tell what his influence is going to be. And yet I don't think these guys are blowing it out of proportion too much. He's on a roll with this single-push thing—he's really taken it to a pretty extraordinarily high level of commitment and boldness. But I'm leery of putting too much expectation on someone like that. I think it has the potential for affecting what the guy ends up doing. Although, he seems to be, so far, fairly immune to that kind of pressure."

OKAY, NOW it's House's turn. As the snow has grown deeper and higher outside the window, so has the pile of mini cassette tapes on the table between us. In terms of who he is and what he's done, I've put him through the wringer, squeezed him dry. But now it's time to talk about the stuff that Steve House wants to talk about: the why. And we will frame it in terms of two more monumental climbs, one that he's already done, and one that he dreams of attempting.

In the summer of 2000, House, Twight, and Backes made climbing headlines with their 60-hour, single-push ascent of the *Czech Direct* (5.9X M6 WI 6+) on the south face of Denali. Carrying only basic climbing gear, belay jackets, energy gel, and two stoves, they launched up the massive 9000-foot wall in a sort of kamikaze assault. Hopefully, in the not-too-distant future, House, Twight, and Rolando Garibotti will try to take this to another level by attempting the soaring, unclimbed, 7000-foot south face of Nuptse, a 7855-meter peak adjacent to Mount Everest, in a similar style. The Nuptse project, whether it comes to fruition or not, is certain to provoke similar notions of recklessness and unjustifiable risk. Just why are these guys sacrificing safety for speed?

What House wants people to know is that they aren't. In fact, the exact opposite is true. "I think one of the biggest misconceptions of single-push climbing and one of the biggest misconceptions about our climb of the *Czech Direct* is that we were really out there," House says. "I will not disagree with anyone who says what we did was dangerous. If something had gone totally wrong, we certainly could have been killed. For us, it was a better solution to climb the *Czech* in a single push than traditional alpine style because it was safer—if for no other reason than because we were on the route only a third the time." That's a lot less time in the shooting gallery, a lot less time for a storm to develop, a lot less time exposed to all the objective hazards of the mountain environment.

Of course, there is a trade-off. If things go wrong, he admits, you've reduced your options. But when people don't see a huge pack full of gear, they tend to think there aren't any options—or planning. And that frustrates him. House and company prepared for this climb like a moon shot: Every ounce, every calorie, every decision was considered, analyzed, justified. Altitude: They climbed the *West Buttress* first, giving themselves ample time to acclimatize. Weather: They waited until a good, solid window was forecast (and all they needed was a few days). Descent: There's a wanded cattle trail from the summit down the other side of the mountain. The bottom line, at least according to House, is that these guys didn't climb the *Czech Direct* in pursuit of a purer style. They wanted to climb this route, and for them—for *this* team, with their collective strengths, weaknesses, and experiences—this style was the best solution for the terrain.

Nuptse—if and when they get a crack at it—will present a whole new set of problems: an unclimbed route, Himalayan weather and altitude, not to mention the intense cold and long periods of darkness during the nighttime (a key factor largely missing from polar latitude climbs in the Alaska Range). But again, for House and his team, the terrain seems to dictate a single-push solution. But it may not. In which case, they will adapt their style, fail, or go home.

None of this is new. House is quick to point out the single-push style has a history. As an example, he offers up the fourth ascent of the Eiger's North Face in 1950, completed in a single 18-hour push. Granted, early on, these climbs tended to occur more by accident than design. "The climbers carried bivy gear intending to camp," he explains, "but they either couldn't find a place to stop or it didn't make sense to stop." Later, both Europeans and Americans began applying these ideas more purposefully. Mugs Stump, one of House's original inspirations, was one of them. "Mugs had a pretty clear vision from the beginning that that's the way he wanted to climb." House just picked up the baton—and has kept on running.

And in doing so, House is helping to transform alpine climbing itself. Catherine Mulvihill hit the nail on the head: Evolution is what's going on here. That's what they're all up to, House and this brotherhood of his: It's about adapting, experimenting, finding and applying the best solutions to the hardest problems. And this year they have continued the streak. In April, House, Blanchard, and Garibotti put up *Sans Blitz* (V 5.5 WI 7, 2500 feet) on Mount Fay, a route that Blanchard calls "the hardest ice climb that I have done." The crux pitch, of course, fell to House. It's uncanny, say his partners, that House always seems to get the toughest pitches.

"Fate hands Steve the pitches he deserves," says Twight. "Or that he can do, and anything less would leave him unfulfilled. He's going up there for a reason, to find those pitches and climb those pitches that will transform him."

Then, in June, House and Garibotti topped *The Infinite Spur* on Mount Foraker in a 13-hour push (25 1/2 hours to the summit). "This was a first for me," House reports. "I realize now that I've made 'the step.' Climbing routes this way is no longer intimidating or frightening. Knowing that it works…knowing that we can deal with just about anything that might happen up there and be OK."

Finally, there is one other significant advantage of moving fast and light, and if Steve House has a message, this might be it: "The simpler we make things, the richer the experience."

"There are memories," he says, talking once more now about the *Czech Direct,* "of big periods of time when it was nothing but fun." Thinking back on it still makes him smile. He and his partners led blocks of four consecutive pitches each. House somehow, once again, ended up with four crux pitches in a row, and was in hog heaven. "It's like taking all your favorite pitches and stacking them on top of each other. What could be better? It's what we all dream of, right? The perfect route that goes on and on forever."

Originally published in CLIMBING, *No. 209, 2002.*

Epics

Rescue party going over the edge of El Capitan

STRANGE TRIP ON "THE TRIP"
A Minnesota Climber Is Center Stage in a Comedy of Errors

W HILE TRAPPED or injured climbers cannot rely on outside help, many epic mountaineering stories have culminated with the timely arrival of the cavalry. But sometimes the rescue itself can add a few chapters—as Dave Mital discovered during a solo attempt on El Capitan's *Tangerine Trip*.

Everything was going like clockwork until early on the fourth day. That morning, Friday the 13th in fact, Dave was cleaning the 11th pitch when the rope dislodged a granite boilerplate with his name on it. The block must have just grazed his head (a more direct hit would have spattered his brains halfway to Fresno) but even that was enough to knock him senseless. When he regained consciousness, severe head pain, disorientation, blurred vision, and the fact that he seemed to be carrying most of his blood on the outside of his body convinced Dave to shout for a rescue.

Within an hour Yosemite park rangers were assessing and reassuring him through a bullhorn while a Navy helicopter ferried rescue equipment between El Cap Meadow and the summit. By mid-afternoon YOSAR specialist "Bob" had been lowered 900 feet to the level of Dave's portaledge. On almost any other part of El Capitan, Dave's rescue would have been a basket ride from over, but the continuously overhanging geometry of *Tangerine Trip* left Bob dangling 70 feet out from his objective. Luckily, he had come prepared. Using a pressurized line-gun, Bob repeatedly attempted to bridge the gap. Heavy winds—coupled with the fact that Bob was spinning like a rotisserie on the end of his thread—made for some complicated ballistics, but even with Dave locked in the crosshairs the projectile was yanked off target when the line came up short. After refitting the unit with a longer rope, Bob fired a shot that would have made Annie Oakley proud, landing the missile right in Dave's lap. Clutching the Styrofoam projectile like a new puppy, Dave felt a wave of relief—until he realized that the rescue line was streaming off into empty space. Regrettably, Bob had neglected to secure his end. Bob had the gun, Dave now had the only projectile; after a few spirited but futile attempts to throw Dave another rope, Bob was reeled up.

As evening arrived, the Navy took over. The helicopter rescue crew—whose previous missions were limited to plucking injured hikers and fishermen—was gung-ho for a chance at a high-angle job. The fact that *Tangerine Trip* was inverted only added to their enthusiasm and creativity. With a crewman dangling 200 feet beneath the chopper, it maneuvered close to the cliff and began rocking. Penduluming wildly, the rescuer rode a giant tire swing toward the stranded climber. Meanwhile, Dave watched with growing concern as the rotor blades drifted to within inches of the cliff face above him. With the swinging airman still some distance away and the possibility of a fiery death for everyone concerned looming closer and closer overhead, Dave frantically waved them off.

Undaunted, the Navy crew quickly implemented a new plan. By alternately rushing the cliff and then abruptly backing off, they set the dangling crewman into slingshot motion. Dave watched with amazement as the tiny figure came bull-whipping toward him out of the dusk, snapping back only 20 feet away from him on the first attempt, five feet on the second, and brushing fingertips with him on the third. Setting up for the fourth and final try of the day, the chopper pilot compensated to a degree that he felt sure would allow his colleague to make contact with the wall. In this respect, at least, he was successful. From only a few feet away, Dave watched in horror as the rocketing rescuer slammed into the granite at about 50 miles an hour. With the unconscious crewman dangling below like a twisted marionette, the helicopter disappeared into the gloom. Delirious from his injuries and distressed that his predicament had now resulted in other casualties, Dave settled in for a restless night.

The next morning, Dave was informed via bullhorn that the Navy helicopter crew had a revised battle plan. In the absence of the buffeting winds which had hampered efforts the previous afternoon, the new scenario called for a dangling rescuer to simply throw Dave a rope, reel himself into the belay, clip Dave in, and slash him loose from his anchors. One important detail, however, had been overlooked: Each time the rope was tossed it arced out less than 20 feet before being redirected straight down by the gale-force currents of the chopper's rotor wash. Stalled at square one, the military was forced to abort the mission and call a final retreat.

In an attempt to implement the same strategy minus the giant wind machine, Bob was once again lowered from the rim. Again, rope toss after rope toss came up agonizingly short. Eventually, as the winds started to pick up, rescuers on the ground, on the summit, and even dangling Bob seemed overcome with frustration and at wits' end in terms of what to do. That's when a dim light bulb clicked on inside the battered cranium of the victim himself. Directing Bob to lower a large U-shaped loop of rope, Dave mustered his strength and then flung the weighted missile from the line-gun outward. Like a miraculous last second shot from half-court, the projectile swished through the hoop and the game was over.

Epilogue: Dave Mital was treated for a severe concussion, broken nose, muscle pulls, and numerous soft-tissue injuries. He eventually got back on the horse, returning to successfully solo *Tangerine Trip*. Remarkably, the helicopter crewman who impacted the rock at high velocity sustained only a pulled groin muscle. For his efforts, the Navy awarded him "Rescue Airman of the Year."

Originally published in CLIMBING, *No. 197, 2000.*

Author's note: Dave's rescue was headline news back in Minnesota. When his mother was asked to comment about her son's seemingly irresponsible and self-destructive behavior, she set the record straight, declaring: "I'd rather have him high on a mountain than high on drugs!"

Storm clouds gathering on El Capitan

ITSY BITSY SPIDERS
Drained on El Cap

THE MERCIFUL THING about death in the mountains is that it usually occurs with the suddenness and swiftness of a bus accident. A roaring avalanche, a plunging fall, a hail of ice and stones—while these fates are not without pain, regret, or horror, at least their durations can be measured in seconds. Outwardly, this may not seem much of a blessing, but on Death Row the real punishment is the waiting. It is the true unfortunate who, like a staked goat, has time to watch and fully comprehend as the butcher sharpens his knives. All my climbing life I've been stepping off curbs in front of buses, but I'm not that lucky. When I finally met God face to face, He was wearing a white apron.

Although every climb has risk, there are some routes so compelling or so notorious that they seem worth dying for. El Capitan's *Magic Mushroom* is not one of them. Low in terms of popularity, middle-of-the-road with respect to difficulty, largely overshadowed by its contemporaries (most notably the neighboring *Shield*), *Magic Mushroom* had my name written all over it. I wanted something big and impressive, something utterly foolproof. And although I dreamed of untamed north faces in my future, for the time being, I was more than content to hide behind the domesticated skirt strings of El Capitan.

My partner was stronger, more experienced, and much truer to his ambitions. As a veteran of numerous Yosemite big walls, including two with me, Dave Mital had all the earmarks of a bona-fide El Cap fanatic. For him, the sweeping expanse of the Valley's greatest monolith was a canvas upon which he intended to sketch an entire climbing career. *Magic Mushroom* would add yet another vertical stroke to his work-in-progress.

Together we made a seasoned and competent team—well up to the rigors of *Magic Mushroom*'s sustained A3 nailing—yet anyone who saw us approach the climb might have mistaken us for the survivors of a routed army. I had twisted an ankle several days earlier leaping from a boulder problem, and the injury had swollen badly, like a fat purple haggis ballooning between my foot and shin. As a result, I had to crawl and hop to the base of El Cap, while Dave wobbled like an overloaded mule beneath the lion's share of our gear. Once we managed to drag ourselves to the foot of the wall, however, we recovered a modicum of efficiency and dignity; oddly enough, standing in slings wasn't a problem for me.

My memories of the climb itself are sketchy. I remember crisp October days spent aiding long, awkward corners of gray-brown granite, and multiple nights smothered in the claustrophobic clutches of my single-point hammock. Any details beyond these superficial impressions are blurred, having been diluted or washed away completely by a geyser of adrenaline during the course of subsequent events.

Perhaps the first inkling of what was to come was suggested in the numerology of our penultimate day. Despite the short autumn days, we had estimated we could finish the route in just under a week and had provisioned ourselves accordingly. Midway through day six, however, we were still six pitches shy of our goal, and so we eventually settled into a final bivouac at precisely six o'clock. At this point, we thought we were merely low on food and water; we hadn't a clue that we were damned.

We bunked that last night on Chickenhead Ledge, an aptly named terrace offering about as much comfort as sleeping on an abacus. Nevertheless, freed from the bonds of my nylon straightjacket for the first time in many nights, I luxuriated in its knobby massage. As I pulled the drawstring of my sleeping bag tight round my face and snuggled in for the night, my thoughts were of appreciation for such a relaxed and incident-free adventure, now only scant pitches from completion, and for the idyllic fall weather that had graced our week, visibly manifested in the panoply of waning summer constellations shining low in the western sky. Dog-tired from the physical and mental exertions of a multi-day climb, Dave and I slept like the dead. Neither of us noticed when sometime during the night the stars vanished.

WE AWOKE to a claustrophobic thick mist that smothered all sound and any trace of the world beyond our solitary ledge. The air was leaden, heavy with the moisture that could spell real trouble so late in the year. The fog itself was alive, swirling, pouring over the rim of El Capitan and into the massive trough of Yosemite Valley. Yet there was not a breath of wind.

This weird cascade of cloud spurred us to action. We packed and racked earlier and faster than any previous morning, and spoke little, if at all. A palpable tension had infected our moods; we were now in a race against deteriorating weather.

The initial pitches went as quickly as could be expected considering the leader was constantly pausing to glance over his shoulder. I tackled the first pitch, Dave the second. Belaying was an exercise in nerve control—the

complete lack of anything other than the ominous murk to focus upon kept me squirming with impatience. I tried to keep optimism alive by imagining that any minute the cloud would thin and we would emerge above it, like castaways on some heavenly shore, clinging to the rocks beside a great ocean of vapor. Instead, the fog seemed conscious of my fantasy and determined to shove it down my throat; the mist thickened, crowding into every surrounding nook and cranny until with each breath it began to fill my insides as well. I exhaled it in frosty plumes. The temperature was falling like a brick.

IT WAS ON the third pitch of the day, the second to last before the summit, when things began to fall apart. The first gust nearly knocked me from my slings. Moments later, the wind rose again with the fury of a moon launch. I clung to my aiders like a fighter pinned against the turnbuckle, praying for the pummeling to end. I was still waiting when the knockout punch landed: a sopping, stinging mixture of wind-driven rain and snow. The sleet quickly penetrated my clothing through every possible opening, and water colder than an arctic sea wicked in along the climbing rope and trickled like icy piss down my crotch and legs. My lead deteriorated into a panicked rush of fumbled gear and A4 placements in an A2 crack. Gradually, a large roof loomed into view that promised shelter. Nestled beneath the overhang I found a belay, but one furnished with its own unique brand of discomfort. Tethered to a bolt, bumping and rocking like a floating minnow bucket in the wild currents of the atmosphere, was a severed human head.

I have been told that a body possesses internal defense mechanisms that shield the brain from situations or events that are too shocking to comprehend. I can now say with absolute certainty that nothing of the sort exists within me. In fact, quite the opposite is true. Whiteout, wind, rain—it all ceased to matter the moment I locked eyes with that leering, truncated apparition. The thing scared me witless, and if I ever meet the genius who carved such a gruesome and realistic wooden icon, and then went through the effort to hang it 30 pitches up El Capitan, I'm going to buy him a drink and have a good laugh—while I watch him writhe in agony from the poison.

Real or not, I was not eager to share a belay with this creepy totem. Its sinister eyes and demonic grin seemed the embodiment of Death itself. The thing hummed with bad vibes. Belaying here would be tempting fate; somehow, tossing it off seemed even more portentous. Squinting into the storm beyond the left edge of the roof I discerned an alternative: a set of fixed anchors in the final easy chimney leading to the summit. With a shudder that was only half hypothermia I turned my back on Mr. Death Head and began the traverse. With hindsight, there is some irony that it was this decision that ultimately placed our necks squarely on the Butcher's block.

Reaching the anchors, however, brought a release of sorts. The storm still raged, the wind still battered, and one pitch still remained, but of the 31 individual segments that made up the *Magic Mushroom* the last one was a throwaway, a mere 5.6 chimney, the home-run victory trot. We could do it backwards and blindfolded if we had to. Hunched against the blizzard, waiting for Dave to clean the Death Head pitch, I took comfort in the fact that at least we would not die on vertical ground.

WHEN GOD puts His cleaver to the grindstone, the resulting spray of sparks can take many forms. For us it began as a persistent trickle in the back of that 5.6 groove. When I first set the belay, it was apparent that the chimney—more of a U-shaped, polished chute than a fracture—was a channel for runoff. The icy dribble was annoying but I was already soaked to the bone and colder than a penguin turd; considering our situation a little more ice water funneling down my shorts seemed the least of my worries.

Preoccupied with hauling the bag and fighting to keep our ropes from spooling out into the tornado, I didn't even notice when the rain/sleet combination, which up until then had pretty much been coming at us from all directions, shifted to a steady overhead drumming. But by the time Dave had joined me at the anchors, the drops had merged into a continuous pounding stream—and the true nature of our fissure was revealed: This was the drainpipe for the upper plateau of El Capitan. Like itsy bitsy spiders we had wandered blindly into this conduit and spun our web. And we didn't have to be up on our nursery rhymes to see what was coming next.

In a matter of minutes the floodgates opened and a thundering cascade developed right on top of us. Yosemite's waterfalls are among the most awe-inspiring natural wonders in the world, but seeing one from the inside out was a frigid torture chamber of raging hydraulics comparable to being dragged through the deep ocean behind a submarine. Except that cutting the rope to free ourselves wasn't exactly an option.

Trying to back out the way we had come was also out of the question. Even if we somehow did manage to clear the waterfall our haulbag was now irretrievably jammed under the flow—the top opening was a brimming, roiling cauldron and high-pressure jets erupted from every puncture and blown seam; it must have weighed a thousand pounds. Without it, retreat back under the overhang would have left us immobilized and stripped of any provisions or shelter.

But staying put was also killing us and it wasn't a lingering death; drowning, exposure and beating were all vying for our souls and it was a toss up as to which would claim the final breath. At a minimum we needed two things to survive: unrestricted movement to run or walk or crawl and in so doing re-ignite a flicker of internal warmth, and we desperately needed to escape the pounding, choking, cryogenic immersion that had all but extinguished those flames from our bodies. Only a hundred feet above us the world leveled off and the atmosphere actually contained more air than water. If we wanted to live, we were going to have to get a line to the top. One of us was going to have to climb this nightmare. I thanked God it was Dave's pitch.

Free climbing was impossible. Dave would have to aid the groove, but first he had to find the rock. The roaring cascade masked all cracks or other climbable features. Thrusting his bare hands into the frigid torrent he groped around until his fingers finally locked in a tapered scar. Hunching over to create an air pocket, he pulled the pin rack up to his face and, using his fingers for reference, selected a piton. Pin in hand, he plunged once more beneath the curtain of foam and hammered blindly. He must have mashed his fingers a dozen times in the process, but finally the pin was in. Fighting to clip his aiders, laboring to stand and brace against the surging current, at last he stepped up. The entire process gained him inches. And yet it was the most heroic bit of climbing I had ever seen.

Again and again, Dave repeated this process until the inches compounded into a foot, and then a yard. Just a few yards off the belay he disappeared from my sight, obscured by a veil of spray, sleet, and mist. My last memories of him are of trembling fingers bent into claws the color of raw cod and a body convulsing from the twin rigors of superhuman effort and cold. And yet, in many ways, Dave was the lucky one.

Alone and staked to the belay, I was dying. At first I tried to keep moving as much as the hanging stance would permit by swinging back and forth, kicking my legs against the rock, and flailing my arms. But any position other than bent forward, head against the rock, knees drawn up under my chest seemed to squander more heat than it gained. The water pounding off my shoulders and back beat the air from my lungs until my breathing was reduced to a series of widely spaced staccato gasps. These were punctuated by violent dry heaves from fear and cold. Over time, all sensation drained from my limbs as the blood flow was rerouted in a last-ditch effort to sustain failing organs. Eventually, I unclipped Dave from the belay. I did not want his struggle for life cut short by a rope jammed in the lap of a dead man. From my hazy world between worlds I reasoned that a belay didn't matter anyway. If Dave fell even once it would stall his inertia—which as far as I could tell was the only thing that was keeping him going. Better for him to die quickly at the end of a long fall than caged and according to the Butcher's whim. My eyes fixed on the bright strand of our rope. Inches from my face the sheath had torn from some trauma during the climb. Like guts spilling from an evisceration the exposed core looked raw and vulnerable. How much easier it must be to die from a sudden and traumatic blow. Or better still, I decided, as my lids drooped, in the warmth and ignorance of sleep.

SOMETIME LATER my eyes flickered open just long enough to see that the rope scar was still there. Deep in the recesses of my brain enough electricity mustered to make a connection. Dave was no longer moving. Either he had finally ground to a halt, or he had finished the pitch. The odds greatly favored the former. Over the din of the waterfall communication had barely been possible even when we shared the same stance, but there had been no tugs, no reeling in of excess slack, no sign at all that he had reached his goal and the way was open for me to follow. Even so, now that his battle had ended one way or the other, I could fight mine.

Despite the determination of Lazarus, I could not convince my arms and legs to return from the dead. Instead, I had to rely on my eyes to direct and confirm each hand movement as I fumbled with the ascenders. Freeing myself from the lead rope was desperate. The knot had tightened into a compacted ball that threatened to keep me chained like a dog to the belay. I finally liberated myself by tearing it apart with my teeth. At last I weighted the rope and began my own slow and tortuous ascent up the downspout. For me, the gauntlet of raging waters paled to the question of what I would find at the other end: a corpse or another chance at life?

I found both. Dave had made the top, but he was sprawled in a death tableau on a snowy slab beside the final bolts. His skin was the color of Kindergarten paste, and from the undisturbed snow on and around his body it was clear that once he had dropped to the ground he had never moved again. Too near death myself to exercise any real tenderness, I poked him with my foot. Against all odds, his eyes fluttered open and a weak smile crossed his waxen lips. "I guess we better get moving," he said.

Even then, by any outside measure we were incredibly screwed—to reach the valley floor, we still had to cover eight miles in rock shoes, much of it over steep slippery trails covered in a foot of fresh snow. But relative to the trials of the past few hours we felt blessed. And not every Fate was conspired against us. The storm was winding down; the snow, wind, and rain were easing off considerably. Although the trail was almost completely obscured, thanks to all his previous trips up and down El Cap Dave knew exactly where to go. And over the course of our week on *Magic Mushroom*, my ankle had healed well enough so that I would not have to coast to safety on another man's back twice in one day.

But the real confirmation of our good fortune occurred just over a week later. On the crest of another spell of fine weather another autumn storm roared into the Valley and dumped another foot of heavy, wet snow. The following morning we walked to El Cap Meadow and surveyed the monolith. We could see the wispy stream that marked the drainpipe pitch once again roaring at full throttle. We knew there were climbers on *Magic Mushroom* and on the *Shield* and we were relieved to see that none of them were anywhere near the final pitch. But over on the *Nose* helicopters buzzed. In the fury of the storm, two climbers had perished on the final bolt ladder leading to the summit. Even with the naked eye we could clearly see the red dots of their parkas perched on the very eaves of El Capitan, itsy bitsy spiders against a background of gray rock and blue sky.

Originally published in CLIMBING, *No. 197, 2000.*

Author's notes: To date, this experience and my skull-cracking plunge down the face of Palisade Head (recounted in "Superior Climbs," page 221) have been the closest shaves of my climbing career—the only times, despite all my worrying and whining, that my life was ever in real jeopardy. The difference is that on Magic Mushroom *I had ample time to consider this possibility. Frankly, I preferred falling 90 feet onto my head.*

Also to date, Dave Mital's frigid swim up the gushing 5.6 exit pitch on El Capitan is still the single most impressive and awe-inspiring bit of climbing I've ever witnessed.

Eldorado Canyon's Redgarden Wall; the Naked Edge *follows the left skyline*

CHEW ON THIS
Cutting Teeth on a Colorado Classic

SCOTT KRAMER was feeling anxious. Whether it was due to the impending storm or the prospect of leading the last pitch of the *Naked Edge* is hard to say. As one of Eldorado Canyon's most celebrated multi-pitch testpieces during the 1970s and '80s, the *Naked Edge* set a standard for hard climbing that made it the subject of magazine covers around the globe, and it remains a coveted Colorado ascent. At the moment, however, all Scott was coveting was the belay that his partner, Mike Dahlberg, was enjoying. Instead, it was left to him to outpace a growling thunderstorm to the top of the thin, overhanging crack that is the final crux, an airy 600 feet off the deck.

The crack gradually widens, and Scott got in a good cam before launching into the homestretch, but somewhere in the No Man's Land between finger locks and hand jams, prayers were spoken as the strength drained from his fingers and arms. Just when it seemed that the gravity toilet was about to flush, a fixed pin appeared in the crack overhead. If Scott could clip it, he'd have a first-class ticket out of Whipperville. With one trembling paw straining to maintain contact with the rock, he managed to free a draw and clip it to the piton. Pulling up slack, gripping the rope between his teeth, he reeled in the last few inches needed to secure his salvation. That's when the hand jam finally blew. Plunging through space, Scott involuntarily clenched his jaw in anticipation of the impact. Unfortunately, the rope was still clamped firmly between his teeth. Traumatic injuries are often surprisingly painless—the victim is anesthetized with adrenaline and shock. Scott was an exception. In the split-second jolt at the end of the 30-foot fall, a mouthful of oral nerves were yanked from gummy slumber and woke up screaming. Awash in the pain of a dozen tooth extractions—blood erupting like scarlet lava from the sockets—Scott had to actually feel his lower jaw with his fingers to ensure it was still attached.

Mike, on the other hand, while alarmed by the gory mass of outwardly bent teeth, still had one eye on the weather. Torn between urgency and compassion, self-preservation won out. Years later, the memory of Mike's first anxious words after the accident can still make Scott smile, revealing two neat rows of reconstructed enamel: "You're still up for finishing the lead, aren't you?"

Originally published in CLIMBING, *No. 197, 2000.*

Scott Kramer, smile right as rain (on right, in the rain), with Hamish MacInnes in Fort William, Scotland

ALL THAT REMAIN

Tragedy Strikes an Ambitious Young Team in the Karakoram

THE SNOWS OF AGES cover the 24,270-foot Haramosh like the blue-white froth of a wind-churned ocean blanketing a rocky shore. Against this dazzling pyramid are two specks below the northeast ridge. They might be isolated outcroppings, black pinnacles piercing the mountain's icy veneer—except they are not motionless. Like gnats stuck to a freshly painted wall, the motes struggle against the whiteness, laboring to escape the monochromatic expanse that has become a prison. Arduously, they creep lower, every inch an act of triumph over physical and mental agony. One is horribly wounded, both are emotionally shattered, there is no trace of the buoyant confidence that permeated the four-man assault party that left high camp three days earlier. They are all that remain.

IN THE EARLY WEEKS, the 1957 Oxford University Mountaineering Club expedition to Haramosh in the Karakoram, Pakistan, was infused with optimism. The era was the golden age of Asian mountaineering, when a small expedition made up primarily of college students on holiday could attempt an unclimbed giant in one of the highest ranges on earth. Haramosh, located at the center of a great triangle formed by Rakaposhi, K2, and Nanga Parbat, was not only unclimbed, it had never even had a serious attempt. It is little wonder that despite the daunting scale—nearly 12,000 vertical feet—and unknown qualities of the objective, the young men from Oxford faced their mountain with unbridled enthusiasm.

The leader of the team gazed upon the northern rampart of Haramosh, with its massive rock barrier and complex glaciation, and instinctively formed a more tempered assessment of the expedition's goals and likelihood for success. At the age of 31, Tony Streather, an officer in the British Army, had already amassed enough high-mountain experience to satisfy a lifetime. In fact, his first climb ever would have been a fitting capstone to a brilliant alpine career. As a young officer stationed in Pakistan, Streather had become intimate enough with the local people and language that in 1950 he'd been recruited to supervise porters on a Norwegian mountaineering expedition to Tirich Mir, an unclimbed 7706-meter peak in the Hindu Kush region. Incredibly (both because his role during the expedition was solely to facilitate the movement of supplies and because he'd never climbed anything before in his life), he summited the peak.

Three years later, Streather's luck seemed to reverse itself when he was one of six tangled climbers dragged from their steps during an epic fall on K2—until the last man standing arrested the entire team. And in 1955, Streather joined the elite ranks of climbers to have bagged the first ascent of an 8000-meter peak when he reached the top of Kangchenjunga (8586 meters), the third-highest mountain in the world.

To Streather's practiced eye, Haramosh looked to be a tough nut; it was clear that a large part of the expedition's time and resources would be dedicated to simply locating a route. Only when and if a weakness in the mountain's defenses could be found could a serious climbing attempt be mounted. Streather knew summiting Haramosh was a long shot. It wasn't that it couldn't be done. The French had faced much the same problem on the first ascent of Annapurna, and his own successful British expedition to Kanchenjunga had approached that mountain in much the same way. But on Haramosh time was short, and his strongest climbers—while long on energy and skill—were barely out of their teens.

The fact that the rest of the expedition was made up of university students had a simple explanation: Haramosh was their idea in the first place. The trip was the brainchild of Bernard Jillot, 23. Jillot was a classic up-and-comer in the mountaineering world: consumed by climbing, naturally gifted with strength and ability, and eager to make a name for himself. A former president of the Oxford University Mountaineering Club, he had also proven himself as a leader, but he was not one to let ego stand in the way of success. He understood from the outset that his Haramosh venture lacked the experience and credibility needed to have any hope of becoming a reality, and so he had lobbied Streather into leading the group.

The other team members were fellow clubbers and climbing friends of Jillot's. John Emery, a medical student, also 23, would play an important dual role on the expedition, functioning both as a lead climber and as the team's physician. Rae Culbert, a 25-year-old New Zealander, filled out the core of the climbing team. A fourth college student, an American, Scott Hamilton, would function primarily as support climber.

It was this group of disparate but remarkably companionable mountaineers who arrived beneath Haramosh in the autumn of 1957. To varying degrees, each felt hopeful that the next month would result in great things: a successful reconnaissance, superlative climbing, perhaps even the conquest of a virgin summit.

AFTER TWO WEEKS of fruitlessly probing the mountain's sheer and complex northern and western aspects, it became obvious that a direct attack wasn't in the cards. The only feasible way to the top of Haramosh was an end run. To the east of Haramosh proper lay the subsidiary summit of Haramosh II (21,930 feet). Taking the huge glacier beyond this sub-peak, a reasonable line could be followed around and up to the crest of the northeast ridge of Haramosh II and across that mountain, then down again into a broad saddle leading back toward the main summit. It would be a long and complicated business.

During the next week, the climbers established and stocked camps on the glacier beneath Haramosh II. Then the weather deteriorated, and over the next few weeks, as the expedition wallowed against seemingly endless snowfalls, the goal of climbing Haramosh gradually gave way to the goal of reaching Haramosh II, which in turn gave way to the goal of simply cresting the northeast ridge and glimpsing first-hand the route up Haramosh proper that now belonged to some future expedition.

On the morning of September 15, the last day of climbing before their schedule dictated retreat, Streather, Culbert, Jillot, and Emery left their high camp in a last-ditch effort to top the ridge at 21,000 feet. Culbert and Emery had broken trail some distance above camp the day before, and the climbers advanced quickly to the previous high point. Although the ridge above them was hidden from view, they steered toward a bulging snow formation they dubbed the Cardinal's Hat which they felt sure must be situated on the ridge crest. At last, Streather hacked through a final cornice, and found himself gaping across at a spectacular, unrestricted view up the main peak. He shouted down to the others, "Come on up. You can't imagine what you'll see when you get up here!"

Their long weeks of labor at an end, the men relaxed atop the ridge and soaked up the hard-earned vista. Surprisingly, the route ahead—the trough between the two peaks—was not the straightforward snow slog they had envisioned. Instead, it was a mad jumble of seracs and crevasses that might well have defeated them even if the weather hadn't. But all that was behind them now; the expedition was over. They'd made a good reconnaissance, pushed forward despite atrocious conditions, and would leave with important information for any future attempts. All that remained was the descent.

Jillot, however, had one last ambition. Throughout the day, the pinnacle of the Cardinal's Hat had dominated their view; they had fixed on it like a summit. Before they left, Jillot was determined to scamper the remaining 100 feet or so to its top. He convinced Emery to rope with him, and together, they moved up the final pitch.

"Keep well back from the cornice," Streather shouted up to them. "It's one of the biggest I've seen."

"We'll keep well down," Jillot answered.

"I'll sing out if it looks as though you're getting too close."

"Right."

The men had almost reached the top when there occurred one of those moments when time seems to stand still—or perhaps it is the mind itself that seizes with the realization that in another instant nothing will ever be the same. With a loud crack the slope beneath Jillot and Emery severed its frictional bonds with the mountain. A sickening tearing sound filled the air as the tons of snow began to slide. Seconds later, a deep rumble erupted as the churning mass emptied into the abyss.

Streather and Culbert could only look on with disbelief and horror as their two companions swept past, engulfed within the chaotic white cloud. And then they were gone, carried beyond the sheer drop at the bottom of the slope, beyond the limit of sight, beyond all hope. The two men on the ridge crest strained to follow the course of the avalanche. Eventually, a thousand feet below, the leading edge came into view again, fanning out across one final snowfield before draining over Haramosh's 8000-foot north face. Belayed by Culbert, Streather moved out onto the freshly scoured slope and peered into the void, desperately scanning the battered surface of the lower basin. Suddenly, his attention riveted upon a speck of colored nylon within the debris. Incredibly, it moved. And then, like a cell dividing, the one moving speck became two. Somehow, against all odds, both Jillot and Emery were still alive.

EMORY WAS a mess. From the moment Jillot tugged him from the wreckage of the avalanche that was clear. His thigh was twisted at an unnatural angle and the slightest movement or pressure on it produced searing pain. To the young doctor-in-training, it was clear that his hip joint had dislocated during the fall. "I can't move, Bernard," he moaned.

Looking up at the steep walls surrounding them, their only possible route back to safety, Jillot told his friend the simple truth, "You must."

Tracing the path of the avalanche back up the mountain, the two men found it difficult to believe that anyone could have survived such a drop. After carrying them down the steep slope below the ridge—a distance of maybe 500 feet—the slide had emptied over a sheer ice cliff nearly 300 feet high. The initially steep, gradually tapering angle of the snowy basin had cushioned the impact of their fall, and the two had slid and rolled to a stop another several hundred feet below. In the turbulence of the avalanche, both men had been stripped of their ice axes. Emery had lost both of his gloves; Jillot was missing one.

The basin itself was perched on the brink of the north face, hemmed on all other sides by steep ice and rock. Twisting his body to survey the surroundings, Emery felt his hip snap, and the pain began to subside. The

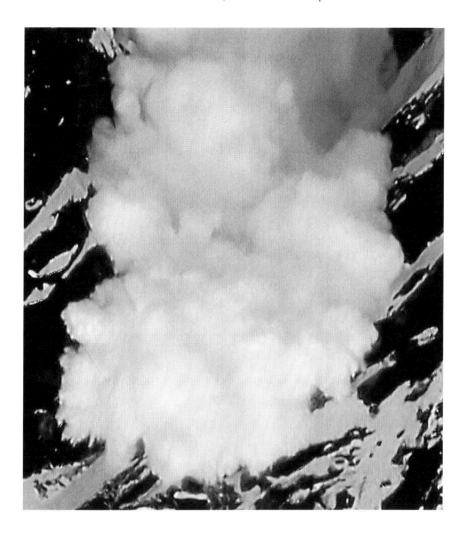

ball of his hip had settled back into its socket. Now the climbers could begin trying to find a way out.

There was never any thought of attacking the ice cliff directly; instead, they attempted to sidestep it along the right edge where it tapered into steep snow. Without axes, even this proved to be too much for them, and it wasn't long before they took another fall back down into the basin. With darkness coming on fast, the battered and dejected men stomped out a platform and braced themselves for the long, cold night.

AS SOON AS Streather and Culbert saw that their friends had survived the avalanche, their emotions quickly ran the gamut from incredulity, to joy, to foreboding. Rescuing them from the snowy basin would be a dangerous, perhaps impossible task, yet it was one they were duty-bound to undertake. "I can't see how we're going to get them out," Streather said despairingly. "This slope's terribly steep and it's in a treacherous state. They're almost certain to be hurt. I can't see how we'll do it."

Culbert tried to be reassuring. "Don't worry, Tony, we'll get down to them." The younger man's optimism was heartening, and Streather's anxieties gradually gave way to steely determination as the two formulated a rescue plan.

Because of the late hour, and in anticipation of the mighty effort it would require of them, they reasoned that the best course of action was to return to their high camp where they could eat and drink, maybe even catch a few hours of sleep, and then return at dawn, well fueled and supplied. Before they left, however, they stuffed extra food and clothing into a pack and pitched it down the slope toward the basin, hoping it just might land within reach of their stranded comrades. The pack seemed the embodiment of their spirits as it suddenly took an unexpected turn, fell lower and lower, and finally disappeared into a dark crevasse.

In fact, Streather and Culbert were back at the ridge crest by 10 p.m. Worry over their partners' exposed condition had prompted them to begin the rescue effort as soon as possible. Belaying each other in turn, all through the night the two toiled to kick a ladder of steps down the 60-degree slope.

When dawn broke, they could see Emery and Jillot in the basin below them. The pair were gesturing and shouting—something about moving to the right, but the distance made their precise meaning difficult to grasp. Soon enough, however, Streather and Culbert understood perfectly. The slope beneath them suddenly dropped away and they found themselves perched on the eaves of the 300-foot ice wall. The only option was a traverse.

Streather began the lateral passage above the ice cliff. He dreaded the first steps beyond the avalanche track, fearing that on undisturbed ground he might trigger another slide. These fears turned out to be unfounded, although the reality was, in some ways, even worse. The slope outside the track was composed of bare, flint-hard ice. Kicking steps into steep snow was one thing, chopping hand and footholds into solid ice was quite another. The two men hadn't slept in over 24 hours, and now they faced one of the most arduous tasks in mountaineering—and they would have to do it sideways. They had no protection and no belay anchors except their axes.

All day long the rescue team labored on the traverse. Near the end, as Culbert lifted his foot from a hold, Streather saw something dark in the hollow. "Rae, hold on. You've left a crampon in that last step!" Culbert brought his leg back and his motion brushed the crampon from the ice. It fell down the slope and disappeared into the bergschrund. This was a serious development. With only one crampon, Culbert was crippled. The line between those bringing assistance and those needing it was blurring.

As the afternoon waned, the pair finally completed the traverse, and then wearily kicked one last line of steps down several hundred feet of steep snow to the bergschrund. While Culbert belayed, Streather advanced to the lip and maneuvered a rope down. Soon, the haggard but immensely relieved faces of their friends greeted them.

"Thanks, Tony. Thanks, Rae." For Jillot and Emery, the gratitude owed to these two who had labored so long and hard to reach them was overflowing. But any fuller expression of it would have to wait. With evening coming on, there was little time for anything other than quickly tying everyone together and starting back up. While Streather shepherded the two without axes, Culbert began leading the party back up the line of steps. He had almost reached the level of the traverse again when his naked boot jetted from an icy hold and he tobogganed down the slope, bowling into Streather, and pulling the others from their steps. The whole team tumbled back down into the basin. Again, remarkably, no one had been seriously injured, but now they had lost Streather's ice axe as well. Using Culbert's axe, Streather took the lead and carefully retraced their steps, belaying the rest of the group to a good stance after every ropelength. But as he approached the traverse, a mighty tug from below suddenly wrenched him from the face. Jillot had fallen asleep on his feet, slid from the stance, and pulled the whole group down after him. Once again, the entire team found themselves tangled in a heap. Once again an ice axe—their last—had disappeared.

Darkness had fallen. Attempting another run at the face now, in such an exhausted state and with no axe, would only invite disaster. With resignation, the four men crawled into the bergschrund for the night. The hours passed slowly, and the men had ample time to reflect on their miseries. After losing his crampon earlier in the day, Culbert had removed the insulating overboot to improve his traction, and now his foot had gone numb with cold. Emery's hands were also almost certainly frostbitten. Jillot, possibly concussed during one of the falls, talked gibberish in his sleep.

The next morning dawned bright and clear. Punching and kicking the slope to rebuild the steps wiped out in last night's fall, Streather led the way. None of the men were roped. Without an axe, it was more dangerous for them to rope together than to climb as individuals. If anyone fell off today, at least he would not take the others down with him. It was grueling, knuckle-busting work, and eventually Emery took over the lead. Nearing the previous night's highpoint, he made a joyous discovery. Streather's ice axe was still planted where he'd come off the night before. Streather climbed through, and began chopping holds up the last steep, icy section before the traverse.

"You hang on there," he told the others. "This last bit is the worst part. When I get to the platform, I'll drop the rope to you and bring you up one by one."

The security of the rope, however, was short-lived. Even with an axe, it would be far too risky for them to rope together across the traverse. While Emery belayed the others up to the platform, Streather moved out onto the traverse and began clearing spindrift from the line of steps and holds that he and Culbert had sculpted the day before. One by one the other men followed, moving carefully and deliberately.

As Streather neared the end of the traverse, his spirits rose. The snow slope above, while steep, offered much greater security. Just when it appeared that they might all get out in one piece, Emery called out to him, "Rae's in trouble." Despite having only one crampon and a frostbitten foot, Culbert had doggedly followed the others across the treacherous traverse, but now he had come up against a tricky spot where the steps angled down for a section, and he simply dared not move without a belay. After stringing him a rope, Streather told Culbert to stay put while he finished the traverse and worked up-slope as far as the rope would allow. Planting the axe and stomping out footholds, Streather secured himself as best he could, and then shouted for Culbert, who was off to the side, to climb. Tentatively, Culbert tested the next step, but almost as soon as he weighted the cramponless foot it rotated off the hold and he was sliding. Streather braced himself, but the shock generated by Culbert's weight plunging over the ice cliff and accelerating in a massive pendulum was too much. Streather was ripped from his stance, rocketed down the slope, and vanished over the lip of the precipice.

NIGHT HAD FALLEN once again. In fact, it had been upon them even as Culbert and Streather tumbled into the void. Afterward, Jillot and Emery had spent hours clawing and kicking their way up the steep slope to the top of the northeast ridge—their determination fueled by the realization that the roles had now reversed. Streather and Culbert were stranded in the snow basin, and it was up to Jillot and Emery to reach camp, refresh themselves with food and drink, and return to help the others. But even now on the ridge, reaching camp was not going to be easy. Over the last several days, the track had drifted in with windblown snow, and the darkness compounded their difficulty. In his eagerness to reach camp, Jillot gradually pulled away from Emery. Jillot wasn't concerned; camp was not far off, and he was leaving an unmistakable path. At some point Jillot deviated from the old trail, but by instinct and good fortune managed to evade any hidden crevasses. He knew from various landmarks that by moving in a certain direction, he would reconnect with the original track somewhere near the ridge crest, just above their tents. He had no idea that

"At some point Jillot deviated from the old trail…"

he'd already crossed over it again until the ground suddenly opened up beneath him. And by then it was too late.

Emery also never made it back to camp that night. Somewhere in the dark he misjudged an icy patch, slipped, and was swallowed by a crevasse. When he regained consciousness, daylight was filtering through the icy-blue walls that encased him. Thankfully, it was just possible for him to worm up and out one end of the crack. Blinking in the daylight, Emery could see that the old track was a safer and more direct alternative to the fresh line of footsteps Jillot had left during the night. Trudging downward, he observed Jillot's path trending toward an intersection with the original trail just above camp. However, he was puzzled by the fact that the track leading to the tents was not freshly broken. And then he saw how Jillot's footprints crossed over the old path, and marched inexorably out to the ridgeline where they suddenly ended. There was only one way to read it—and there was no question as to the result. The fall line funneled into a massive crevasse, which in turn emptied out over the valley 6000 feet below. With a sinking heart, Emery realized that the life of one friend had been extinguished, and with it, probably any hope of saving two others.

INSIDE THE TENT, Emery was in despair. His hands, which had been exposed to the elements for three continuous days, were deeply frostbitten. His feet probably weren't in much better condition. He was dehydrated, starving, and at death's door with exhaustion. And yet the physical pain was nothing compared to the mental agony he was suffering over the fates of his companions. That Jillot was gone was a terrible shock, but at least his ordeal was over. What could he possibly do to help Streather and Culbert? Were they even alive? At this point, after struggling and failing to open a tin, barely managing to light the stove, and too weary even to remove his crampons, Emery wasn't even sure that he could save himself.

As yet another day transitioned into evening, there was a sudden crunching noise outside the tent. Moments later, the flaps opened, and the drawn and worn face of Streather peered in at him. The man looked a wreck, but he was still lucid enough to realize that Emery was alone. "Where's Bernard," Streather gasped.

"He's gone, Tony."

"Gone? Gone where?"

"He's dead."

Streather was stunned. And he alone understood the full significance of this tragic development—because he was also alone. Both Streather and Culbert had survived the fall into the bowl, and had spent the night huddled together in the bergschrund. The next morning, Culbert had fallen twice more from the snow slope below the traverse. At last, Streather had continued on alone, shouting promises to Culbert that he would return with help. The climb back to camp had taken every ounce of his strength and will. Now, after learning that Jillot was dead and finding Emery a virtual invalid, Streather glimpsed the final, awful truth. There was no help to return with.

EPILOGUE: Haramosh was climbed in 1958 by an Austrian party via the route reconnoitered by the team from Oxford University. For the survivors of the earlier expedition, however, the tragedy of Haramosh did not end on the mountain. John Emery's frostbite injuries resulted in the amputation of all his fingers and toes. Thanks to some skilled surgery and great determination on his part, he was able to walk, and eventually even to climb again. Just as his life had seemingly been cobbled back together, fate intervened. He was killed in a fall on the Weisshorn in the Swiss Alps in 1963.

Tony Streather lectures annually about the Haramosh expedition at the Royal Military Academy, Sandhurst (Britain's West Point equivalent). Streather made a trip back to the Karakoram a few years after the disaster, in part to place a memorial to Culbert and Jillot. He then gave up climbing big mountains altogether. And although he has led a full and productive life (he helped found World Challenge Expeditions, a program that works with schools to send youth expeditions to developing countries around the globe), Streather is still haunted by that decisive moment high on the northeast ridge of Haramosh, just before Jillot expressed his desire to climb the Cardinal's Hat, when turning around and calling it a day—and bringing a happy ending to a fine expedition—was all that remained.

Originally published in CLIMBING, *No. 206, 2001.*

Author's note: A full and compelling narrative of the 1957 Haramosh expedition is presented in The Last Blue Mountain *by Ralph Barker, a principal reference used in the preparation of this article. Special thanks also to Lt. Col. HRA Tony Streather for his kind assistance.*

Home Turf

Little Crag on the Prairie: the climbing scene at Blue Mounds State Park, Minnesota

WHAT IT'S LIKE TO BE
A CLIMBER IN THE MIDWEST
My Reality Made Planar

I'VE OFTEN SAID that Midwestern climbers are hungry lions living in a country of mice. We spend a lot of energy chasing diminutive prey, our appetites must be satisfied with tiny morsels, and when we finally travel to someplace where we can gorge ourselves, we may never go home again.

But the fact is, most of us do. Family, jobs…our roots—these are the things that cause even the most passionate and gifted flatlander mountaineers to turn their backs on Nature's grandest cathedrals and return to a scattering of three-pew crags tucked amid the corn rows and bean fields. And so we become ascetics, our religion twisted slightly out of the climbing mainstream.

Let's start with the whole toproping thing. Partly because of a legitimate urgency to stake a claim to our precious rock and ice ahead of the other weekend warriors, and partly because we rationalize that our bitsy outcrops have too much groundfall potential for lead climbing, a popular Midwestern trad crag such as Devil's Lake in Wisconsin or Minnesota's Taylors Falls will be festooned with slingshot belay set-ups by Saturday sunup. Often the most valuable real estate is hoarded by groups asserting squatter's rights. I've watched parties spend an entire day lapping a single classic line rather than risk yielding their ground. Thus, heartland cliffs have objective dangers all their own: The last time I encroached upon someone else's territory—by hanging my rope two feet to the side of one that had gone unused for hours—that someone nearly took a poke at me.

As a result, we Midwesterners resort to behaviors that, to others blessed with more generous climbing topography, might seem, well… countrified. For example, it is not unusual for us to beg, barter or steal to get on a pre-rigged climb ("Hey, Zeke, I'll trade you a run at *Farm Accident* for a turn on *Hog Heaven!*"). Of course, any bona fide cliff here is almost certainly the centerpiece of a state park where bolts are *verboten*, so taking a spin on

someone else's toprope rig means trusting his or her anchor. After years of climbing up to discover everything from single-nut set-ups to slip-knotted clotheslines that came apart with a tug, I finally fled the zoo.

I got lucky. The North Shore of Lake Superior, where I now live and climb, is ice and jamcrack rich by Midwestern standards, and still relatively uncrowded. It's well off the beaten track—four to five hours from the nearest metropolitan center. For most lowland city folks, unconventional or artificial outcrops are the only practical alternatives to the mob scene. And I'm not talking about the climbing gyms. In southern Minnesota, active quarries, roadcuts, even a single erratic boulder can merit a guidebook or a slideshow. Similarly, grain silos, bridges and skyscrapers have been clandestinely bolted or climbed.

But there are those of us who simply cannot survive on a diet of canapés—no matter how creative, exclusive, or tasty these may be. We are the Road Warriors. It should surprise no one that to folks like us, Lewis and Clark's single journey west seems like a milk run. I had more miles on my last van when I sold it (to another climber) than Apollo 11 did when it landed on the moon. Even today, for me, 26 hours behind the wheel traveling to and from Devils Tower is just the price of doing business for a weekend of multi-pitch climbing. After all, making it in the Big League, "Out West," is what many of us in Middle America aspire to.

Which brings me to one feeling I suspect nearly all Midwestern climbers, young and old, urban and rural, have in common: a deep-seated inferiority complex with respect to "mountain people." That's also our edge. Our insecurities often push us to try harder, or our naiveté allows us to succeed on things that someone with a more developed, intimate mountain sense wouldn't attempt. Plus, we enjoy the freedom to climb hard without the pressures of being in the limelight or meeting high expectations: Few people imagine that Backwater Bill from Minnesota or Wisconsin is capable of doing much of note outside the borders of Flatland—until one of us makes the first ascent of the lethally runout *Superpin* in the Black Hills (in 1967!), or climbs the *Czech Direct* on Denali in a 60-hour continuous push. The truth is that a lot of damn fine climbers live on the prairie.

And when this notion finally arrives, it's the best and most uniquely Midwestern feeling of all—the realization that it isn't the mountains that make the mountaineer.

Originally published in ROCK AND ICE, *No. 135, 2004.*

Author's note: This short essay was solicited for an issue themed: "What It Feels Like." Other contributions included "What It's Like to Fall While Free-soloing" and "What It's Like to Get Hit by Lightning." You get the picture: a bunch of dreaded climbing misfortunes—like being born in the Midwest.

The Fool's Progress *(5.11) at Palisade Head; Shovel Point in background*

SUPERIOR CLIMBS

Falling Head Over Heels for Minnesota's North Shore

T HE WIND IS SLAPPING ME against the rock face like a tetherball. Above, malignant gray clouds have opened their floodgates, drenching me with alternating sheets of rain and sloppy wet hail. Between my feet and flapping etriers I glimpse the roiling surf of Lake Superior—a stewing, hissing pit of angry white serpents—and I speculate that my belayer might be in real danger of drowning, except that I don't have one.

I'm not sure how I got here. I know it has something to do with a woman. More precisely, it has something to do with a woman's less-than-enthusiastic response to a particularly heart-felt declaration. But remarkably, that all seems pretty trivial right now. What I'm most consumed with at present is the fact that every placement I have made in the past 50 feet is crap. Case in point: The last one is gone, brushed away by a touch of the rope just as I unweighted it. Somehow I have managed to solo aid climb an astonishing ladder of imaginary micro-nuts and tenuous hook moves to a point 90 feet above Palisade Head's wave-battered talus. And yet there is no feeling of victory here, because everything below me is junk and the next placement looks even worse.

In fact, I have come to a dead end. I can't help thinking that things cannot possibly get any worse, but, of course, such thoughts only seem to usher forth utter and conclusive disaster. Scant moments later, a realization strikes me like a brain embolism: Slowly, yet persistently, the flake to which I'm attached is expanding. The cams that support my sopping, miserable carcass are opening, and I am about to be flushed into the swirling chaos of wind-driven rain and surf.

With mounting desperation I run trembling, waterlogged fingertips over the rock face searching for another crack or nubbin or any kind of feature that might accept a nut, a hook, my car keys…anything to defuse the time bomb that is rapidly counting down under my weight. But the wall is smooth, overhanging, and, except for the ironing-board-sized piece of it that I am inevitably prying off, utterly featureless.

I am doomed. Yet there isn't even time for real despair. Before my bowels can unload, the camming unit does. And I am gone.

THE NORTH SHORE: FABULOUS ROCK AND ONE GREAT LAKE

There are those who will tell you that the only climbing adventure possible in the American heartland involves dressing up in a superhero costume and clinging to the side of a skyscraper. These people watch too much television.

It is an understandable misconception. After all, the continental ice sheets that have repeatedly steam-rolled the Midwestern countryside have pretty much eradicated anything resembling mountain topography. And yet the region is not all cornfields and Great Plains: In northeastern Minnesota, along the North Shore of Lake Superior, the geologic legacy has been kinder to climbers.

Eons ago, under smoky Precambrian skies, a feisty infant planet Earth burped and spat gooey pools of pinkish lava onto the surface of primordial Minnesota. In the cool ancient air, the lava rapidly solidified into a thick scab of rhyolite bedrock. Over countless millennia the forces of erosion have whittled away at these flows, but a few stalwart remnants managed to tough it out even through the Great Ice Age. When the glaciers withdrew they left in their wake a number of broad ridges, sculpted knobs and the Greatest of Lakes. In post-glacial times, Lake Superior has tirelessly nibbled away at the base of these landforms, undercutting enormous sheets of rock and causing them to periodically collapse, simultaneously giving birth to extensive talus slopes and a multitude of steep and exposed rock climbing surfaces.

The most popular climbing crags are at Palisade Head, which rises some 300 feet above Lake Superior, and at the nearby peninsula of Shovel Point. Although both formations originated from the same rhyolite lava flows, the comparisons really end there.

Palisade Head lurks defiantly above the lake like some forbidding citadel. Its walls are relentlessly steep and laced with formidable cracks. There is no way to walk out from the thin strip of talus at its base; once you rappel down, you must climb out—one reason toproping is so popular here. In contrast, Shovel Point presents a sunny, inclined wedge of rock that tapers almost apologetically into the lake. The wall is perfectly positioned to maximize the sun, and its lower-angled slabs are host to an abundance of friendly face, crack and stemming problems. Shovel Point's intimidation factor, if there is one, comes from the fact that most of the cliff drops straight into the lake without encountering any sort of talus, beach, or ledge system. Needless to say, toproping is also popular at Shovel Point. Unlike in Britain or the south of France, climbing on soaring "sea cliffs" such as these is genuinely rare in this country. Thundering waves,

Palisade Head, viewed from Shovel Point

screeching gulls, and stiff breezes often drown out climbing signals. The vast expanse of the lake—an inland sea if there ever was one—stretches beyond the horizon and reflects the moods of the fickle and often dark weather that it creates.

***

MY FALL DOWN the face of Palisade Head is disquietingly uneventful. This is no free climb with long stretches of nothing between protection points—an aid climb this thin and steep demands a placement every few feet. So even if the gear is as bad as I hope it isn't, I should be feeling a multitude of sickening jerks as I rip it free. Instead, I am experiencing an uninterrupted free fall.

In the accelerated manner that is only possible with a brain spiked full of adrenaline I attempt to reason this through, and the conclusion I arrive at is not good. Earlier in the climb I had taken several modest falls. In each instance, my self-belay functioned perfectly, stopping me after less than 20 feet of air travel—barely long enough to realize what was going on before it was over. But now I am thinking about the jagged roof I surmounted low on the route: the overhang with the evil, serrated edges that the same part of my rope has dragged across during all these falls. And suddenly it all makes sense.

My rope has parted, of this I am certain.

But even this sobering revelation quickly loses priority. Just as my body has pin-wheeled through nearly one perfect revolution and my head is coming round again to the 12 o'clock position, I suddenly find myself face to face with the only significant ledge on the route. Literally. My forehead slams into the rock like a cantaloupe hit with a bat. The impact is powerful enough to crack my helmet—if I'd remembered to bring it along.

The fact that my rope has probably been severed doesn't seem that important anymore.

ARE YOUR HANDS CLEAN?

The North Shore is a traditional climbing area. There. I said it, and I'm glad I said it. But before half of you 86 this article and flip to the comp results, you should know that there are some excellent clip-up routes on the North Shore. A contradiction in terms? Perhaps, but the term "traditional" as used on the North Shore has more to do with environmental sensitivity and preserving access than it does with old climbers with old ideas doggedly determined to remain in the past.

The climbers who live on the North Shore have a history of respect for their spectacular surroundings. They pick up trash, establish trails so the woods leading to and fro between outcrops aren't randomly trampled, and discriminately clean climbs—that is, scrub away just enough lichen and loose rock to make a route safe and enjoyable.

This minimum-impact attitude has helped to create an exceptionally unspoiled and beautiful place to climb, as well as a shared sense of purpose among local climbers. Perhaps most significant, though, is the reputation for responsibility that the North Shore climbing community has earned from local land managers. In Minnesota, as in many places around the country, rock climbers are facing increasing regulation. Both Palisade Head and Shovel Point are administered by Tettegouche State Park, and issues such as the impact climbers might have on nesting peregrine falcons have made some park managers anxious about rock climbing at these locations. Presently, most park officials seem to recognize and appreciate the sense of responsibility of the North Shore climbing community, and, hopefully, will be less likely to regulate such a group.

Over the past 25 years, a local climbing ethic has evolved encouraging people not to use white chalk here. Additionally, fixed anchors should be placed thoughtfully by hand, and only in locations where they are not expressly prohibited by local land owners or park managers. The thought of climbing without chalk has made a lot of climbers wary of the North Shore, and its climbing community. But this is not traditionalism run amok—the idea is not to control anyone's experience or impose traditional rules on others. Rather, it is an attempt to protect an experience and a level of freedom that is important to everyone. And so far, it has worked quite well.

***

IN FACT, my rope is still in one piece. I know this because I am finally noticing a gradual deceleration, despite the numb grayness that now shrouds my perception. I know I should be relieved, but my head is probably spilling brains and, about this time, I hit the ground.

Perhaps "visit" the ground is more accurate, since I am not there long enough for my feet to do more than plant themselves firmly on a wet boulder before I am yanked into the air again as the rope's stretch is reabsorbed back into its length. I finally come to rest, a battered yo-yo, spinning some 20 feet above the talus. All told, I have traveled well over 100 feet in less than five seconds and the only piece of gear left on the route is the one that finally arrested the fall.

SUPERIOR CLIMBS

The North Shore is a dead ringer for the coast of Maine. In fact, it looks so similar that when 20th Century Fox needed a dramatic location to shoot the final cliff-top fight sequence for the Maine-based feature film *The Good Son,* they came to Minnesota and tossed the kid from *Home Alone* off Palisade Head. It is doubtful that many climbers were fooled, however, because they know there are no sea-cliffs this big along the East Coast (and also they would actually have had to see this turkey of a movie). So, Midwesterners looking to experience a rugged, New England coastline environment need travel no farther than northern Minnesota.

Climbers who visit the North Shore will undoubtedly want to focus their attentions on Palisade Head and Shovel Point. Both crags are easily accessible, both look out on Lake Superior, and both have plenty of do-not-miss routes.

The weather is an important factor when deciding which place to visit. The shadowed cracks at Palisade Head are best avoided on cold mornings or after rainy spells, while Shovel Point is always a delight as long as the sun is shining. Climbing ability is another consideration. Palisade Head has very little to offer beginners, with almost no quality routes easier than 5.8.

Approaching Palisade Head couldn't be easier. A short paved road winds up the backside to a parking lot situated only a few feet from the brink of the cliff. This parking area is located directly above "the amphitheater," an indented curtain of rock containing some of the most popular routes at "the Head." On any given weekend, novice climbers can be found here coming to grips with the wide fissures of *Superior Crack* and *Quetico Crack* (both 5.8); *Bluebells* (5.9), a superb dihedral crack climb; and *Phantom Crack* (5.9), the area's premier hand-crack problem.

Adjoining the amphitheater on its north side is *Driving in Duluth* (5.11b), a brilliant, zigzagging line that utilizes a number of traverses to connect crack systems. As the name implies, route-finding on this devious climb is very much like motoring in a town renowned for its steep hills and one-way streets.

Adjacent to the amphitheater on the south side, situated directly beneath a small stone retaining wall, is *Rapprochement* (5.10b), a sustained crack and stemming classic with multiple cruxes and good rests. Highlights farther south include *Danger: High Voltage,* a multi-pitch 5.8 that roughly follows the lightning cables grounding the 300-foot radio tower atop Palisade Head (definitely *not* recommended during inclement weather), and *Scars and Tripes Forever* (5.10b)—a wonderfully diverse crack route on stone surrounded by clinging potato chips of rock tripe lichens. Near the southernmost fringe of the main cliff face is the striking line of *Laceration Jam* (5.l0b), a beguiling hand crack with an unsettling appetite for human flesh. Do yourself a favor and tape up!

The northern section of cliff at Palisade Head is a second broad amphitheater characterized by pumpy cracks and steep face climbs. A classic example is *The Poseidon Adventure* (5.11d), a sustained dihedral pitch with spectacular position.

THE APPROACH to Shovel Point is also straightforward. After parking at the Tettegouche State Park visitor center, it is a 15-minute hike along a well-marked trail to the overlook atop the cliff face.

The sunny walls here contrast sharply with Palisade Head. Perhaps most notable is the vast slab of *Dance of the Sugar-Plump Faeries.* At least four distinct face climbs ranging from 5.7 to hard 5.10 wander up this 75-degree flatiron. Nearby are *Balance of Power* (5.11c), a muscle and thought-provoking crawl up an exposed spine, and *Ross's Crack* (5.10b), a popular stemming problem attributed to British climbing legend Paul Ross who spent time in northern Minnesota over 20 years ago as a consultant to the Voyager Outward Bound School.

Nestled within 40 feet of one another are *Sacred Biscuit* (5.11a/b), *A Study in Scarlet* (5.10c), *A Dream of White Sheep* (5.9), and *Straw House* (5.11b/c), some of the finest face climbs on the Shore. Completing this judges' row is *Narcoleptic Epic* (5.11d), a flawlessly smooth dihedral that is one of the most desperate non-strenuous routes a climber will ever encounter.

Farther down the point the cliffs diminish in size, and here novice climbers will find several moderate classics, including the old Outward Bound trade routes *Out on a Limb* and *The Great Yawn* (both 5.6). Although the cliffs are shorter here, the waves are still deceptively far below. An instructor friend of mine was leading a youth group on an introductory climbing course when one of the students stunned him by suddenly leaping off at this spot, ignoring a number of key factors: The rockface leans at an angle considerably less than vertical, the drop here is still almost 80 feet,

A Study in Scarlet *(5.10c), Shovel Point*

the water of Lake Superior averages a bone-chilling 39 degrees Fahrenheit year-round, and the nearest beach is 100 yards away. The kid survived, but, obviously, the deck is stacked against anybody tempted to try something this stupid.

* * *

MY FACE has no feeling, anesthetized with trauma. After a quick damage survey, my hands come away looking like I have crawled through a slaughterhouse. Since I have no way to treat or even evaluate my injuries, I perpetuate the day's long line of stupid decisions by grimly pulling my stocking cap down over my head in the hope that it will at least hold things together. Slowly, painfully, I extract myself from my gear and lower to the ground. The rain and hard spray from the pounding surf are pelting me like gravel. Fortunately, the waves have not yet engulfed the area beneath the cliff, and my eyeglasses—stripped from my head during the fall and essential for the long drive back to town—are lying intact and in plain (fuzzy) sight only a few feet away.

The immediate problem now is that while I am safely at the bottom of the cliff, my car is on top. Since the thin boulderfield along the base of Palisade Head is cut off at either end where lake meets wall, the only way out is straight up. Fortunately I had the common sense (or blind luck) not to pull my rappel line earlier in the day. The 100-foot jug out nearly puts me into a coma, but at last I crawl up to the car.

With great trepidation I adjust the rear-view mirror and finally get a look at myself. One side of my head has swollen horribly and blood is seeping from beneath my cap and caked to my face and clothing. I am afraid to look under my hat, so I don't.

I really wish I had health insurance.

GREEN CHEESE AND OTHER CLIMBING MEDIUMS

Although the North Shore climbing experience is mainly defined by the lakeside venues of Palisade Head and Shovel Point, it is not limited to them. Scattered throughout the region, typically within several miles of the lake's shore, are eight other significant crags.

Unlike the smooth, frictionless lavas that make up the sea cliffs, places like Mystical Mountain, Section 13, Sawmill Creek Dome, and Carlton Peak feature a more extraterrestrial geology. These rocks—a rare form of anorthosite gabbro—are the closest match on Earth to rocks brought back from the moon. In fact, "Minnesota Lunar Simulant," a substitute that scientists study when real moon rocks are not available, is quarried from a climbing crag (a peerless mixed-climbing playground called Casket Quarry) in Duluth.

Casket Quarry in Duluth

The most significant thing about anorthosite for climbers, however, is its abrasive qualities; the rock's crystals are as hard as steel and as sharp as broken glass. Carelessly thrusting a hand inside an anorthosite crack is like reaching inside a lawn mower. But what bites the hand usually delights the feet—the frictioning properties of anorthosite are unparalleled.

The high northern latitude of the North Shore makes the free-climbing season relatively short (May through October), but in darkest winter, when the low sun peers like an anemic eyeball between bony trees and bitter winds beat the lake into seething gray froth, the gloves go on, the tools come out, and it's a whole new ball game. In the shadowed ravines and river canyons along the North Shore, the crumbling overhangs above frozen streams become the dark gums for gleaming ice fangs, pillars, and shrouds.

North Shore ice climbing samples a variety of unique locations, from the frozen spillways of the hydro stations near Duluth to the dark corridors of the Manitou River. The area's premiere ice route is *Nightfall,* a 200-foot frozen seep situated in a deep couloir along the Devil Track River. The mile-long approach, with its numerous crevasses and delicate ice bridges along the frozen river surface, is an exercise in glacier travel Minnesota-style.

***

THE DRIVE back to Duluth is a nightmare. For 60 miles I am weaving in and out of consciousness, not to mention all over the road. And I'm not even sure where I am going. I am in need of medical attention, but my lack of insurance makes an emergency room a last resort. Suddenly an answer occurs to me. And it is such an exquisite, masterful solution that I momentarily consider whether my entire ordeal has been pre-destined to this end. The woman I love—the very female whose rejections have gotten me into this mess (remember, I have taken quite a blow to the head)—is a health-care professional. Not a doctor, true; not even much of a nurse really—only a few weeks out of nursing school in fact—but to my battered faculties she is Florence Nightingale incarnate. She will patch me up. And perhaps, I strategize, my situation might even elicit some propitious sentiments from her, sympathy perhaps—maybe even tenderness.

She is not sympathetic. In fact, she screams at me in horror. To be fair, however, this is an understandable reaction to the bloody and wobbling Frankenstein monster ringing her bell on such a wild and Gothic night. Once she discovers who it is beneath the gore, and why I am in this state, she exhibits a bit of the Creature herself. I am an idiot, she assures me, and the immaturity she has always accused me of possessing has only been confirmed by this incident. She does patch me up, however, although tenderness never enters the picture.

And in the end, after all her rough harangues and ministrations, she finally reveals a softer side by tucking me beneath crisp sheets and warm blankets, and turning out the light.

As my bruised mind wades out into the dark, silent waters of sleep, I reflect on two thoughts: Although no one in his right mind would go seeking the kinds of things I've been through today, anyone who says that climbing adventure is not possible in the Midwest has never been to the North Shore. And secondly, there must have been an easier way into this woman's bed.

Originally published in CLIMBING, *No. 151, 1995.*

Author's notes: This head injury could explain a lot. To this day, I have a tendency for repeating myself that I'd like to believe is more than a penchant for hearing myself talk. This head injury could explain a lot.

For a more detailed account of filming the movie The Good Son *at Palisade Head, see "That's a Wrap!," page 239.*

Finally, it is important for me to emphasize that the woman described in this story is not the person I ended up marrying. I made a number of inexplicable choices on the relationship front before my wife, Dina, swooped in and saved the day. This head injury could explain a lot.

THE LONELINESS OF
THE LONG DISTANCE CLIMBER
For a Flatlander, the Crux May Be Just Getting Home

*T*HE CLIMBERS WHO LIVE in the heartland of America are captives of a cruel geography. There are no mountains and only a few cliffs. Ancient glaciers long ago planed them into cornfields and then, with heartless irony, melted away, transforming a plethora of spectacular ice-climbs into the flattest surfaces possible: lakes.

The unfortunate inhabitants who experience the urge to climb rocks are thus confined to a scattering of humble outcrops that somehow managed to elude the Ice Age. These climbers would drool over the most modest Colorado roadcut. It is little wonder then, that they come to feel a bit like fish out of water and train their sights on the great ranges and distant walls that lie beyond the fringes of the Central Time Zone. Consequently, they periodically flee the confines of Minnesota, Wisconsin or Iowa and travel to far away places blessed with a more precipitous topography.

Restriction of time and finance often necessitate that the vast distances to mountainous lands be traversed at breakneck speeds and in vehicles of questionable constitution and prehistoric vintage. The epic nature of these long and harrowing crossings to and from the golden West often overshadows the actual climbing adventure.

This is the chronicle of one such journey.

6:02 A.M. - GORDON ST., BOULDER, COLO.

Alarm clocks are mean little bastards, perhaps with good reason. They are conceived to perform one task. When they do it well they are greeted with the same enthusiasm and gratitude accorded a dentist's drill. And so they become mean. This one is certainly no exception.

I am waiting for it, dreading it, and praying it will malfunction so I might prolong these final moments of peace and relaxation. Miraculously, it appears as though it has—a bleary glance at my watch reveals it is overdue. I am just sliding back into the serenity of slumber when the son-of-a-bitch explodes the silence of the house like an air raid siren in a library.

In a bewildering display of almost Olympic speed and choreography, Laurie leaps from bed, sprints across the room, silences the blaring intruder, and is back asleep under the blankets without missing a snore. I suspect that this woman oversleeps a lot.

With far less agility and sense of purpose, I rise and foggily begin to collect my things. I nearly trip over Craig who is asleep on the living room floor. My fellow couch-surfer is entombed in a fat sleeping bag and in the darkness resembles a monstrous slug that has slithered down the chimney and lies waiting for a puppy or small child to convert into a sinister snack. I am confident that if I were a three-year-old in search of a glass of water I would not have survived the encounter. I tiptoe around him gathering my gear and bags as he patiently endures the motion and noise of my preparation.

At last the car is packed. I go in to say goodbye. Laurie is still out cold, and Dave's bed has not been slept in. Gifted with an enthusiastic pituitary and irresistible personality, he has undoubtedly roosted in some coed's dorm room, divorcee's double-wide or some other amatory nest. As I pass back through the living room I am startled to see a clutching hand protruding from the mouth of the worm. Fighting an impulse to grab it and drag the undigested portion of my friend from the gullet of the beast, I curb my imagination long enough to clasp it in the gesture of farewell that was intended.

I will miss these people, but to dwell on such sentiments now will only exaggerate the already staggering task at hand. It is time to go home.

6:40 A.M. - ARAPAHOE AND 28TH ST., BOULDER, COLO.

I am stopped at a traffic light. In my rear-view mirror the Flatirons gleam with the wetness of a misty dawn. Before me there is only smooth horizon. I am situated exactly on the most well defined boundary of geological contrast in the United States. To the west is a land of intrinsic wonder, the earth wrinkled into great peaks and colorful deserts. To travel through this region is a delightful exercise in logistical navigation while experiencing constant sensory overload.

The other way is madness. It is a vast province of unrelenting grasses and grains. It is limbo: as big as the sky, as empty as the wind, and as interesting as a pail of dirt. Attempting to drive across it alone represents a battle against monotony and fatigue akin to Lindbergh's solo flight across the Atlantic, except the ocean isn't as boring or as flat.

The light turns green and I roll forward, acutely aware that according to all logic and reason I am facing the wrong direction.

7:20 A.M. - FORT LUPTON, COLO.

The car seems to know what I am going to do to it. It senses that this is no merry jaunt in the country, but rather the beginning of a piston-pounding marathon across a sizeable swath of continent. The peculiar vibrations that plague it at moderate speeds have increased in both intensity and duration during the last fifty miles, as if to protest the extreme effort that I will require of it.

To compensate, I attend it like a surgeon watching over an unstable patient. I meticulously monitor the levels of all essential fluids and keep one eye glued to the various gauges, lights and dials. The radiator is running a little hot, but other than this mild fever and the occasional bouts of spasm the patient seems to be clinging to life.

7:40 A.M. - KEENESBURG, COLO.

I am already falling asleep at the wheel. This threatens to erode my will, undermine my purpose, and kill me outright, so I must nip it in the bud. I decide to pull over and seek metabolic and blood sugar stimulants. Still under the influence of the vaguely hypocritical Boulder mindset—*your body is the fragile repository for all that you are, treat it gently and thoughtfully, nourish it with healthy and natural foods grown in the rich earth, then stuff it with all the brain-altering chemicals you can afford*—I purchase an apple and a cup of coffee that is black as tar. Laurie would be so proud. The apple tastes like candle wax and after one sip of the day-old asphalt I pour it on the paving where it belongs. I go back inside and get a Twinkie and a Coke. Laurie would be so disappointed.

9:00 A.M. - STERLING, COLO.

The radio is my friend. It is my sole source of external stimuli while driving the prairie treadmill. It talks to me, tells me the news, and engages me in sing-alongs with everyone from Bach to The Talking Heads. And I discover that if I get sleepy, with four independently controlled speakers and a Bevada power-boosting system, I can crank the volume so high that it sets up a standing wave in the fluids inside my brain.

10:00 A.M. - JULESBURG, COLO.

The enormous distance I have left to cover is weighing on my mind like a lead hat so I attempt to adopt the same mental attitude that I use to survive multi-day rock climbs. I resolve to never look farther than one hundred miles down the road at a time. The psychological impact of making many little trips seems far easier to cope with than contemplating one impossibly immense journey. I keep telling myself that the way to eat an elephant is one bite at a time.

10:30 A.M. - OGALLALA, NEB.

I have just entered Nebraska—a state shaped like a Westinghouse steam iron. This is appropriate since the entire surface of the planet here looks like it was yanked out of the wash and pressed while still wet. This place must have been scheduled for late on the first Saturday of Creation, because it feels as though after a long week of sculpting and molding the earth's intricate features, the inventive hand of God either ran out of ideas here or simply clocked out.

12:15 P.M. - NORTH PLATTE, NEB.

Just forty-five minutes beyond the state line I stop for gas and wander inside the station to stretch my legs. The clock on the wall confuses me until I realize I have just crossed back into the Central Time Zone. Thanks to the Earth's rotation and a temporal universe that progresses in only one direction, I have been cheated out of an hour. Now, no matter how fast I drive, I will always feel like I am trying to catch up. I burn out toward the freeway, cursing the obstinacy of general relativity and the ghost of Einstein.

2:00 P.M. - GRAND ISLAND, NEB.

Maintaining a constant 85 miles per hour, I am amazed at the conspicuous absence of the Highway Patrol. This is the major trucking route through the heart of America, and perhaps the police here have better things to do than slow the wheels of commerce. A steady procession of cattle trailers are the corpuscles of this artery as the ranchers and stockmen of the plains transport their herds to the vast meatpacking concentration camps of St. Louis, Chicago, and Omaha. The cattle still grazing free beyond the highway fences are pathetically oblivious to the fact that they are doomed to end alongside baked beans and potato salad, smothered in ketchup and heaped on a paper plate at some church picnic in Kansas. Or perhaps they have just grown complacent from the years of genetic tinkering that has made their brains and bodies well marbled and ideally suited to the purposes of their carnivore overlords.

I'm not sure if it's the relentless vibrations of the road or this line of thinking that is making me queasy, but I decide to pull over for a break. A set of glowing neon arches rivet my attention, and I am drawn like a helpless moth to the yellow bug-light of fast-food cuisine. Road-fatigue, loneliness and innate gluttony incite a mindless feeding frenzy, and I greedily gorge myself like a starving shark in a tank of bleeding dolphins. It is hard to tell which leaves me feeling more wretched: the gassy indigestion, or the horror at my hypocrisy.

3:30 P.M. - LINCOLN, NEB.

Lincoln is the midpoint in my journey. It would be psychologically devastating to view this fact with even a shred of pessimism so I keep telling myself that the glass is now half-full, the elephant is half eaten. And I'm not the only one trying to outflank his brain: On the radio, Huey Lewis is screaming about wanting a new drug. Okay Huey, I'll meet you halfway— I switch to psychedelic rock, crank up the volume and rip through Nebraska's capital city like a rocket sled on greased rails.

4:30 P.M. - OMAHA, NEB.

Another gas stop, and with the needle pegged on "E" I am lucky to find a mom-and-pop pump at a lonely exit on the outskirts of town. Any relief is short-lived, however. I've depleted all my cash, and when I drop my battered plastic on the counter, the attendant startles me by warily eyeing me up and then produces a fat ledger filled with the names and cards of fraudulent transactions. While he compares the numbers, I stand shifting uncomfortably, sweating like a fat man under hot lights. I am guilty of absolutely nothing, but am nonetheless paranoid that due to some cruel typo I will be bludgeoned senseless with tire-irons by the unsavory mob of oily mechanics that has gathered to bar the only exit. At last the grumpy attendant slams his book and reluctantly accepts my card. The surly gang shifts to let me by and I dash for the car, vowing to stick to main roads from now on.

4:45 P.M. - COUNCIL BLUFFS, IOWA

As I cross into Iowa I am engulfed in a violent thunderstorm. The tempest intensifies into a typhoon-like deluge until I realize I am tailgating an eighteen-wheeler and its wheel splash has been fire hosing my windshield point-blank for at least fifteen minutes. As I brake to put some distance between us, the sun reappears and an astonishing double rainbow paints the heavens. I am mesmerized by its awesome beauty and for the first time since before leaving Colorado...I smile.

5:45 P.M. - BRAYTON, IOWA

I am at ground zero in the radio-free wasteland of western Iowa. I lost the last station just outside Council Bluffs and I know from experience that I will not find another that doesn't specialize in Johnny Cash and Slim Whitman tunes until Des Moines. I begin to wonder about the name of that city. My rudimentary knowledge of French makes only a rough translation possible, but it can't really mean "some monks," can it?

7:00 P.M. - DES MOINES, IOWA

There are no friars here, but "fried" and "frayed" aplenty. Darkness, the thing I fear most, is upon me. I must summon all my energy and creativity to remain conscious. To wit: I attempt to allow one side of my face to sleep at a time. I find that my eyes are too powerfully interconnected for this trick, however, because I cannot close one for very long before the other mindlessly follows suit. The radio is operating at airport decibel levels, but I soon discover that even bruised eardrums are no guarantee against falling asleep. To make matters worse, cloying and maddeningly repetitive retro-pop songs are a monopoly of the Iowa radio stations. I vow that if I hear Phil Collins sing "One More Night" one more time I will steer my car into the nearest telephone pole or concrete bridge abutment.

9:15 P.M. - MINNESOTA BORDER

My soul has been eaten away by the demon of the road. My head is an empty shell staring catatonically into the oncoming headlights through lidless fish eyes. I am knee deep in paper cups and burger pods, gripping the wheel instinctively and steering solely by reflexive action. I no longer hear the radio, but its presence is made known by sheer vibration. I may be clinically dead.

1:30 A.M. - DULUTH, MINN.

I'm not sure how long I've been idling at the curb outside my house before the mental fog thins, the nightmare ebbs and realization dawns: After 1,080 miles, it is done. My joints are popping like sniper-fire as I pry my ruined body from its seat cushion mold and stagger out beyond the bug-splattered paint and glass, beyond the blistering waves from the engine block, out and up and into a deliciously dark and static environment where I hit the mattress like two hundred pounds of dead fish impacting a concrete slab. My eyes are stuck open and I am trembling like a mountain of jello in an earthquake. I know that sleep will come. Like a great black whale it will come and swallow me whole in one sudden gulp.

Until then I am fated to lie, and wait, and suffer the lingering effects of my journey. But there is a spark of contentment amidst the arcing neurons of trauma. I have successfully completed a grueling rite of passage. I am not sure what it will mean to me tomorrow, but at this moment it feels as though I have reached out and managed to touch the Grail. I know what it is to have eaten an elephant.

Originally published in CLIMBING, *No. 102, 1987.*

Author's notes: Unless the goal is free-soloing vertical mud in the Fisher Towers, driving cross-country is doubtlessly fraught with more perils than any other aspect of a Midwesterner's climbing vacation. These include ready access to cheap and delicious artery fudge (fast food), epic boredom (i.e. the Dakotas), and breakdowns both mechanical and mental. During the dreaded graveyard shift between midnight and 5 a.m., I have lost hours in the blink of an eye and nearly flipped the car swerving to avoid vivid hallucinations (washouts, trees across the road, charging elephants). Closest call: I once drove an eight-hour shift, then passed the baton and crawled into the very back seat of a 12-person van for a well deserved snooze. Ten minutes down the road, just as I was drifting off, I came to the terrifying realization that everybody else in the vehicle, including the driver, was already sound asleep. I could only watch helplessly as the van launched off the freeway like a satellite bound for orbit. My personal entry for the Road Warrior Hall of Fame: Duluth to Yosemite, 2000 miles in 29 hours with four guys and enough gear to fix El Cap stuffed into a 1979 Volkswagen Rabbit.

Since publication, this story has undergone modest revision to fine-tune the narrative and correct minor inaccuracies in the chronology.

Cast and crew of The Good Son *filming at Palisade Head on the North Shore*

THAT'S A WRAP!
Alright Mr. Wiggins, I'm Ready for My Close-up

I'M NO STRANGER to the dirt: sleeping under tarps, mining ditches for aluminum cans, subsisting on a dreary diet of Ramen noodles and abandoned leftovers scarfed from picnic tables and cafeterias. I could have drifted more quickly into the main current of society, finished school on the four-year plan, poured my time and energies into achieving financial success and security. But I was hooked on climbing. Instead of squirreling away money for the future, I frittered away my youth living close to the soil in places like Yosemite's Camp 4 and the Tetons. The only squirreling I saw involved the critters themselves begging potato chips and other snack-food detritus off tourists. Even though the rock-hobo lifestyle was my choice, I envied those rodents and their easy lives. Nobody ever tossed me so much as a Cheeto—until the spring of 1993, when Tinseltown came calling.

"Dave, it's Earl Wiggins," the message said. "I've got a job in your area. I need a local climber with time on his hands, and your name came up. Are you interested?" Well, yes, I was interested, and not merely because I apparently topped the list in some mysterious slacker database. Mostly, I was excited because a call from Earl Wiggins could mean only one thing: Fat times were just around the corner.

Earl is something of a legend in climbing circles. His name can be found on numerous hard and classic routes, from the first free ascent of *The Cruise* in the Black Canyon to the first ascent of *Supercrack* at Indian Creek. Earl's real claim to fame, however, is that he's one of a select few climbers who've succeeded in making the transition from dirt to pay dirt, by parlaying his expertise with ropes and heights into a lucrative career as an aerial rigger for TV and motion pictures. Earl was part of the team responsible for Captain Kirk's trek up El Cap and Sly Stallone's cliff-hanging in the Dolomites, and now he was bringing his big dollar, Hollywood smoke-and-mirrors operation to my neck of the woods.

In fact, 95 percent of Earl's latest project—a formulaic "good-versus-evil" feature film—had already been shot on the coast of Maine. The ending, however, had hit a cinematic snag. The climactic scenes called for a dramatic sequence in which two boys wrestle atop a sheer sea cliff. The denouement comes when one boy plummets to his doom onto the wave-battered rocks below. The problem now facing the moviemakers was this: Kids leap for fun off the biggest ocean cliffs in Maine. Hence, the scramble was on for another location with a drop high enough to ensure that when their child actor did take the plunge, he wouldn't be back for the sequel. After searching coastlines from Big Sur to Cornwall, the studio finally settled on the obvious choice: Duluth, Minnesota.

I got my first glimpse into the Hollywood mindset during this "scouting phase." Earl had recruited me to shepherd the key filmmakers to the impressive cliffs fronting the shoreline of Lake Superior just north of Duluth. The group's initial confusion upon deplaning amidst boggy marshes and pine-covered gravel flats vanished the minute they saw the rugged scenery along the North Shore. "This looks more like Maine than Maine!" the director gushed. The cliffs were perfect, too: "Easily big enough to kill a child," the location manager declared with satisfaction. However, since Hollywood must always improve upon perfection, changes would have to be made. "Of course, most of these forests will have to go," the art director mused, and then turning to me, "Who do we have to pay to get that done?"

Thankfully, the filmmakers found their "must-have" rock face at Palisade Head, a promontory within the jurisdiction of a state park. Though this meant that indiscriminate pruning and any other environmental "enhancements" were out of the question—at any price—the production team was undeterred. For the few "reverse angle shots sans forest" (movie-speak for the equally perplexing "Position the camera so that it's looking at the trees we don't want to see"), they devised a simple alternative. They would create a second film set by manufacturing a life-size replica of the Palisade Head clifftop and perching it on a less vegetated outcrop a few miles down the shore.

Thus, my second job on the movie project was to rig safety lines for the workmen while they assembled this precarious, Ark-sized contraption. When I showed up with a sack of old webbing and timeworn equipment, Earl frowned and led me to a massive footlocker. The box contained enough ropes, carabiners, and cams to shackle Marley's ghost—along with all the other dead misers in history. The gear was shiny and unblemished, most still in the original packaging. "Use *this* stuff," Earl commanded. "Our insurance requires that any gear used has to be new." Then, noticing the foamy trickles of drool forming at the corners of my mouth, Earl narrowed his gaze, closed the lid on this treasure trove, and waited for my eyeballs to settle back into their sockets. "You remember that scene in *Cliffhanger* where the climber's harness blows apart and she falls about a million feet?" I had the distinct impression that this question had less to do with movie trivia than with the perils of yielding to base temptation. "Never forget," Earl said, "I made that happen. And I can do it again."

The third phase of the production was the filming itself. Once the cast and crew began arriving, the circus *really* came to town. Any floodgates on fiscal restraint that had not yet fully opened were simply torn from their hinges by the Niagara-like outpouring of cash. In lieu of personal trailers, fully furnished Quonset-like structures were erected on-site to shield million-dollar faces from brisk lake winds, and toilets were airlifted by helicopter to the cliff edge. In the catering tents, lavish gourmet meals were laid out in endless succession. Earl's crackerjack rigging crew (a veritable "Who's Who" of the Camp 4 elite) also pulled out all the stops.

At Palisade Head, Earl's crew constructed a false lip over the actual cliff edge, outfitting it with the cable and breaking mechanisms needed to send actors and stuntmen winging into space and then reel them up again. The riggers also erected an enormous mast sporting a gyro-controlled camera platform that could be maneuvered out over the cliff edge to track the action from above. Once again, I managed to extend my employment—and secure a job for my climbing buddy Tom—by toadying up to the riggers. As "safety officers," Tom and I were responsible for making sure that anyone who approached the cliff edge wore a length of seatbelt webbing buckled securely around their middle and that the carabiner tethering them to a bolted anchor was locked. For this, we were paid like airline pilots. Most of our time, however, was spent sipping designer cocoas, sampling freshly made pastries, and marveling at the seemingly endless resources of the moviemakers (e.g. the fleet of rented fishing launches that circled endlessly offshore in order to produce an ocean-like surf).

After the final day of shooting, the movie company hosted a wrap party for everyone involved with the production. It was a fete worthy of a coronation with food made from plants and animals utterly foreign to citizens of northern Minnesota. I found myself face-to-face with such exotic delicacies as Russian caviar and rare chocolates wrapped in gold leaf. Live lobsters scuttled back and forth inside a rowboat filled with crushed ice, and the bottles of fine wines and spirits could be measured by the case—a method of packaging I had previously assumed was unique to canned beer.

For climbing bums like Tom and myself, it was the party of a lifetime, a Roman bacchanal of heretofore unimagined decadence and self-indulgence. But the Hollywood folk had seen it all countless times before and so it wasn't long before they began slipping away, either back to their private lounges and suites or in airport-bound limos to jet off to their next multi-million-dollar extravaganza. Only an hour or two into the party, Tom and I found ourselves utterly alone, surrounded by the largely untouched banquet feast and a hoard of abandoned liquor.

I'm not ashamed to say that we did what any resourceful squirrels would have done. Tom backed his car up to the service entrance and we loaded up everything that wasn't nailed down. After all the glamour and the glitz, one simple truth remained: You can take the climber out of the dirt, but you can't take the dirtbag out of the climber.

Originally published in CLIMBING, *No. 219, 2003.*

Author's note: Throughout this month-long spectacle, the producers of the movie were sweating bullets worrying that Palisade Head's nesting pair of peregrine falcons would return from their winter migration, in which case the filmmakers were contractually obligated to pull the plug. As if scripted, the day after filming wrapped, the falcons arrived. And...scene.

DUST STORM
What Happens When Ethical Conflicts Mushroom out of Control?

M Y HOME CRAGS on the North Shore of Lake Superior are an ethical powder keg. White powder, that is. Thirty years ago, the use of climbing chalk was a hot potato throughout the country. Magnesium carbonate's visual impacts (not to mention how it illuminated the problem-solving aspects of a climb) were wildly controversial. Today of course, chalk squabbles are passé.

Everywhere except on the time-capsule cliffs of Lake Superior's North Shore. For those of us who live here, it's hard to think of the North Shore as a hotbed of anything. Life in this remote corner of northern Minnesota is a seemingly endless struggle against sub-arctic cold and winds stiffer than a frozen walleye. When June finally rolls around and the overcoats, earflaps and mukluks come off, we make a mad dash for the lakeside cliffs at Palisade Head and Shovel Point, hoping to get in one or two good weekends of climbing before the black flies and mosquitoes hatch. It takes a special mindset to willingly live here, in a climate where Santa himself could die of exposure. Perhaps this explains a lot about our attitude toward the white dust: Chalk is a remedy for sweating—something so rare for us that when it happens we regard it as something of a miraculous stigmata, and embrace it like a blessing of heaven's own dew.

We northern Minnesotans are by nature a solitary folk. It's not that we're unfriendly—just wary of anyone to whom we can't relate (or, perhaps more accurately, to whom we're not related). And so when outsiders, climbers sporting immodest, form-fitting clothing made of fabrics not found in nature, first began to invade our crags in the early 1980s, we eyed them with a mixture of curiosity and trepidation. In fact, their arrival sparked a cultural collision on a par with Pizarro and the Incas, except these visitors carried their plague in small pouches dangling from their waist-belts.

In the beginning, we sought to understand their chalk addiction, but its magic was beyond our experience. For us, a humble swipe on the seat of our woolen trousers or against the homespun fabric of our flannel sleeves had to suffice. Our abstinence (and obstinacy) with respect to chalk wasn't (and isn't) based upon a fear of new ways, new methods, or the newcomers themselves. The bottom line was that these chalk-carrying conquistadors were making a frickin' mess of the North Shore.

While struggling to prevent our backyard from becoming a Polka-dot Palisade, we took a bold gamble and did the opposite of what any defending army should do when its home turf is threatened: We gave away the blueprints to the castle. We published a guidebook that opened the floodgates to an ocean of road-tripping Midwestern climbers. But this also allowed us to include a manifesto detailing our anti-chalk ethics and a "request" that everyone who climbs here follow suit. I've been holding my breath ever since. Asking Joe Chalk Bag to go cold turkey is a touchy situation. He might comply, or he might tell me to take a flying leap. Or he might try to help me along with that flying leap, at which point I might try to feed him a rack of Stoppers. This escalation is what I fear: "cliff rage."

Such conflict was presaged in the early 1970s when Royal Robbins' ethical opposition to the unprecedented bolting on Warren Harding's *Wall of Early Morning Light* route on El Cap caused him to sanctimoniously chop the lower pitches. Thankfully, rather than physically taking Robbins to the mat, Harding wrestled with him in print. A later incident, in the 1980s, was elevated to high farce when Todd Skinner's free-climbing efforts on *City Park* at Index, Washington, were temporarily thwarted after disgruntled locals troweled axle grease into the crack—Skinner eventually triumphed, but only after burning out the offending goo with a blow-torch. But on the other side of the country, tensions reached felonious levels in the 1990s with Ken Nichols' bolt-chopping shenanigans at Rumney, New Hampshire and Ragged Mountain, Connecticut. If this trend continues, one of these days an "ethical" controversy seems destined to end in disaster—the kind in which everyone loses.

In a classic Cold War treatise, political scientist Herman Kahn outlined how two divided camps could go from trading words to lobbing missiles. He described an "escalation ladder" in an ever-deepening crisis leading up to, and including, total mutual annihilation. Although Kahn's model was designed for conflicts between nations, I believe these same rungs can apply to any dispute—even one as mundane as two climbers at odds over a chalk bag. As a warning, and an example, I offer this quasi-fictional North Shore scenario, framed within the rungs of Kahn's ladder:

RUNG 1: OSTENSIBLE CRISIS

Dusty Mitts, who has gone seriously off route on his way from Boulder to the New River Gorge, pulls into a parking lot high atop an intriguing lakeside crag. Perusing the local climbing guide (shoplifted from the park visitor center), he is stunned to discover that he's not in West Virginia.

"What the hell is this?!" Dusty exclaims, reading from the guidebook: *On the North Shore, the white chalk that climbers commonly carry to blot perspiration from their hands is not used.* As unsettling notes from a banjo filter through the pines, Dusty realizes that he's stumbled into some kind of backwater Twilight Zone of traditional climbing.

Dusty: "Are they serious? Who do these people think they are?"

RUNG 2: POLITICAL AND DIPLOMATIC GESTURES

Dewey Palms, a North Shore local, alerted by the raised hackles on his chalk-sniffing sled dog, approaches Dusty, who is painstakingly scrutinizing the cliff face below in an attempt to locate "Even a single goddamn bolt hanger!"

Dewey: "Hello, excuse me. I couldn't help noticing your chalk bag. I wonder if you're aware of the fact that we don't use chalk here on the North Shore? Now, I can see by your face that you've got some questions, so let me explain our thinking: Chalk is unsightly—there's no denying that. And the local climbers here have traditionally avoided marking up the cliffs with it—all part of our appreciation for this wild, unspoiled setting."

RUNG 3: SOLEMN AND FORMAL DECLARATIONS

Dusty: "Bite me."

RUNG 4: HARDENING OF POSITIONS—CONFRONTATION OF WILLS

Jaw set, feet firmly planted, chalk bag riding like a six-shooter against his hip, Dusty squares off with Dewey. Squinting at the sport climber, Dewey mirrors the *High Noon* pose—except he's wearing bib-overalls and a Whillans harness. Dusty is first on the draw: Clapping his hands loosens enough residue from under his fingernails to raise a provocative white cloud.

Dewey: "So that's how it's going to be, eh, Sporto? Look, I've tried to be decent about it, but the bottom line is that you can't use chalk here. So if you won't climb without it, why don't you crawl back into whatever gym crapped you out and connect the dots in there—kapeesh?"

Dusty (sucking down a packet of energy gel): "Look, Goober, how 'bout I connect my foot with your ass? Now stop bothering me or I'll squeeze your head like this packet of GU."

RUNG 5: SIGNIFICANT MOBILIZATION

Dewey calls out to other locals climbing nearby: "People, looks like we've got a troublemaker over here!"

The other climbers begin to gather round Dusty—their '70s-era tube chocks clanking like cowbells as they press for position. Soon, Dusty's is the only bare head in a crowd of orange and red Joe Brown helmets.

Dewey: "It's time for you to pack up and go back to Chalk-orado, man."

RUNG 6: HARASSING ACTS OF VIOLENCE

Breaking free from the group, Dusty skulks off in the direction of his vehicle. Believing they have triumphed, the North Shore locals celebrate their victory by breaking out the moose jerky and a thermos of Molson Canadian. But Dusty, now out of sight, begins methodically defiling their routes with various sundries from his pack. The locals discover his desecrations when one of their comrades, smeared with chalk and protein powder, manages to claw his way to the cliff top where he collapses in a hazy puff.

Dewey (calling out to Dusty a short time later): "Gosh, I hope this isn't your SUV in the parking lot. All four tires going flat at once—man, what are the odds of *that* happening?"

RUNG 7: DRAMATIC MILITARY CONFRONTATION

Rushing back to defend his truck, Dusty finds he is too late. Blind with rage, he wildly rummages through the Kevlar duffel in his trunk until he unearths a telescoping carbon-fiber cheater stick. Brandishing the implement, he screams at the locals: "You *hicks* come anywhere near me or my chalk bag, I'll crack your skulls! What's with this time warp, anyway? No wonder there aren't any hard routes around here!!"

RUNG 8: BREAKING OFF OF DIPLOMATIC RELATIONS

Dewey: "I'm done talking to this moron. If he won't give up that bag of devil-dust, we'll have to take it from him."

RUNG 9: NUCLEAR ULTIMATUMS

Further skirmishes result in the complete destruction of a boombox and some localized bruising sustained during hand-to-hand combat from quickdraws wielded like nunchuks. Hopelessly outnumbered, Dusty retreats to a bunker of boulders at the bottom of the crag. At his cliff-top command post, Dewey addresses the troops: "He's got an endless supply of stones down there in that talus, but we've got the high ground. If he starts to score any hits, we'll have no choice but to jack loose that huge block above him. I realize it may take out some of the key holds on *Superior Crack* on the way down, but that can't be helped."

Then, calling down to Dusty: "We didn't want this, but you've brought it upon yourself. We're prepared to take this as far as necessary to get you to hand over that chalk bag! By the way…"

RUNG 10: SPECTACULAR SHOW OR DEMONSTRATION OF FORCE

"…the spare tire seems to have come loose off the back of your truck. Let me return it to you…Oh, tough bounce—right into the lake!"

RUNG 11: "JUSTIFIABLE" COUNTERFORCE ATTACK

A stone whizzes up from below. A husky yelps.

Dusty: "Gee, I didn't mean to wing your dog. I guess that rock just took a 'tough bounce.' But now you know that I mean business too!"

RUNG 12: NUCLEAR WAR

Dewey: "Okay boys, this is it: One, two, three, heave! There it goes…"

(As the impact of the massive trundled boulder shakes the ground below, it triggers a deep, shuddering rumble of shifting bedrock within the escarpment.)

Dewey: "Shit! The whole cliff edge is collapsing! Get back, get—no! Oh my god, *noooo…*"

Above the crystal blue waters of Lake Superior, an enormous dust cloud of pulverized stone rises. The thunderhead of suspended particles swirls silently over a massive swath of newly calved talus and now-quiet rock walls. It finally drifts back to earth, where it settles over everything— like a coating of fine chalk.

Originally published in ROCK AND ICE, *No. 118, 2002.*

Author's notes: This piece has been slightly revised from its original form (e.g., the more satirical names "Dusty" and "Dewey" are used here, an edit I submitted too late to change before the magazine went to print). Also, credit where it is due: The idea was inspired by a story called "Crab Apple Crisis" by George MacBeth.

After my story ran, Rock and Ice *published a letter from another North Shore local decrying this "very controversial article." By this person's reading of it, both the message and my motivations for writing it were suspect: "In short, the article leaves you with the impression that if you use chalk on the North Shore, we (the locals) are going to throw rocks at you, slash your tires, and even go as far as throwing you off the cliff!…It's creepy and it makes me think that [Pagel is] exposing too much of what may simply be a sick fantasy of his."*

Mountain Profiles

The Southeast Face of Nelion; Batian in background

SHIPTON SELECT: MOUNT KENYA
Africa's Perfect Penultimate Peak

*L*IKE A SCAB OF SNOW on a sheet of pan ice, the continent of Africa caps a drifting fragment of planetary crust that geologists call the African plate. One of many pieces in an ever-shifting global mosaic, the African plate has spent the last few hundred million years jockeying for position in a kind of continental demolition derby. But unlike the buckling impact between India and Asia that has thrust up the Himalayas, or the massive upheaval along the Andean spine where an ocean plate is being driven under South America, the African plate has largely escaped any of the earth-shattering head-on collisions that result in spectacular mountain building. Despite its tremendous geographic diversity and vast size (second only to Asia in area), the continent of Africa is markedly void of great ranges.

This is not to say that Africa does not have great mountains. In the mid-1800s, tantalizing glimpses of distant, snow-capped peaks dumbfounded early missionaries and elicited skepticism from high-brow European geographers—for decades the various reports of "snows on the equator" were summarily discounted or discredited. By the dawn of the 20th century, however, the first-hand experiences of numerous explorers, scientists, and mountaineers confirmed that one of the world's largest dormant volcanoes (Kilimanjaro, 19,340 feet) and one of the highest volcanic remnants (Mount Kenya, 17,058 feet), complete with fat mantles of snow and even glaciers, were situated almost squarely upon the line of zero latitude.

The origin of these lofty equatorial peaks is in fact linked to movement of the Earth's crust, but not a continental collision. The Great Rift Valley, a network of fractured depressions extending 4000 miles from the Red Sea to Mozambique, is a landscape in the process of tearing itself apart. Here, diverging plates have produced a massive laceration across the face of Africa, along with rugged earthquake-jumbled terrain and vast lava plains dotted with volcanic mountains and pinnacles. Both Kilimanjaro and

Mount Kenya were born of molten rock erupted from the fiery tumult within the rift.

The similarities end there, however, because while Kilimanjaro is a bulging hog-pile of relatively young flows, Mount Kenya is a bony, crystalline skeleton—a volcano stripped to the core by the jackals of erosion. This transformation has cost Mount Kenya dearly in terms of elevation (it was a 25,000-foot elephant of a mountain before the glaciers got their teeth into it). And this erosion has forever relegated Mount Kenya to "also-ran" status in terms of climbing popularity. Compared to the thousands that flock annually to the continental highpoint of Kilimanjaro, Mount Kenya is like afternoon Mass on Superbowl Sunday—there's just nobody there. For serious alpinists, however, it is precisely this reworking from ashy cupcake to rocky thorn that has made Mount Kenya the most interesting and significant mountain in Africa.

The first adventurers to probe its flanks were frustrated to discover that, unlike every other major African peak, there was no easy path up. Every ice-cleaved facet of the mountain was a sheer battlement. Furthermore, Mount Kenya's situation high atop an ancient plateau meant that the altitude was also a serious impediment. Swooning in the thin air, the earliest explorers barely managed to penetrate the mountain's inhospitable zone of ice and rock. The bitter cold and hostile winds that defined its uppermost slopes belied the fact that the peak virtually straddles the equator. It's not surprising that it was a full decade after Kilimanjaro was conquered before the summit of Mount Kenya yielded to mountaineers. What is surprising is that it didn't take a lot longer.

HALFORD MACKINDER'S 1899 expedition to Mount Kenya was extraordinary from the start. When the young Oxford-based geographer first decided to scale Mount Kenya, he wasn't even a climber, but he soon made himself into one. Several seasons in the Alps gave Mackinder the basic skills, and a fierce commitment to succeed along with some excellent planning compensated for the lack of depth in his mountain résumé. Key among these preparations were the two veteran Italian alpine guides, César Ollier and Joseph Bocherel, who Mackinder hired to accompany him to Mount Kenya. Together, the trio methodically reconnoitered the mountain, finally settling upon the steep walls around the southeast ridge as the best choice for a concerted assault. After two failed attempts—during which they endured nearly every sort of high-mountain epic imaginable—the climbers had only enough time and supplies for one last run at the peak. High on the mountain, they made a bold gamble.

"We were obliged to drop on to the hanging glacier to our left which descended from the col between the summits," Mackinder wrote in his official report. "To cut steps across this glacier direct to the higher summit

was the only way left to us. It took three hours to cut our way across this hanging glacier to the farther side of the gap between the two summits, and I gave it the name the Diamond Glacier. At first we traversed the ice obliquely upward, each step requiring thirty blows with the axe…The glacier was steep, so that our shoulders were close to it. Had we fallen we should have gone over an ice cliff on to the Darwin Glacier several hundred feet below."

For Mackinder and his party, the precarious traverse opened the door to the summit rocks of Mount Kenya. At that time, their route (East African Grade 4), which incorporated bold, technical rock and ice climbing at impressive altitude, was very likely the highest-standard mountain climb in the world.

Mount Kenya would be Africa's most technically challenging mountain if the route pioneered by Mackinder's team was the only way up. Of course it isn't. In fact, it isn't even the standard way. Thirty years after Mackinder's climb, Eric Shipton forged a new line up the Southeast Face (Grade 4) and bagged the second ascent of the mountain. Shipton was one of an adventurous group of colonial British farmers who immigrated to Kenya between the wars. Others included Bill Tilman and Percy Wyn Harris, who both partnered with Shipton on Mount Kenya climbs.

On their descent from the mountain in 1929, Shipton and Wyn Harris had little to say about their own adventures. "What impressed them most was Mackinder's courage," wrote Vivienne de Watteville, a Swiss woman who was living at the base of the mountain at that time. "They said that they would have tackled any kind of rock rather than go the way he went, passing that perilously canted stretch of ice hanging over the void."

But Shipton's route was no walk in the park. His line threaded an intricate path up the sweeping 1000-foot face, brilliantly linking clean cracks and corners via wildly exposed traverses. With its high-quality rock and solid in-cut holds, Shipton's route on the southeast face quickly became the mountain's *voie normale* (today it is even called the *Normal Route*).

And so it continued: A third route was added in yet another British *tour de force* when Shipton and Tilman climbed the striking *West Ridge* (Grade 5) over one long day in 1930. Even during the darkest years of World War II the mountain continued to inspire the human spirit when a trio of Italian POWs escaped from a nearby prison camp with the express purpose of climbing Mount Kenya. Using homemade climbing gear, two of these stout-hearted escapees actually started up the Shipton-Tilman *West Ridge* before a nasty snowstorm forced them down.

In the years following the war, the torch of new-route development on Mount Kenya passed to Nairobi-based climbers, where the prolific and important Mountain Club of Kenya was gradually taking form. From these ranks came the amazing Arthur Firmin, a gifted alpinist who added a handful of fine routes before his death in the Himalayas in 1955. Advances in climbing equipment and techniques allowed succeeding generations to push the standards on Mount Kenya's steepest ice gullies and alpine faces.

Finally, in the mid-1960s, came the inexhaustible Ian Howell, whose relationship with Mount Kenya is probably best described as a love affair. He even built the mountain a house.

HOWELL WAS PART of a generation of ambitious British mountaineers who traveled the globe seeking out unplucked alpine plums. The very first time he climbed Mount Kenya, Howell sensed that his appetite could be sated on what he has called "this perfect mountain." The rock was excellent, the equatorial weather was friendly and predictable, the altitude was challenging without being debilitating, and the potential for new, cutting-edge routes was vast. "No wonder I fell in love with it!" exclaims Howell.

He spent the next decade and a half in alpine hog heaven, exploring every nook and cranny of the mountain and ferreting out major new routes like *North Gate* (Grade 6) on the north side of the mountain, and *Diamond Buttress Original Route* (Grade 7) and *Equator* (Grade 6+ A1) on the Diamond Buttress. Howell, now age 66 and still rock climbing at a remarkable standard, says his passion for Mount Kenya was inspired by two things: good partners and an exceptional mountain.

"It wasn't so much planned," he explains, "as it was an obsession I had with wanting to climb existing and new rock routes on the mountain that just kept going for over 10 years. Iain Allan was my main partner over this period and certainly his climbing ability, eye for a line, and endless energy kept me going as much as anything." Whatever the reason, Howell's prolific climbing record here speaks for itself: There are currently 33 major alpine routes on the mountain; one third of them were first climbed by Howell.

And yet it was early on in his relationship with Mount Kenya that Howell dreamed up what would, in some ways, become his most impressive contribution to the mountain. Logistically, many of the routes

Howell was doing on Mount Kenya required a high bivouac. After observing the massif's unique weather pattern (afternoon storms that arrived with such predictability they put Old Faithful to shame) and enduring a few cold nights out, Howell concluded that all this mountain really lacked was a proper high-altitude hut. So he single-handedly built one on the summit.

Actually, he built it in his garden first. Using the lightest, most durable materials he could get his hands on, Howell engineered an ingenious four-person bivouac shelter that must have raised a few eyebrows in the neighborhood as it took shape. With its shiny aluminum skin, porthole windows, and hatch-like door, it was decidedly more space capsule than garden shed. Once the refuge was finished, Howell disassembled the structure and bundled it into parcels that he arranged to have airdropped onto the glacier beneath Mount Kenya. Finally, and most remarkably, he ferried the bundles to the summit, one by one. He accomplished this by soloing (up and down) Shipton's *Normal Route* with pieces of the hut strapped to his back. It took him 13 round trips to get everything up, reassembled, and firmly anchored to the summit rocks. But he was forced to spread it out a little.

"The concentration got to me after a few days," he admits, "so I descended the mountain and went to Mombasa for a few days where I was able to totally switch off and relax on the beaches. Then back to the mountain for a few more carries." Every climber who has ever dived inside the Howell Hut to escape the afternoon storms nipping at their heels or spent the long equatorial night on top of Mount Kenya squirreled away in sheltered comfort rather than on exposed rock ledges, owes a debt of gratitude to Ian Howell. Some owe him their lives.

IF HALFORD MACKINDER could step forward through time and see the mountain as it exists today, the Howell Hut is just one of the things he would probably need a stiff drink and a few long minutes to comprehend (to be fair, it has the same effect on many modern climbers). He could empty a bottle or two contemplating the various changes and amenities that now make Mount Kenya so accessible to climbers: the development of a national park around the peak with organized mountain-rescue capabilities, the well-worn approach paths, mountain huts located on all sides of the peak, and the ready services of porters and guides.

But what has not changed is that Mount Kenya still stands alone among the great African peaks as the summit that must be climbed, rather than hiked, slogged, or scrambled.

It was Mackinder himself who gave the names Batian and Nelion to the twin summits of Mount Kenya, and it is to his credit that these were not European monikers, but the names of local African chieftains. The two

Peak comfort: the amazing Howell Hut on the summit of Nelion

peaks are separated by a deep gap he dubbed the Gate of the Mists, but they are so evenly matched in terms of elevation that it is difficult to discern which is highest, even when standing on their summits. In fact, Batian, the point reached by Mackinder, is 36 feet taller. It was a lucky thing for him, since Nelion is the more technical summit to tick—although that may not be true for much longer.

A rapid loss of snow and ice due to global warming is rewriting the faces of Africa's mountains. Legendary ice routes like Mount Kenya's *Diamond Couloir* (Grade 6) are still occasionally climbed, but the chossy, melted-out gullies and discontinuous seams of rotting ice are a far cry from the stupendous classics of only a few decades ago. Another casualty is the Gate of the Mists itself. Until recently it was a matter of course to climb as Eric Shipton did to the summit of Nelion, descend into the Gate and then continue up Batian. Today, as the snow and ice in the Gate rapidly recedes, this traverse—particularly the return climb back up Nelion—is becoming increasingly problematic. As a result, more and more climbers are contenting themselves with a summit 12 yards lower than the mountain's true highpoint.

On Mount Kenya, however, with its fine rock, superb technical climbing, challenging elevation, and reliable weather (not to mention the unique experience afforded by a bivouac in the Howell Hut), it is hard to imagine anyone leaving the summit of Nelion feeling disappointed—even without surmounting Batian. After all, the fact that a climber has chosen this particular African mountain implies an understanding that reaching a highpoint is not everything.

Originally published in a CLIMBING *Special Edition: "Super 7," 2002-2003.*

Author's note: This article was prepared for a special issue of the magazine that profiled "The Real Seven Summits: The Toughest Mountain On Each Continent." Whenever somebody contrives to compile one of these highly subjective (and popular) "lists," it opens a can of worms. For example, in this case, the argument could be made that rock climbs on the Hand of Fatima in Mali lead to more inaccessible high-points. But is a cluster of lowland desert spires a mountain? In the end, it was decided that according to the criteria, Mount Kenya reigned supreme in Africa. Nonetheless, the fact that this 5.7 peak ranked alongside such hard-won summits as Torre Egger and K2— coupled with the reality that Kilimanjaro (a walk-up) is queen bee here in terms of elevation—is proof enough that in terms of truly difficult mountains, the massive and majestic continent of Africa needs to grow a pair.

On the Eiger's summit ridge

CLIMB OF THE GODS

So You Want to Climb the Eigerwand? One Shmoe's Advice:

W HEN I FIRST STARTED CLIMBING back in the Paleozoic, it was assumed that someone who had climbed the Eiger's North Face possessed three qualities in abundance: 1) fitness on par with that of an Olympic athlete, 2) courage, enough to piss in a lion's den, and 3) consummate mountaineering skills. Indeed, for decades after the first successful ascent in 1938 by Anderl Heckmair's Austrian-German team, you could confidently count any Eiger veteran among the world's finest mountaineers. The Eiger, after all, has long been regarded as alpine climbing's "final exam." And so, years later, when I found myself considering this vast sweep of black limestone from the unlikely perspective of its summit ridge, one of my first thoughts was, "Boy, how times change."

Over the course of three, fine autumn days, my climbing partner and I visited the Eiger's legendary landmarks: the Difficult Crack, Death Bivouac, the White Spider, etc., and experienced a revelation. True, we were exceptionally lucky—the weather was nearly perfect, stonefall was minimal, and we found no rotting corpses to rattle our nerves. But weaned since our alpine cradles on an endless succession of Eiger horror stories, we had come prepared to engage in an ultimate struggle of Good vs. Evil, a "Climb up To Hell" on the "Wall of Death." Instead, we encountered something markedly less epic. While the climbing was interesting and challenging, it was not desperate. The crux was getting past the exaggerated demons haunting every crack and couloir. Clearly, in good conditions and with modern techniques and equipment, the Eiger no longer qualifies as a final exam. It is no pop quiz, either.

Despite the indignity of my successful ascent, the Eiger wall—or Eigerwand, as it is known locally in the Swiss community of Grindelwald— still retains a near mythic aura of difficulty and danger. It is a reputation born of a sensational history. Throughout the middle part of the 20th century rock-and-roll singers flying in small airplanes were probably better insurance risks than aspirant Eiger climbers. In those days, venturing onto the North Face was akin to entering another world—one of complete isolation and commitment. Because the Eigerwand's path of least resistance (now known as the *Heckmair Route* or the *1938 Route*) meanders circuitously back and forth up the face, the prospect of retreat—with rudimentary gear and engulfed in storm—was a formidable proposition. For injured climbers, sprouting wings was more likely than a rescue party.

Today, sprouting wings is entirely plausible; helicopters, winches, and copious beta have shrunk the face to more manageable proportions. Yet most of the dangers that have figured in countless Eiger tragedies remain undiminished: Violent storms still occur with alarming frequency, stonefall still rakes large portions of the mile-high alpine face, the route is still long and sustained, and the rock is still crap. In short, while completely buying into the Eiger's "Wall of Death" reputation may be a recipe for psyche-out and failure, taking this climb too lightly can still spell disaster.

THE SETTING

The base of operations for climbing the Eiger North Face is the picture-postcard village of Grindelwald. This modestly sized tourist town is located in the Bernese Oberland region of south-central Switzerland, near the city of Interlaken. You can easily reach Grindelwald by either car or train. European-style campgrounds (cramped, but with superb showers, laundry, and so forth) are found in four locations around town, and signs are posted to direct campers.

Switzerland has three peculiar cultural oddities: a near-manic obsession with order and public neatness, high prices, and a rifle under every bed. Camping costs are calculated by the number of people in a site, plus an additional surcharge per tent, plus a surcharge for a vehicle, and so on. Two people with a car can expect to pay a premium per night, including the nights you're on the Eiger.

You'll either have to bite the bullet and pay the going rate (unauthorized bivouacking anywhere around town violates the neatness obsession and is a good way to get a closer look at those rifles) or forego the bakeries, cafes, and other pleasures of Grindelwald. Camping or bivouacking several miles away in the pastures beneath the Eiger is the traditional alternative for cash-strapped climbers. If this sounds like you, stock up on groceries in town, and hike or take the train (no cars) to Alpiglen, wander up to the base of the face, and stake a claim. Secure unattended gear: Curious cows have been known to wreak havoc on campsites, even to the point of trampling tents and devouring money, passports, and return airplane tickets. Yet another low-cost lodging option is to rent a hayloft from farmers near Alpiglen for a few francs per night. The local folk consider Eiger North Face candidates a bit deranged, so you'll likely be asked to pay in advance.

Since you'll probably spend some time waiting for a good slot of climbing weather, you might amuse yourself by checking out some of the local color and amenities. Sport shops and eateries in Grindelwald are pricey and tourist-oriented. If you have a car you're better off bumming around Interlaken's shops, restaurants, and movie theaters. A worthwhile side trip is the Reichenbach Falls, the spectacular waterfall Arthur Conan Doyle used as the site of the final showdown between Sherlock Holmes and his arch-nemesis Dr. Moriarty.

When the clouds break and you finally get a chance to see the Eiger, don't be surprised by its oblique, unfamiliar appearance. You'll have to leave Grindelwald and go to Kleine Scheidegg, just up the tracks from Alpiglen, for the classic perspective. Here, you can use the incredibly powerful coin-fed telescopes on the terraces to study the face. These are the same optical devices that the tourists will be using to scrutinize you as you climb (they'll know when you're flipping them off). And, on your first clear night in the area, don't be fooled into thinking that the light burning in the middle of the face is the world's largest headlamp. It is the bizarre inset windows of Eigerwand Station, a popular tourist stop along the Jungfrau railway that tunnels up and through the very heart of the mountain.

WHEN TO CLIMB

Storms smack the Eiger like ocean waves all summer. You can spend days poring over Eiger chronologies like *The White Spider* trying to determine the most opportune month to sneak in an Eiger climb (most parties require two to three days for an ascent). Almost all the early ascents occurred in July and August, but so did most of the disasters. The realities of the summer months are that long, settled spells are rare, warm temperatures increase the rockfall potential, and running water is everywhere. During my second tempestuous summer trip to the Eiger, my constant bitching about the rain elicited this illuminating tidbit from a Swiss citizen: "Too bad you are not here in autumn when the weather is much better." Needless to say, my next trip was timed to extend well into September, and I finally hit the jackpot.

The flip side of climbing in the fall (or spring) is that the conditions will tend toward wintry. We wore crampons and thin gloves continuously from the Difficult Crack to the summit. In addition, any late-season storms are likely to be doozies ushering in cold temps, lots of snow, and icy conditions. Throughout the year, weather forecasts are posted daily at the guide's bureau in Grindelwald, but keep in mind that unexpected storms often develop on the Eiger's North Face while the rest of the region basks in sunshine.

EQUIPMENT

Modern climbing gear has helped to bring once formidable alpine testpieces like the Eiger into the realm of possibility for shmoes like me. One thing that never ceased to amaze me during our climb was how Heckmair and his companions managed some of the more tricky passages with such primitive gear—Heinrich Harrer, who would write the Eiger classic *The White Spider,* didn't even have crampons, and none of the party carried more than a single ice axe. How they clutched and chopped their way up pitches like the Ice Bulge is beyond me.

As for our climb, we went pretty light, especially in terms of protection: just a few nuts and pins and one small cam. Our reasoning, based on our experiences elsewhere in the Alps, was that fixed gear would be plentiful. To our dismay we found only one or two old pins per pitch. A few extra pins and cams on the rack would have been worth their weight in gold. An extra pick for your ice axe is another smart addition. I bent one of mine by clunking it into solid rock and spent the rest of the climb wishing I had a spare. For ice protection, we brought four screws, which proved adequate. With the exception of the short Ice Bulge, the icefields and other ice pitches are moderate and can be simul-climbed with an occasional screw for pro. One final note on protection: We encountered old, tattered, fixed ropes on many of the key pitches. While I wouldn't advise relying on such relics, we occasionally clipped them for quick, easy, better-than-nothing protection. I also might have pulled on one or two of them, but only because I knew I could've done the moves without them. Really.

The traverse to the Difficult Crack

REQUIRED SKILL LEVEL

What does it take to climb the Eiger North Face? On our climb, the hardest technical moves were probably 5.8. But, on an 8000-foot alpine route where you climb in crampons, wear a pack, and reef on rock of dubious integrity in a wet and/or snowy, cold environment, numbers tend to lose meaning. Another problem with trying to quantify something like this is that everyone who climbs the face seems to describe the various pitches and cruxes differently. The fact is, conditions can change in minutes, and will radically alter the nature of the climbing. I can only say that to attempt the Eiger you need solid climbing skills, good judgment, honed route-finding instincts, and above all, competence in the face of the sudden and unexpected adversities that are common in the alpine environment. In short, you should have quite a bit of mountain experience on lesser peaks under your belt. But you don't need to be a Superman— label me exhibit A.

I will give Anderl Heckmair, that brilliant architect of the first Eigerwand ascent, the last word here. He has written the best piece of advice I can imagine for an Eiger hopeful or, for that matter, any alpine climber: "I often had very bad weather conditions—on the Eiger, the *Walker Spur,* etc.—but it didn't bother me a lot. To the contrary, bad conditions made me more animated and active and I said, 'Now, more than ever, I shall succeed!' I never had the feeling of dread or fear, because, you see, fear doesn't help."

ROUTE DESCRIPTION FOR THE EIGER NORTH FACE— HECKMAIR (1938) ROUTE

Approach: The Grindelwald to Kleine Scheidegg railway runs right along the base of the face. Most climbers take the train to Kleine Scheidegg and walk back downhill a mile or so on a good path that traverses just below the start of the climb. We opted for a more direct route and disembarked at the tiny station at Alpiglen located squarely beneath the face. We then climbed on top of the concrete bunker that protects the train tracks from avalanches and walked this smooth pavement a quarter mile or so until we could make a short traverse up through the cow pastures to the start of the climb.

The Climb: The lower third of the face is characterized by rubble-strewn slabs, ledges, and gullies. Ice, snow, or running water may also be present depending upon the conditions and season. Although the terrain here is neither steep nor difficult—it is typically third-classed in a few hours—fatalities and many near-misses have occurred here. Countless route variations are possible up the lower face. The key is to follow the path of least resistance, and a general course dictated by some of the major features

Moving across snowy ledges on the Traverse of the Gods

of the wall. The most prominent of these is the First Pillar, an enormous triangular buttress projecting from the base of the Eiger. Begin climbing to the right of this feature where the scree, snowfields, and tapering rock bands converge to form an obvious weakness. Wander up on slabs and gullies using ledges to make an occasional end run around any of the short, vertical rock steps. Above the level of the First Pillar is a lesser, more eroded buttress known as the Shattered Pillar. Pass this feature also on the right. You are aiming for the base of the Rote Fluh, the sheer wall looming ominously overhead.

Most parties rope up in the general vicinity of the Gallery Window (or *Stollenloch*), where the face steepens precipitously. This infamous doorway—originally used to jettison rock while tunneling the Jungfrau railway—has figured prominently in many Eigerwand escapes and rescues. Not far above the Gallery Window is the Difficult Crack, the first really technical bit of climbing. Probably the hardest thing about this crack, however, is identifying it—there are a lot of false pin lines in the same area. We traversed right to reach the base of the Difficult Crack. A small overhang at the beginning and the fact that it is largely in a right-facing corner should help confirm the correct line. It also had a fixed rope in place when we were there, but we saw ropes dangling in a lot of weird, off-route places, too. The crack itself is a 60- to 80-foot dihedral that is probably 5.7, but packed snow or running water can make it seem much harder.

Several easy pitches above the Difficult Crack you will dead-end at the Rote Fluh. A short traverse left leads to the key passage of the Hinterstoisser Traverse. This 70-foot horizontal jog across a steep slab is apparently a pendulum/tension affair in warmer conditions. We found it covered with a thick layer of firm névé, and we kicked and chopped our way across quite easily. This is also one place where old fixed ropes are almost certain (though they may be entombed in ice or snow in wintry conditions). At the other end of the Hinterstoisser, a short flake leads up to the Swallow's Nest, a popular, albeit cramped and damp, bivouac niche.

A traverse out of the Swallow's Nest deposits you onto the First Icefield which is inclined at about 55 degrees and exposed to stonefall. Three hundred feet up the Icefield is the Ice Hose, a steep runnel that gets you through the rockband above. Normally, the Ice Hose consists of tricky mixed climbing and has some fixed gear. We found it packed with unconsolidated snow and absolutely unprotectable (the crux of the climb for me). The Second Icefield was more reasonable, at least in the beginning: several hundred feet of 55-degree ice to the top where an overhanging rock barrier necessitates more than 1500 feet of calf-flaming sideways front-pointing to the opposite end of the Icefield (severe rockfall risk here, especially in the afternoon). As you near the end of the Icefield traverse, the level platform of the Death Bivouac is clearly visible atop the protruding buttress of the Flatiron.

It is probably easiest to gain the top of the Flatiron by breaching the rock band some distance to the right, and then traversing left toward the Death Bivouac. We tried to save time by forcing a more direct line through the rock face, and ended up making things a lot harder for ourselves (the crux of the climb for my partner). From the sheltered nook of the Death Bivouac, move left and down onto the 60-degree Third Icefield. Several hundred feet of traversing up and left leads to the entrance of the long, diagonal cleft of the Ramp. The Ramp is five or six pitches of moderate crack and chimney climbing. The second-to-last pitch in the Ramp is a saturated section known as the Waterfall Pitch, although for us it was a steep corner of spotty ice smears. The final exit chimney is blocked by a 20-foot, yellow-green icicle called the Ice Bulge. Wriggle up the side of this pillar to gain the steep ice slope above the Ramp.

It is critical that you do not continue too far up this icefield. Instead, keep a sharp eye out for a traverse right leading onto the Brittle Ledges. At the far end of this crumbling band is a short, steep corner with fixed gear known as the Rotten Crack (aka the Brittle Crack). A bulging 5.8 move at the top of the crack gains the ledges at the beginning of the Traverse of the Gods. This is a long, exposed, horizontal traverse back toward the center of the face on narrow, downsloping (often snowy) ledges. The traverse finally terminates at the icy lower webs of the White Spider. Beware: This bowl-shaped icefield acts as a collecting basin for any loose material cleaved or sloughed from the uppermost sections of the face; in snowy conditions the avalanche danger here is severe. Follow the central hump of the Spider to its top and the Exit Cracks.

The second couloir from the left (we found anchors with lots of slings) is the correct entrance to the Exit Cracks. The Exit Cracks are a series of technical rock runnels, often icy and snow choked. One notable pitch several hundred feet above the Spider is the Quartz Crack, a problematic offwidth lined with white mineral. Just beyond is a series of large, columnar features. Upward progress terminates in a cul-de-sac atop one of these columns. From this airy pulpit, make a 30-foot rappel or tension traverse left (possible fixed ropes here) down and around a corner to a ledge at the base of a shallow, box-like chimney. Climb two long pitches up this chimney to a belay perched atop an exposed ridge. Move through a rock band, then angle right onto snow and ice. Crampon straight up, threading around the rocks, as the ice and snow gradually spread out to become the Summit Icefield. A seemingly endless plod up the icefield concludes abruptly at sharp crest on the uppermost section of the *Mittellegi Ridge*. A short step up the ridge and then a traverse along the corniced crest leads to the summit of the Eiger.

Descent: Descend via the west flank. This is no picnic—particularly in stormy or snowy conditions. Begin by heading down 40-degree slopes and gradually trending back to a spectacular overlook on the edge of the North Face about halfway down. From here, angle away from the face and down toward the Eigergletscher Station. Although no rappelling is necessary in good conditions, you will likely encounter anchors at several of the steeper rock bands. The descent from the summit to Eigergletscher took us about six hours on a clear, sunny morning.

One final, crucial bit of advice: Slip a credit card into your pack so you can gorge and swill on the terraces at Eigergletscher and Kleine Scheidegg after the climb (we ate full meals at both places). You'll have earned it.

Originally published in CLIMBING, *No. 169, 1997.*

Author's note: In recent years, climate change has wreaked havoc in the Alps, shrinking icefields and melting the permafrost that for centuries has provided the glue that binds these mountains together. Attempting the 1938 route on the Eigerwand during the summer months today is nothing short of suicidal folly due to the extreme stonefall danger. Thus, in addition to autumn and spring, winter has become an increasingly popular time for those seeking optimal climbing conditions on the North Face. Otherwise, the information and advice offered up in this profile, including the route description, are still remarkably accurate and relevant—although lodging options around Grindelwald have doubtlessly expanded and become even more expensive; this is Switzerland, after all.

A climber inches up the profile of Devils Tower

DEVILS ADVOCATE
Wyoming's Devils Tower Is Plumb Perfection

I N A PLACE DEFINED by vertical geometry, I am the lone exception. As a climber of decades, I am no stranger to seemingly insane positions and situations, the kinds of things that predictably and, I admit, satisfyingly cause sightseers to unhinge their jaws. Dangling from a jut-browed overhang, posed upon invisible crystals, topping out on a pinnacle with my arms outstretched like an eagle king, I relish not only the joys of conquest, but the sheer wonderment these exploits elicit from tourists, hikers and other passersby.

This time, however, even the other climbers are gaping. This time, instead of dangling or posed or perched, I am, well…sideways.

And I don't mean facing to one side—but rotated at 90 degrees. You know the little horizontal line braced between the vertical segments of the letter "H"? That's me: spanned out lengthwise, an unlikely spring-tension rod of arms, spine and legs, wedged between two perfectly parallel walls of stone. It takes a bit of doing to upstage the scenery here but, conspicuously, I have pulled it off.

I'm several hundred feet up the side of Devils Tower, a rock formation that is itself a befuddling attraction. An utterly unique fusion of striking symmetry and WTF geology, Devils Tower National Monument draws climbers and non-climbers alike to this backwater corner of Wyoming.

For climbers, "the Tower" (which, like "the Valley," needs no other modifier to set it apart) is among the best climbing locations in North America, and perhaps the world. Cracks at other venues may be longer, steeper, even more uniform (though that would be a knock-down drag-out title fight), but no place can boast such a concentrated assembly. The fact that Nature has raked them so uniformly upon the flanks of a surreal, flat-topped, sky-scraper-sized stump—well, that's what brings the tourists.

Of course, the minute the RV captains and crews get a glimpse of our cliff-side shenanigans, they are riveted, amazed and intensely curious. But no amount of patient demonstrations, no matter how dutifully performed by fully roped and racked park rangers, will ever explain to them what I'm doing at this moment. Strung out like a human hammock, I'm not quite sure myself. But I do know who to blame: a photographer. Or, rather, a photo.

Photojournalists are the porn-peddlers of the climbing world. Their images ignite our desires and passions—lust would not be too strong a word. One iconic shot of Our Hero posed upon an exotic chunk of stone is enough to compel us to bad choices: to spend money we don't have, to put lives on hold—in short, and in the language of addiction, "to suffer negative consequences." I once burned through an entire summer's savings traveling halfway around the world for a single route that had bewitched me from a magazine cover. By the time I finally bagged it, I was already under the spell of another route back home, a siren song from the center spread of a climbing journal printed in a language that I couldn't even read.

My very first ascent of Devils Tower marked the beginning of this pattern. My hometown newspaper had run a photograph of some local heroes on top of the Tower. It didn't look like any summit photo I'd ever seen: no jagged peak, no high point at all, really; just a pile of rocks in a field of weeds. What did capture my imagination was the large wooden signpost that declared, "No Climbing Above This Point." To my adolescent sensibilities, something had finally surpassed MAD magazine as the absolute apex of hilarity. Imagine my disappointment when a year or so later I staggered onto the summit of Devils Tower myself, a brick-like "instamatic" in tow, and found only a couple of other climbers sitting on that rock pile.

"Hey," I croaked, "where's the sign?"

"That way," one of the guys said, pointing west.

"Yeah?" I brightened, shading my eyes in that direction. "I don't see it."

"No," he said with a smile, "not here. It's on top of the Grand Teton now."

Great. A few years later, a guy in the Tetons told me it had been carried to the summit of Mount Rainier. I'm still chasing that sign. And that photo.

Thankfully, my definition of high art has evolved. Today, the most seductive imagery incorporates stunningly unique rock. An elephant-sized flake that is waffle-thin, a corner so clean it surely must have been quarried, the crack that breaks like a flagpole shadow: These surreal angles and shapes burrow like parasites deep into the brain folds to trigger neurons that scream, "Holdup—look at *that*! Where *is* that?!" Which, of course, is only a single synapse spark from, "I've got to *climb* that!" It's all about the stone—the more out-of-this-world, the better. And there's only one place on Earth where no matter which direction you point a camera, you frame columns that embody an alien landscape.

The superlative hand jamming treadmill of Assembly Line *(5.9)*

Another killer photograph: That's what's gotten me in over my head. Except that's not quite right. No part of me is actually over my head. Oddly, there's nothing under my head either. I'm not doing any of the things that might make a grain of sense in terms of explaining why I'm bridged out like a plank over empty space between two stone columns. But I'm definitely attracting a crowd.

There's no place to hide on Devils Tower. A loop of paved trail provides ready access to every aspect of the monument. For climbers, this facilitates quick and easy approaches no matter where you're headed, but it also promotes little knots of ordinary folk who congregate to observe the spectacle playing out on the walls above them. Beneath the deeply weathered southern aspect, they *ooh* and *aah* as climbers rappel any of the several equipped descent routes. Their emotions seesaw beneath the awesome North Face when climbers seemingly give up and descend without reaching the summit (the fact that this is de rigueur for avoiding the loose upper sections of many routes here is baffling to them). The East Face is also a mystery. Here, the tourists are likely to ponder the relative absence of climbing activity, oblivious to the formidable barrier of *The Window*—a double-tiered roof that spans 10 columns. And the West Face: The one displayed above the grandstand of teeming parking lots and the Visitor Center, the one with acoustics that ensure every gasp and whimper is clearly transmitted to the gawking throngs, is the one that I'm stuck smack dab in the middle of.

Of course, even before there were rock climbers, Devils Tower was the scene of some pretty hair-brained stunts that the public devoured like candy. The first, and probably still the hairiest, culminated with the first ascent of the monolith—with nary a rope involved. As a prelude to the 1893 Fourth of July picnic extravaganza at the foot of the Tower, local ranchers William Rogers and Willard Ripley spent weeks hammering a line of 24- to 30-inch wooden stakes up a crack system on the southeast face of the Tower. The pair fixed a continuous rail of wood to the outer ends of the pegs to fashion a crude but fantastic ladder. On the appointed day, before a crowd of a thousand strong, Rogers ascended to the summit and planted the American flag. Perhaps because this was Indian land, the flag promptly blew over and floated down onto the talus. Because they were Americans, the promoters quickly portioned up the flag and sold the bits as souvenirs. As a veteran of a few epic climbs on welded ladders (TV antennas, water towers, etc.) undertaken by necessity in the dead of the night, I shudder at the thought of Rogers under a blazing midsummer sun, pulling nearly 400 feet of fat, shaky rungs.

Perhaps angels watch over Devils Tower. (The name alone begs a watchful eye from on high.) Not counting my current predicament, I have used up at least nine lives here stepping on a rattlesnake, dodging lightning strikes, ascending jammed rappel lines, and being present in a local bar when, in response to a cowboy's drunken declaration that he was none too fond of sharing a stool with us "climber faggots," a friend responded, "Well, then, I guess sodomy is out." And that's just the stuff that wasn't actually climbing. The fact is, approximately 5,000 people registered to climb Devils Tower in 2007, and there have only been five fatalities here. Ever. None of those occurred during the 44-year period before people started using ropes (over two dozen people, including his wife, summited via Rogers' stake ladder during those decades).

In 1937, Fritz Wiessner led the first rock climbing team up an ugly 5.7 offwidth crack that still carries his name and relatively little traffic. Modern teams looking to tag the summit by the easiest path typically opt for the 5.6 trade route pioneered by Jack Durrance the following year (Durrance returned in 1941 to play a part in yet another crowd-pleaser, as leader of the rescue party that brought down a stranded parachutist). After that, the routes at Devils Tower quickly advance up through the grades, with a high percentage of modern classics concentrated in the 5.10 to 5.11 range. One of these is called *El Matador* (5.10), and the cameras love it.

Picture this: a stunning perspective shot straight down a breathtaking three-sided chute, the climber posed with legs forked impossibly outward between the columns, limbs split like a rubber wishbone, torqued beyond the tolerances of ordinary sinews and joints. Don't get me wrong, I'm a master at devising unorthodox rest positions. But like a rare book, my crotch is not something that can be roughly pried without threatening the spine. Yet from the moment I laid eyes on an image of *El Matador,* I've imagined myself as elastic as a cheerleader. Why am I surprised that things have not gone well?

I'm feeling betrayed—by my own stupidity, but also by this crag. Devils Tower is, after all, an old friend. As the closest Western "mountain" to my life-long home in the Minnesota heartland, this was the scene of my first multi-pitch climb, my first hanging belay, my first summit. Time and again, this is where my friends and I would return to savor even just a few hours of Big League adventure, despite the fact that it was over 500 miles away. Devils Tower was both our salvation and our curse. To this day, I question whether the Dakotas really exist because they were never seen. I recall only a fuzzy dreamland of dark grasses and distant lightning that we passed through in fitful half-sleep as our cramped and creaking vehicles traversed the long night separating week from weekend. As Saturday dawned, we tumbled out into the dust beneath the Tower, but by Sunday evening, we were back in our rides again, wheeling east through the nothingness, arriving home with just enough time to bandage our scabs, knot our ties and take our workday seats; sated but scarred—not only in body, but so road-shocked we could not even begin to explain, even to ourselves, how we spent the weekend.

Now, as then, fooling oneself is just too easy. So is blame. Confession is something historically associated with being twisted into bizarre contortions, so it is my turn: It wasn't really a photographer, or a photograph that put me here. Ambition is what has brought me to this place, and to this end. Towering ambition.

At least I am in good company. Names like Robbins, Kor and McCarthy attest to the Tower's longstanding preeminence as a crucible in North American climbing. *El Matador* was originally a dicey nail-up pioneered by the ubiquitous Fred Beckey. In the mid-1980s, Todd Skinner—who applied almost frantic energy to advancing free-climbing standards—lived entire seasons based out of a teepee beneath the Tower, as he methodically plumbed the possibilities between every column. Skinner, who was tragically killed in a fall from Yosemite's Leaning Tower, was also a spirited raconteur. Among his campfire standards at Devils Tower was the story of how he once hired a small boy to confront John Bachar, another 1980s climbing icon, beneath Camp 4's Columbia Boulder. According to Skinner, the kid practically thumped Bachar on the chest as he asked, "Are you John Bachar?"

"That's me," Bachar declared.

Following Skinner's script, the youngster narrowed his eyes in a gunfighter squint and put Bachar on notice: "Someday, I'm gonna blow you out of the water."

But it was Bachar's steely response that brought Skinner to tears: "Go for it, kid."

Skinner loved the idea of a big-name climber matching toes with a child—and he wasn't alone. One morning, as he racked for his daily dance with the Devil, a small boy wandered over from an adjoining campsite. "Are you Todd Skinner?" he demanded.

Skinner responded, "Um...who wants to know?"

Undeterred, the kid issued his challenge. "Someday, I'm gonna blow you out of the water."

Skinner deflated. "Aw, c'mon, kid," he pleaded. "There are other sports."

At this writing, Skinner's record for the fastest ascent of the Tower still stands: 18 minutes via the 5.9 classic *Walt Bailey Memorial.* Of course, he also put a lot of effort into reworking (freeing) the contributions of earlier pioneers. Dennis Horning (aka Dingus McGee) also helped rewrite the book by freeing an impressive number of modern classics, and literally rewrote the book in the late 1970s by supplanting an archaic guidebook with a series of pamphlet-like "Poorperson's Guides" that he practically gave away. "Free" was indeed the mantra at Devils Tower.

For a few short years after its own liberation by Bob Yoho and Chick Holtkamp in 1978, *El Matador* was rated 5.11, the top of the scale for the place and time. Soon, however, the realization dawned that there simply

A human curtain-rod extended across the flaring three-sided box of El Matador *(5.10d)*

isn't a move that hard here. To me, considering the outward uniformity of the cracks at Devils Tower, it has always seemed remarkable that cruxes exist here at all. In fact, there is tremendous variation within these crystalline fissures. Feldspar shards and differential weathering of the gray phonolite porphyry have resulted in toothy pockets and tapers within the seams and fractures—myriad opportunities for all manner of locks, jams and protection. As a result, pitches can be outrageously sustained and pumpy, but there is still quite often a distinct "hardest move."

Except on *El Matador*. Even the current 5.10d rating may be a stretch in terms of pure technical difficulty, but nobody's lobbying to drop it another peg. *El Matador* is a different kind of hard. The climb is the stemming archetype—the one by which scientists calibrate their instruments, and the rating is an attempt to quantify the endurance required to sustain an unconventional and agonizing position for an entire rope-length. From my first, tentative attempts to ascertain *El Matador's* singular demands, my groin threatened to go critical, but I found I could make and hold the stem. And I did—for a while.

It began as a sort of wounded waltz. Foot up, foot out, work the crack, then again. Each time I abandoned the stem in favor of the crack, I knew I was turning my back on convention and exhausting valuable strength, but I'd found a rhythm. The key was to climb as quickly as possible, don't pause, don't overprotect, don't think, just move. Foot-crack-foot…shit, that's not right—I missed something. Crack-foot-rest, no—not rest!

Ground to a halt by flaming calves, smoked forearms and a mental meltdown—fixed in an excruciating pose that no longer afforded a shred of recovery or relief—I played my ace. With both hands locked neatly together in the left-hand crack and one foot stemmed out right, I blindly lobbed my other leg outward toward the right-hand corner. The toe caught, and I shuffled both legs up until the burning began to subside. I experienced a fleeting moment of relief—and then dawning dread at the doomed absurdity of my situation: stretched out at full extension between the columns, both hands on one side and both feet on the other. It was unorthodox. It was creative. It was something I could never reverse.

So it ends here: legs at 3 o'clock, arms at 9. Any relief this position afforded my calves has been replaced by a volcanic burning within my abs. Staring straight down the wide, fluted box of *El Matador* I consider that at least it will be a clean drop—as long as my arms don't give out first and dump me headlong into the chute.

The crowd is getting excited. "Hey, check it out dude, that guy's horizontal!" I do love impressing the tourists.

Soon, very soon, things at Devils Tower will fall back into line.

Originally published in ROCK AND ICE, *No. 175, 2009.*

Author's note: It will surprise no one to learn that El Matador *was not my greatest indignity at Devils Tower. There was the time my climbing partner traded me for a dog. The guy was from North Carolina, weaned on the bald friction of Stone Mountain and the surreal eyebrow pockets at Looking Glass. Abrasive cracks were not a part of his growing up. After just a day or two at the Tower, the backs of his hands looked like pulled pork and he'd had enough. The last time I saw him he was headed west with a stray mutt he'd picked up in the campground grinning at me from my seat. At least he'd had the decency to arrange a ride back to Minnesota for me with some nice folks from St. Paul, who let me hang my head out the window all the way home.*

Don't forget to tape up! Climbers' picnic table at Devils Tower

Perspective

Our Hero

SEEING IS BELIEVING
Thanks to the Blindness of Youth, the One-Eyed Man Is King

THREE CLIMBERS—a mountain guide, an aid climber, and a young gym rat—join up for a game of golf. But the party in front of them is behaving rudely: moving at a snail's pace, whacking balls all over the fairway, and making no provision for anyone to play through. Finally, their patience at an end, the trio seeks the club manager to get these hackers kicked off the course.

Instead, the manager reproaches the climbers for their insensitivity. "Surely," he says, "you noticed that those gentleman are blind."

The guide, who has spent years honing his people skills, is mortified, and resolves to exercise greater compassion. The aid climber, who prides himself on keen powers of observation, vows never again to leap to a conclusion.

The kid asks, "Then, why can't they play at night?"

WHILE I WON'T pretend to have a lot of empathy for the younger generation (in my day, any plastic we pumped was wrapped around an iron barbell, and the only piercings we flaunted were battle scars earned the honorable way: with ice tools), I can appreciate flouting convention. Fringe thinking is a trait shared by climbers of all ages—although one measure of maturity is knowing how and when to apply it. In a broad sense, this is what first attracted me to climbing. In my own youth, I was captivated by the eccentricities of explorers. The maverick spirit of mountain climbers and other nonconformist adventurers seemed a welcome alternative to the ox-like tedium of conventional athletics and coaches who, quite frankly, scared me half to death with all their yelling. Mountaineers in particular seemed a breed of rather independent thinkers, focused on goals that were, by their very nature, both romantic and delightfully absurd. And they seemed to have a damn fine time doing it.

My first climbing hero was Anderl Heckmair, the pioneering German alpinist who led the first successful climb of the Eiger North Face, and who once walked out on Hitler because the *Führer* was more committed to sending young men off to war than sending them off to climb Himalayan mountains. I'm not sure which act of Heckmair's was more dangerous, or admirable.

Heckmair's adventures and philosophies, spelled out in his autobiography *My Life as a Mountaineer,* propelled me along a worthy path, and even up some remarkable climbs. He was a terrific role model (although the only thing I've ever walked out on was a job). Now, however, after some 25 years of buzzing around on the periphery of the climbing spotlight, I realize that the mountains are full of great characters—both in terms of the people and their mettle. And I've found that an unexpected bonus of being a climber is that rubbing elbows with Big Names is not uncommon. Golf enthusiasts can only dream of teeing off with Tiger Woods, but in the mountaineering world, anything can happen.

To wit: Teton legend Paul Petzoldt once bought me dinner. I've bought Heckmair dinner—twice. I've shaken hands with the great alpine pioneer Walter Bonatti. Photographer Beth Wald's first Nikon was stolen out of my car (you've never seen the photos she took of Todd Skinner climbing Colorado's *Sphinx Crack;* now you know why). I've held super-alpinist Scott Backes' rope. Bouldering guru John Sherman has held my rope (along with a pretty spectacular fall). And yet, despite all these brushes with greatness and (albeit mostly dubious) honors, very few of these people would know me from Adam. I am something of a Teflon spoon in the great stew of famous climbing talent. Nothing sticks.

But I'm not alone. Even great climbers can go unnoticed. It would be easy if they were all like Heckmair: courageous, talented, and instantly recognizable when we see them. I know from personal experience, however, that this isn't always the case.

Some years ago, I camped on a nude beach in the South of France with an international assembly of climbing bums (no pun intended). Besides my partner and I, the only other Americans were Alex and Joe, two strapping lads from somewhere "out West." The limestone fjords of the French Riviera are renowned for their pocketed climbs and boulder problems, and the four of us were determined to crack a nut called the *Hemming Traverse,* a 100-yard lateral passage across one wall of the inlet, just above the high-water mark. The *Hemming Traverse* is named for Gary Hemming, an American beatnik mountaineer who took Europe by storm in the late 1960s. Hemming was a tragic figure, a tortured soul who eventually took his own life, but also a gifted climber—in fact, downright ahead of his time judging from the crux of the traverse he put up along this sea-cliff in the *Côte d'Azur.* Besides being ripping hard, a fall off the thing lands you square in the aquamarine waters of the Mediterranean. This means swimming back to shore and drying off thoroughly before you can even think about making another attempt. To minimize the trauma and turn-around time, and because the local custom was *au naturale,* we all tried this thing wearing nothing more than the day we were born—and one after the other we all dropped like big naked babies into the bath.

Except for Alex. He insisted upon tackling it in his shorts, T-shirt, rock shoes, and chalk bag. So great was his confidence that he never even considered the repercussions of falling. And so we all laughed twice as hard when he inevitably peeled into the saltwater, emerging some minutes later on the beach looking every bit the drowned rat. In the years that followed, Alex Lowe's determination and confidence never wavered.

Yes, indeed, there have been times when greatness has been right in front of me, the signs staring me in the face, and I didn't have a clue. But the exact opposite also occurs: mediocrity in disguise. Seeing is believing—except when your beliefs turn out to be a misguided bucket of bushwa. Like the three golfers (or two of them anyway), I learned this lesson in an unexpected place, and in a manner that is par for me: the hard way.

Racking up in the parking lot at Colorado's Eldorado Canyon State Park one summer morning, my partner and I were nearly run over by a battered station wagon that was taking the narrow and potholed gravel road leading into the canyon like the home stretch at Le Mans. Fishtailing to a stop in a cloud of dust, the vehicle nonetheless remained in motion, rocking to the vibrations of a tape deck pushed to the breaking point. The exterior was coated in a thick layer of grime into which copious amounts of finger-drawn graffiti had been scrawled—lewd phrases and drawings, many exhibiting a level of vulgarity that would make a Navy SEAL blush. In this way (and some others) the car reminded me of a backwater toilet stall.

"Kids," my partner grunted.

Sure enough, moments later the doors of this weathered punkmobile spewed open and half a dozen whooping, braying teenage boys were ejected into the dirt. Half deafened by the raw, throbbing noise grinding from their boom-box, my buddy and I watched aghast as these miscreants heedlessly shattered the serenity of the park, wrestling, bouncing against adjacent vehicles, and shouting obscenities at one another, completely oblivious to anyone or anything around them. We shook our heads. Do kids these days—kids like this—even have heroes or role models? If so, I was sure I didn't want to know who they were.

A day or so later, while lazily paying out rope high above the canyon floor, a scuffling noise below me heralded the arrival of another party hard on our heels. As I shifted to make room at the belay, my heart sank when a purple-haired, pimple-faced adolescent suddenly pulled over the edge. It was, of course, one of the delinquents from the crapper on wheels. Forced to stand shoulder to shoulder with the little felon, I braced myself for anything from profanities to a belay ledge slam-dance. Instead, he surprised me with polite conversation—just the sort of reverse psychology trick a young ruffian might employ to get me to lower my guard. The whole time he was speaking, I fixed him with what I hoped was an alert and menacing stare.

It turned out that he and his friends were engaged on their first cross-country climbing road trip, and had driven here nonstop from their home in Arizona. Their ultimate destination, however, was Devils Tower, a place he and his pals believed to be the pinnacle of "rad." I don't often get the opportunity to impress others—even children—with my climbing achievements, so I took the opportunity to warily mention that, as one of the nearest Western crags to my native Minnesota, I had climbed many times at "the Tower." Genuinely excited to be in the presence of someone who had actually been to this "killer" crag, he eagerly pressed me for details. Perhaps because of the way he was toadying up to me, I warmed to this kid, and started rattling off the routes I had done at Devils Tower. When I named one route in particular, he nearly knocked me off the ledge with excitement.

"That's the climb we're going there to do!" he babbled. "It's the whole reason for our trip!" I'm certain that somewhere deep within my swelling head the warning bells were sounding, but with the windbag now blowing at gale force, I was deaf to everything but my own voice. Puffed up like a turkey, I told him that not only had I done the climb, I'd once written an article about it for *Climbing* magazine.

"No way!" he shouted, eyes popping. "Are you...*Dave Pagel?!*" And then, drawing back from me, as if the simple act of physical contact with such a being was too overwhelming for him, he bowed his head, and I'm certain that if space had allowed, he would have kneeled at my feet.

"Dude..." he stammered, "My friends and I...your story is our Bible, and you are our *God!*"

I realize now that there are different kinds of heroes. There are the kind who fall into the sea, but truly deserve our admiration. And there are those who, for one reason or another, we elevate to great heights, even though they are really just everyday Joes or Josephines, doing what they love, and in the process managing to gather enough speed to make a ripple or two once they hit the water. And for the hero worshipers, the difference really isn't important.

And I know something else now. Everyone—even strange, obnoxious, punk-ass kids—deserves the benefit of the doubt. They are, after all, the heroes of tomorrow.

But why can't they climb at night?

Originally published in CLIMBING, *No. 204, 2001.*

THE TRUTH IS OUT THERE
Climbing Paranoia Is Just a Click Away

I WASN'T ALWAYS a conspiracy freak. Having been raised in the Midwest, I grew up believing that it wasn't polite to ask questions. Lately, however, I've been spending a lot of time on the Internet, and now I'm having trouble ending a sentence with anything other than a question mark? It all began with an innocent search for information about tent flies. I typed in "FLIES" and hit the search button. But because my fingers typically dance across the keyboard with all the dexterity of a chimp's, what I had really entered was "LIES." What came up on my screen was website after website dedicated to exposing the truth about everything from Roswell to WHAT THE GOVERNMENT DOESN'T WANT YOU TO KNOW ABOUT MOPS. (Sadly, this last site's field reporter was silenced before he was able to finish filing his report.) What I had stumbled onto was the mother lode of secret information that THEY are keeping from us.

On a whim, I decided to post a few queries on various mountaineering-related topics—things that I've always blindly accepted without question as fact. What I learned has got me peering through the blinds:

Mount Everest. Tallest mountain on Earth? Not even close. In the mid-19th century, the glory of the British Empire was at its zenith, a point from which history had proven it could only, and must inevitably, decline. The British were already anticipating the partitioning of Pakistan out of their hands, and with it, bragging rights and probably access to what the Great Survey had revealed was the highest mountain on Earth: K2. But with India—that vast launching pad to the Himalayas—firmly under their thumb (or so they thought) the British government pressured the Surveyor General to "fudge the numbers." Everest was given an exaggerated altitude safely out of reach of anything likely to crop up in the Karakoram, and thus began the "saga" of Mount Everest, an exclusively (surprise, surprise!) British affair. It turns out that what we have come to accept as high drama, was in fact, high theater. Through a series of carefully orchestrated expeditions, all with scripted, predetermined outcomes, various explorers and mountaineers played out decades of reconnaissance, assault, and conquest. The successful ascent of Everest was originally slated for the early 1940s, but the war necessitated a postponement. Afterward, the Swiss almost ruined everything by sneaking in a couple of very strong expeditions from Nepal. John Hunt, Hillary and company arrived in the nick of time and saved the day—and the summit of Everest has been Britain's Tranquility Base ever since. Of course, modern geographers and cartographers are all wise to the truth, and are paid fat sums to keep it under wraps.

Mallory and Irvine. Oh, they made it all right. But that wasn't part of the plan (see above), and when they wouldn't play ball and threatened to blow the lid off the whole Everest sham (Mallory's furtive attempt to alert the outside world to the conspiracy—"Because it is there!"—was sadly misinterpreted), the POWERS THAT BE stepped in and took drastic action. A mysterious and suitably poignant disappearance was devised, and the pair was secretly hustled off to Australia where they lived out their days confined on a remote sheep ranching outpost. And what about the corpse and other artifacts unearthed on the mountain a few years ago? All part of a vast media plot to sell magazines, television documentaries, and a mountain of books (who didn't get suckered in by that?). And I have only one thing to say about those macabre pictures: PhotoShop.

The Yosemite Decimal System. Ridiculous—but then we all knew that. What is not common knowledge is that all the world's rating schemes are a lie. Or at least they have been since the early 1990s. That's when an unidentified climber (the name has been censored) put up the hardest route in the world (location similarly expunged). Not just for that time, but forever. The climb—clocking in somewhere in the upper 5.12 range—has since been scrutinized by the world's top experts from the fields of anatomy, physics and mathematics, who have scientifically proven it to have the smallest holds to which the human body is capable of adhering. Game over. Of course, a major outdoor industry (along with all its associated revenues) depends on the illusion that rock climbing superstars continue to push the limits and standards. Point of fact: The echelon of top climbers is a very small and economically challenged group, meaning that they, along with any associated misinformation, are easy to control. To this end, an international Star Chamber meets once a year to consider who has climbed what, and what difficulty ratings will be applied. Meaningless, arbitrary, and ever higher numbers are applied to any new route that it is judged 99.999 percent of the world's climbing population will never be able to get up anyway.

Fred Beckey. No such person. Fred was originally invented in the 1940s by climbers in the Pacific Northwest as a sort of campfire tall tale, a "been everywhere, done everything" mountaineering bogeyman. In the ensuing decades the legend grew: People claimed to have seen Fred, met him, even climbed with him—until things spun out of control and exceeded the limits of rational credibility. As a result, today hundreds of crags and mountains across the country sport a "Fred Beckey" climb or two. Recently, the story has quieted down a little; after all, the guy would have to be getting pretty old. But a lot of folks, with a wink and nudge, insist that Fred is still out there, tramping around the alpine backwaters, ferreting out new routes and pulling down. Of course, the fact that Fred doesn't really exist isn't much of a revelation, most of us outgrew him along with the Tooth Fairy and Santa Claus. Anyone who honestly believes that one man could have done all the climbs in all the places attributed to Beckey should come and see me. I've got a bridge I'd like to sell you.

Energy Gel. This stuff is just what it looks and tastes like: shampoo. A few years back, a couple of world-class alpinists got suckered into eating hair gel at a drunken tradeshow party. Some marketing people were present, and the rest is history. In terms of delivering any nutritional value, it turns out that with all the protein and vitamins in shampoo, the goo really works. But I still say no soap. Back in the mid-1980s there was an attempt by the hair-care product industry to market shampoos with beer in them. If this trend ever comes back into vogue, call me. Until then, I'll stick to chocolate.

The Eiger Sanction, Cliffhanger, **and** *The Vertical Limit.* Everything you saw in those movies was real.

Climbing protection. Not long ago, word leaked out that ice screws are actually most secure when placed in a downward-angled orientation. Similarly, nuts are most secure in open flares, camming units are safest when only two of the cams are engaged, and bolts, no matter how or where they are placed, must never be trusted.

Chalk. Street names: *poof, dip, white courage.* Turns out that it's addictive for a reason. Laced with something other than magnesium carbonate (precise formula suppressed), climbing chalk is the original designer drug. Manufactured in top-secret military labs and disseminated to an unwitting climbing population, chalk is specifically formulated to give the user exaggerated feelings of strength, confidence, and a delayed adrenal kick. In fact, it turns out that any euphoria experienced while climbing is due entirely to the white stuff—government studies show that rock climbing by itself delivers no buzz whatsoever (quite the opposite, it leaves a person feeling kind of bewildered and foolish; since I don't use chalk, I've been onto this one from the start). But before half of you dash off in search of your chalkbag and a spoon, let me caution that any narcotic effect from climbing chalk is dermally activated—absorbed through the skin (you can't snort a toad, ditto for chalk). Frankly, you all should have read the clues— think back to the very first time you tried chalk: Did you buy it, or did someone give it to you? The first bag is always free.

SO THERE YOU have it—just a few of the things that THEY don't want you to know. And there's a lot more where that came from. I've cracked the lid off the jar of lies, exposed the tip of the iceberg, but the rest is up to you. My wife has banned me from the Internet. She claims it's for my "own good," but her determination to keep me out of the loop, along with all the thinly veiled muttering about me "finally starting to lose it," has got me wondering whether or not she isn't part of the plot. In the meantime, I've discovered another equally authoritative and reliable source for finding out about what's really going on out there: AM radio.

Originally published in CLIMBING, *No. 206, 2001.*

Author's note: As this book goes to print in 2014, the legend of Fred Beckey persists. Even now, over ninety years after this fanciful yarn was first spun, a considerable number of people insist that Fred is not only real, he's still climbing. Preposterous!

SHIFTING GEAR
Reflections on the Evolution of Climbing Equipment

"Every tool carries with it the spirit with which it has been created."
—WERNER KARL HEISENBERG
Physics and Philosophy (1958)

I HAVE COME, to borrow a phrase from George Mallory, "because it is there." In this case, however, the "it" is not Mount Everest, but one of Everest's most famous and enigmatic artifacts, now housed within a hallowed hall in London.

In 1933 the British came as close to reaching the summit of Everest as anyone ever had. Unless, of course, the mountain had already been climbed nine years earlier by Mallory and Irvine. One of the goals of the 1933 expedition, the first since that ill-fated attempt, was to seek clues of the two vanished mountaineers. In this regard, it was successful. High on the North Ridge, lying as if Mallory himself had only minutes earlier set it down upon the rocks, the climbers discovered a solitary ice axe. For 66 years it remained the only tangible evidence of the doomed pair. Today, I hope to encounter this same axe.

The relic is kept in England's venerable Alpine Club. I had imagined it nestled in satin or mounted above a great stone hearth, the focal point in a room decorated with elephant tusks and other adventure trophies, where wizened mountaineers puff a haze of pipe smoke from high-backed leather chairs. The reality is decidedly less genteel. The old men are here, but they are rooting around in a crammed basement, rummaging through over-stuffed boxes of antique climbing paraphernalia. The only puffing is from exasperation. It seems the axe—*the* axe—has been temporarily misplaced.

In the meantime, I am left to contemplate the history scattered about me. Despite the clutter, these closets and shelves are the Smithsonian of mountaineering. Names like Norman Collie, Edmund Hillary, and Joe Brown can be seen scribbled on the tags affixed to various items. I reach for a long staff that looks more like a shepherd's crook than a mountaineering tool.

Relics of climbing history in the cellars of the Alpine Club

"Ah, yes," an elderly curator exclaims. "Whymper's alpenstock. If only it could speak, eh?"

I am speechless. Edward Whymper was the Victorian artist and mountaineer who started it all. Mountain obsession, mountain fame, mountain narrative—if Whymper did not invent these things, he at least elevated them to new heights. His conquest of the Matterhorn was the first mountaineering episode to grip the general public through a sensational sequence of events that remains highly marketable to this day: a triumphant ascent, a disastrous descent. And now I am gripping Whymper—or at least a palpable appendage of the man.

It's a fascinating tool, fully five feet in length with a spiked ferrule on one end and a curved black chamois horn adorning the other. Spiraling down the shaft are the carved names of the Alpine bases that Whymper visited throughout his career: Chamonix, Zermatt, Grindelwald, etc. What impresses me most, however, is the fact that in deft hands, this staff was a state-of-the-art aid for negotiating mountain terrain, doubtlessly requiring techniques and methods now lost to the ages. Turning it over in my hands, I am as clueless to its intricacies as Whymper might have been if some time traveler had materialized in 1865 and handed him a bent shaft with a banana pick.

Would he even care about the new technology? How important was equipment to the business of climbing during the Golden Age of mountaineering, and would pioneers like Whymper admire modern innovations, or would they simply shake their heads at the level of obsession their descendants invest in things like clothing and equipment? Standing in the museum-like bowels of the Alpine Club, surrounded by the ghosts and gear of climbers past, I cannot help but wonder which has changed more through the years, mountain equipment or the mountaineers themselves.

ROPES: FROM HANDLINES TO LIFELINES

"I do not believe that the use of the rope, in the ordinary way, affords the least real security upon ice slopes."
—EDWARD WHYMPER
Scrambles Amongst the Alps (1871)

The old adage "the leader never falls" probably had less to do with an ideal of competency as with a healthy skepticism of early ropes. The best rope available to Whymper and his contemporaries was manila, a three-strand braided cord made of fibers garnered from exotic leafstalks. Lesser quality ropes made of ordinary hemp were also common-place. Ropes like these, composed entirely of vegetable material, had distinct disadvantages. For starters, both manila and hemp were prone to rotting if put away wet. They also ran the risk of being snacked upon by rodents in huts or on

BEALE & CLOVES,
Late JOHN BUCKINGHAM,
194 SHAFTESBURY AVENUE, LONDON, W.C.,
ARE THE ONLY MAKERS OF THE CELEBRATED

ALPINE CLUB ROPE

WHICH IS ALMOST EXCLUSIVELY EMPLOYED
BY THE **LEADING MOUNTAINEERS** OF THE TIME.
THIS ROPE IS MADE OF THE BEST MANILLA HEMP, AND IS MARKED
BY A RED WORSTED THREAD TWISTED WITH THE STRANDS (SEE THE
REPORT OF THE SPECIAL COMMITTEE ON ROPES, ETC., IN VOL. I.
NO. 7 OF THE **ALPINE JOURNAL**), AND IT CAN BE
OBTAINED ONLY FROM THE MAKERS,

BEALE & CLOVES,
Late JOHN BUCKINGHAM,
194 SHAFTESBURY AVENUE, LONDON, W.C.
Beware of fraudulent imitations.

Beware of fraudulent imitations: an advertisement for climbing ropes, circa 1900

bivouac ledges. For mountaineers, however, these shortcomings were eclipsed by a greater concern: Even a new or well-maintained rope was woefully inadequate for supporting much more than a static load. Top belays, glacier travel, the occasional steadying tug—these were the principal applications of early climbing ropes. Such ropes were not and could not be expected to hold the weight of a falling leader. Of course, for the rest of the party, with no intermediate protection or even belay anchors to keep them from being yanked into oblivion, a broken or cut rope was about the only chance of salvation if a leader suddenly became airborne. Whymper himself was likely spared an early grave by a snapped rope. After the tragedy on the Matterhorn, he wrote that he was horrified to discover that the rope that parted between the three survivors and their four "unfortunate companions, sliding downwards on their backs, spreading out their hands, endeavoring to save themselves" was a lightweight line, one that "should not have been employed for the purpose for which it was used." Lucky for Whymper that it was.

By the 1920s, when Mallory and Irvine disappeared on Everest, ropes made of flax were also in use. While somewhat stronger and more supple than manila, these ropes, like other natural-fiber cordage, came up short with respect to durability.

The real revolution in ropes came about in the way of so many significant advances in technology: as the result of war. Nylon was first developed in 1938 and the outbreak of World War II accelerated its production and applications. It wasn't long before the first synthetic climbing ropes began to appear. Strong, light, and flexible even when wet, nylon ushered in a new degree of confidence for climbers. For the first time, the idea of taking a significant fall seemed less than suicidal, and men like Hermann Buhl, Lionel Terray, and Walter Bonatti boldly pushed the standards in the Western Alps and abroad. Climbs like the East Face of the Grand Capucin in the Mont Blanc massif and the first ascent of Fitz Roy in Patagonia proved that nothing was too steep and no conditions were too demanding for the new cords. The earliest nylon ropes still consisted of three braided strands, but by the 1950s ropes appeared featuring a more sophisticated, woven construction. The famous French guide Gaston Rebuffat initially pooh-poohed such innovation. "Three-stranded ropes are preferable," he advised, "…because, in contrast to woven ropes, which are smooth, they have a rough surface and thus offer a better grip to the hands." The advent of kernmantle ropes during the 1960s must have given poor Gaston a stroke. Slick as a whip, the new ropes raised the bar even higher in terms of strength and durability by virtue of a unique dual design: an external sheath woven around a core of twisted nylon cordlets. The extraordinary strength of these ropes set the stage for more changes in climbing trends and attitudes, including long runouts, worked routes, and sport climbing. In less than a century, climbers' concerns had shifted from the integrity of the rope to the integrity of style.

THE GREAT DEBATE: ROCK PROTECTION AND ETHICS

> *"Supposing it was the regular thing for all mountaineers to use pitons on their climbs, would it not be a sign of the degeneracy of man?"*
> —FRANK SMYTHE
> Leading British climber of the 1920s and '30s

Ethical squabbles among climbers are in no way unique to modern times, and perhaps no aspect of mountaineering has remained so consistently controversial as the methods and types of climbing protection. During the early years the issue was moot simply because the tools had yet to be invented. Whymper himself devised an early form of artificial protection in the form of an iron claw that could be set from the tip of an alpenstock or flung grapnel-like with the aim of "hauling oneself up."

By the turn of the century, however, the bane of everything the purists held dear had reared its Cyclopean head: the piton. In truth, the earliest forms of the piton had no eye at all. These were rough iron spikes or hooks over which the rope was simply draped—a serious liability if a slip sent the leader skittering in the wrong direction. The deficiency was soon corrected by the addition of a ring with a loop of cord through which the rope could be threaded. Clipping quickly to protection would have to wait a few more years until the advent of the snaplink carabiner.

Initially, pitons were hammered in as anchors to help safeguard descents, a fact that helped keep any grumbling from the old guard in check. It wasn't long, however, before inventive and ambitious alpinists began using pins—including a design by the Tyrolean guide Hans Fiechtl featuring a vertical blade and a forged eye—to develop new techniques that provided access to increasingly improbable terrain. Tension traverses, artificial handholds and footholds, even short falls were all part of the new order. With their widespread application, malleable iron pitons became one of the first pieces of specialized equipment to radically alter the established style of climbing, and the floodgates of traditionalist contempt burst open. Of the epic climbs taking place on the north faces of the Eiger, Matterhorn, and Grandes Jorasses—routes at the cutting edge of the new methods and unthinkable without the new equipment—London's *Alpine Journal* offered this haughty assessment: "The most revolting and unsportsmanlike travesty of mountaineering yet reported."

The end of the war ushered in a brave new world, and one in which the spirit of innovation was pervasive in all societies. Still, another reality of pitons—that most were left in situ—remained contentious. Attempting to remove the soft-iron pitons of the day often resulted in badly deformed and dangerously fatigued metal. It was therefore easier, safer, and certainly more helpful for subsequent parties to simply leave them in place. As a result, the mountains, some critics felt, were beginning to look like they had been machine-gunned with metal.

Surprisingly then, the next step in protection evolution did not begin in the Alps, but half a world away. In 1947, an immigrant Swiss blacksmith named John Salathé decided to apply his mountain skills and his trade to the goal of climbing Yosemite Valley's Lost Arrow Spire. Salathé knew that conventional pins, designed for limestone, wouldn't last long in the bullet-proof California granite, and he understood that he would have a hard time carrying enough of them for such a long and technical route. So he fashioned a new type of piton: a hybrid of classical styling and ultra-strong carbon steel, that could be hammered in by the leader and then smacked back and forth by the follower until it popped free. Salathé's reusable pitons got him up the first ascent of Lost Arrow and opened the door to the classic big-wall routes on Half Dome and El Capitan. Years later, when the torch passed to another young smithy named Yvon Chouinard, he called one model of his pins "Lost Arrows" in deference to Salathé's inspiration and resourcefulness.

But even as Salathé labored at his anvil, a new controversy was being forged. In the beginning, climbing had been a maverick sport that attracted only a very limited number of people. Few mountaineers believed that any route would ever see more than a handful of ascents. In fact, the ranks of climbers were swelling exponentially with each passing year. And if the machine-gun analogy with regard to pitons had once been an exaggeration, it was now distressingly on the mark. Rock damage resulting from repeated pin placements threatened to permanently scar the medium and the experience of climbing.

It was the British—the old adversaries of the peg—who offered an alternative. Early on, British rock climbers had experimented with hammerless crack protection in the form of jammed stones around which a sling could be looped. Later, the stones evolved into slung machine nuts, and finally into the myriad forms of specialized climbing protection called "chockstones" or "nuts" to this day. The spread of chockcraft beyond the British Isles was hastened during the early 1970s by several American champions. In the 1972 Chouinard-Frost equipment catalog, Doug Robinson wrote an eloquent and persuasive how-to essay on nutting titled "The Whole Natural Art of Protection." Yosemite climbing icon Royal Robbins had observed first-hand the virtues of clean climbing during a tour of English crags, and also advocated "safe and silent" protection in his instructional books *Basic Rockcraft* and *Advanced Rockcraft*. Both writers saw nuts as an essential step for preserving the rock and for the progression of climbing as an art form. "Clean is climbing the rock without changing it," Robinson wrote, "a step closer to organic climbing for the natural man." Such heady thinking was probably wasted on many of the drifters and dopers living in Camp 4, but nuts were nevertheless embraced because they provided fast, versatile, and secure climbing protection. However, even clean climbing gear, when taken to the next level, could not escape controversy.

In the late-1970s, rumors spread through Yosemite Valley of a secret weapon, a new form of protection that was so effortless to use it was almost mindless, so multi-faceted it could work in parallel-sided or even flaring cracks, so utterly different that it would redefine climbing racks the world over. Remarkably, the rumors were true. The Oppenheimer of this secret weapon was an engineer named Ray Jardine; the device was a spring-loaded camming unit code-named the "Friend." The secrecy was an attempt by Jardine, who knew he was onto something big, to protect his patent. Once the gadgets became available to the general climbing population, some began to speculate that they made protecting *too* easy, almost to a point of cheating, and thus compromised the style of an ascent. Even Royal Robbins, a staunch supporter of clean climbing, feared things had gone too far. In a letter to *Climbing* magazine, Robbins pronounced, "The use of chocks on established climbs was usually a step upward—the use of Friends on established routes is a step downward."

The Author models state-of-the-art climbing hardware (and the height of mountain fashion), circa 1979

Time, of course, has quelled these debates. Cams, having intricacies and shortcomings of their own, have neither dominated nor diminished climbing the way some feared. On most routes, cams and nuts share equal space on the climbing rack—assuming a rack of anything other than quickdraws is even needed. The explosive popularity of bolt-protected sport climbing means that modern climbers now have the option of freeing themselves entirely from the complexities and worries of placing protection. The luxury to concentrate exclusively on technical challenges has produced routes of astonishing difficulty. Ironically, it also means that a growing segment of today's climbing population probably has less experience placing gear than at any time since the Golden Age.

CLIMBING HIGHER: CLOTHING ADVANCES, FROM WOOL TO SYNTHETICS

"Carry a light woollen sweater and a very light woollen muffler, about one foot wide and six feet long at least. In very cold weather, or if sleeping out, pass this tight twice round the stomach and fasten with safety pins."
—GEOFFREY WINTHROP YOUNG
Mountain Craft (1921)

The prevailing attitude among Victorian society was that people who aspired to climb mountains were sheep headed off to slaughter. In terms of how mountaineers were dressed, this observation was dead-on. Wool raiment was universal. By virtue of its absorbency and its ability to trap an air layer near the skin, wool could keep a climber warm in chilly, damp weather, and also cool once the sun burned through the clouds. Cotton was sometimes used for underwear and windshirts because of its comfort, despite the material's heat-sucking properties when wet. The standard alpine outfit included stout, loose-fitting wool pants or knickers, a flannel shirt, an unlined woolen waistcoat (vest), and a heavy tweed coat. Mountain women could only envy such functional attire. In 1871, when Lucy Walker became the first of her sex to climb the Matterhorn, she did it despite the impediment of billowing skirts.

Little had changed by the time Mallory made his fateful bid for the summit of Everest. When his body finally turned up in 1999, the vintage layers of cotton and wool beneath a canvas wind jacket—astoundingly lean apparel for 28,000 feet—provided the first clues to his identity. Goose down, which even today remains an unrivaled form of insulation (when dry), was stuffed into the sleeping bags of the early Everest climbers, but the practice of baffling it into clothing had not yet been perfected.

Thanks to the new materials and designs that emerged in the wake of World War II, Edmund Hillary and Tenzing Norgay had something a little more substantial around their middles. Wool still comprised the innermost layers of their Everest clothing, but to this was added a down suit and finally a cotton/nylon wind shell. In his description of the final climb to the summit, Hillary voiced his pleasure with the outfitting: "Insulated as we were in all our down clothing and windproofs, we suffered no discomfort from cold or wind." Such entries are conspicuously absent from the journals of tweed-era expeditions.

The space age resulted in even more exotic textiles. One of the cornerstones of the Patagonia clothing company was a synthetic climbing sweater called the "pile jacket." The man-made fibers—essentially spun plastic—had the insulating properties of wool but were lighter and didn't absorb water or sweat, and thus dried quickly. The company's 1977 catalog hailed this polyester pelt as "the most significant advance in cold-weather undergarments since the union suit." Pile and similar fibers enjoyed such phenomenal cross-market success that climbers soon began to grump about "their" label showing up on regular people. Words like Capilene, Polartec, and Microfiber became part of the expanding language of insulation.

In the late-1970s, W. L. Gore & Associates began marketing a new outerwear fabric touted as both breathable and waterproof. The key to this technology was a skin-like Teflon membrane developed for arterial grafts, hernia patches, and other surgical procedures. It featured pores too small for a water droplet to pass through, but large enough for water vapor to permeate. By laminating the membrane to a layer of uncoated nylon, Gore gave clothing manufacturers a material that could keep rain out, while still allowing steamy perspiration to escape. Gore-Tex and its spin-offs have dominated the shell clothing industry during the final decades of the 20th century.

Other than down, the materials worn by contemporary climbers are largely inorganic. There is, however, one circumstance in which the synthetically outfitted modernist is more disadvantaged than his wool-draped forebear. In the event of a lightning strike or stove flare-up, there is a tremendous advantage in clothing that smolders rather than melts into fiery glue.

A STICKY SOLUTION: CLIMBING FOOTWEAR

> "No doubt for very high work some Polar foot-gear would be better…but a piece of blanket wrapped over the whole boot and held in place with a large pair of [crampons], or by the boot-nails as they wear through, ought to be an efficient substitute."
>
> —T. G. LONGSTAFF
> Regarding footwear for the Himalayas (1921)

On the first ascent of Chamonix's Grepon in 1881, Albert Mummery had something new in his rucksack. The climb was a series of stiff rock pitches culminating with a nasty fissure now called the Venetz Crack in

Contemplating the first "sticky rubber" rock shoe, circa 1984

honor of one of the two guides who led Mummery up it. When it came Mummery's turn to climb, he had changed from his nailed leather boots into a pair of rubber sneakers smuggled along in anticipation of just this kind of crux. Determined to ascend with no aid from above, he leapt upon the crack where, with the help of his nimble shoes, he made steady progress. While Mummery struggled with one particularly hard move, however, his guides lost patience with all the tomfoolery and pulled him up. "I was hauled onto the top," he wrote, "where I listened with unruffled composure to sundry sarcastic remarks concerning those who put their trust in tennis shoes and scorn the sweet persuasion of the rope." Mummery, at least, was a man ahead of his time.

Sturdy leather boots were the tradition in the early days. For purchase on snow and rock, metal cleats or nails were driven into the smooth soles (a single hob for friction, a row of sharp tricounis for edging), and a thorough knowledge of boot nailing methods and patterns was an essential alpine skill. Other than some improvements in materials and designs, boots changed very little over the next few decades. Although, in the spirit of Mummery, some rock technicians experimented with less cumbersome, more sensitive, higher friction alternatives such as felt, rubber, or hemp (in 1937 Fritz Wiessner and Bill House wore canvas shoes soled with concentric strands of rope during the first rock climb of Devils Tower).

Finally, on the eve of the Second World War, two innovations appeared that would eventually send hobnails the way of the alpenstock. The Italian bootmaker Vitale Bramani invented a sole with a hard, tire-like tread. His "Vibram" sole would form the foundation or model for nearly every modern mountain boot. And an inventive French climber named Pierre Allain began marketing a lightweight, specialist rock shoe named with his own initials. PA's were the first in a long evolution of rubber-soled friction shoes which eventually included EB's and the RR's (imaginative marketing people were apparently in short supply at the shoe companies).

By the early 1980s, however, any forward thinking in rock-shoe design seemed to have stagnated and the different models all looked and performed pretty much the same. It took a Spanish company to set the climbing world aflame. By virtue of a new type of rubber that practically glued itself to the rock, the Boreal Fire could add a full grade to a rock climber's ability just by slipping it on. Overnight, ratings and techniques were turned upside-down, and heated ethical debates concerning the use of "sticky rubber" raged. Just a few years later the arguing was over, the dust had settled, and everyone was again dancing to the same tune—and in the new shoes.

Today the only debate over rock shoes is how to choose one from the myriad options lining the shelves. Do you go for slippers, lace-ups, or the Velcro models? Cambered toe or straight? Stiff soles or soft soles? Consumerism rules, and it's the climbers who benefit from ever-improving technology.

ICE WARS: CRAMPONS AND OTHER TERRORS

"Nor do I think that any benefit is derived from the employment of crampons."
—EDWARD WHYMPER *(1871)*

Cutting steps in ice and snow is a lost art. The methods of the ice-axe swing, angle of attack, and sizing of the steps were all skills that the early climber honed to perfection. It was hard work, but a mountaineer proficient in the techniques could chop a staircase up a thousand-foot slope in just a few hours. During the late 1800s and early 1900s, when step cutting was primarily the labor of guides, the axe for the job was long and stout, a combination of the alpenstock and the basic woodsman's tool. The adze, a neglected appendage in modern times, was a crucial feature. In a pinch, the pick could be thrust into a slope or crack for security, but the primary function of the axe was chopping.

Crampons—or, as they were called at the time, "ice claws"—were little more than a spiked bar lashed to the underside of the boot. These offered a degree of security, but since the flat-footed French technique of twisting the ankle to penetrate the slope had not yet been developed, step-cutting was still required. Whymper considered crampons superfluous for this reason. "Such adventurous aids are useless," he reasoned, "if you have not got a good step in the ice to stand upon; and if you have got that, nothing more is wanted except a few nails in the boots."

Around 1910 another Englishman named Oscar Eckenstein developed a set of 10-point flexible crampons with spikes arranged uniformly around the outline of the sole, as well as techniques for using them that all but eliminated the need for steps on moderate slopes. The gear and the methods were met with the usual resistance from traditionalists, but the ice climbing revolution had begun. In the early 1930s, the Italian equipment maker Larent Grivel added front points to Eckenstein's basic design, an innovation that made moving up alpine couloirs as straight-forward as kicking a boot's toe into the slope. Soon after, the Austrians began welding a bar across the hinge, creating a rigid crampon that was even more suited to the calf-busting rigors of front pointing. Also during this period, specialized but sketchy protection in the form of steel pitons for ice were used on the frigid north faces of the Alps by the Bavarian climber Willo Welzenbach, sometimes referred to as "the father of modern ice climbing."

Axes, meanwhile, were becoming shorter, sleeker, and also more specialized. The classic piolet as crafted by such famous firms as Simond, Charlet Moser, Grivel, and Stubai featured a flat or gently curved adze, a thigh-length hardwood shaft, and a straight, dagger-like pick. These axes were well suited to the tasks of hacking and arresting, but were almost useless for steep ice. The pick offered little more than a balance point, and so a climber either chopped handholds or risked toppling backwards. To push standards, that pick was going to have to bend. In 1966, Yvon Chouinard began testing every existing ice axe he could get his hands on...and then he made one that was all his own. Chouinard found that by dramatically shortening the shaft of an axe and applying a curve and teeth to the pick, it could be swung hammer-like into vertical ice—and stick there. Even the name had the feeling of a new beginning: the Model Zero.

Almost simultaneously, in isolated Scotland where an appropriately hardy and independent brand of ice climbing had developed, Hamish MacInnes had the same revelation. MacInnes, the first to replace an axe's traditional wooden shaft with metal, took his own famous hammer—known throughout the Highlands as "The Message"—and drooped the pick at a radical angle. He called this new incarnation the "Terrordactyl," while others dubbed it a Terror for it's knuckle-bashing shaft.

Armed with the new technology, ice climbers of the 1970s experienced a new Golden Age. Steep alpine plums were picked clean while frozen waterfalls and treacherously vertical icicles became climbing routes in their own right. The 1980s saw even more innovation in the form of crampons with step-in bindings and axes with modular components, including the now-standard reverse-curve picks. In the 1990s shafts were bent, front points became mono for more precise mixed work, and ice screws, which had previously been stubborn metal tubes requiring an ice axe to crank in, sprouted user-friendly handles and knobs so that they could be spun into hard ice with only two fingers.

TODAY'S GEAR is a far cry from the relics scattered about the basement of the Alpine Club. I am still waiting for the appearance of the Everest axe, but in lieu of that I'm fingering the summit of Mount Everest itself— some British expedition has actually pinched the highest rock in the world and carried it back to England.

Suddenly, from behind one of the stacks comes an enormous clatter, as if someone has overturned a bag of golf clubs, followed by a triumphant exclamation. The curator emerges brandishing a simple, reddish-colored piolet. Beaming, he presents it to me as if it were the sword Excalibur. I run my fingers over the antique wood and metal, darkened by a patina of age yet gilded with history, and I can almost see Mallory and Irvine, scratching over the rocks in their hobnails, scratching beneath the canvas and tweed in their wool, powered by sheer grit up and into the mists of legend.

What if by some wrinkle in time they could walk out of the cloud and find Everest as it is now—dotted with fantastically colored, nylon-swathed, and plastic-shod apparitions? To do new things with the best gear is what mountaineers have always done. But to do old things with new gear—the concept really didn't exist in his day. How would Mallory react?

I suspect the first thing he would do is to get his hands on a good down jacket.

Originally published in CLIMBING, *No. 192, 2000.*

Author's notes: One sure way to drive an insurance adjuster insane is to file a "stolen property" claim for a haul-bag filled with climbing gear. After this happened to me (see "Down and Out," page 321) my agent spent weeks pulling out his hair trying to calculate the monetary worth of such perplexing items as "Hexentrics" and "etriers" and, perhaps most mystifying of all, "Friends." In the end, the company paid full retail value for all the soft goods like ropes and webbing, but deducted a percentage for "wear and tear" on all the hardware. Goofy. But not as ridiculous as I felt when I showed up at the crag dressed head to toe in my spanking new replacement gear. It turns out there is one timeless aspect of mountaineering equipment that climbers respect and revere above all else: battle scars.

Interested in even more historical context about the progression of gear and style set to music? I thought so: "We Don't Make the Rules," page 362.

GRAND AMBITION
Sometimes the Price Is Just Too High

I HATE THE NORTH FACE route on the Grand Teton. It's a wandering line on loose, crappy rock. During a wet year it streams with water, during a dry year it whistles with stonefall. It features such infamous pitches as the Guano Chimney, an 80-foot vertical swim in bird shit. And it's the kind of route where bad weather can sneak up on you, snaking around from the opposite side of the peak like a viper with fangs bared. But the main reason I hate this route is because of what it has cost me, and what I was willing to pay.

To this day, I've never climbed the Grand; it has resisted my attempts to finish it off with Rasputin-like tenacity. By now, I probably could have climbed every other ridge and face on the mountain. But I've squandered my time and energies entirely on the North Face, in futile pursuit of this single alpine trophy.

The route has been called the "Eiger of North America." Comparisons between the Alps and Tetons are mostly wishful thinking on the part of the Wyoming Department of Tourism, but there's no doubt that even by Swiss standards the 13,770-foot Grand Teton is a jewel, and the North Face is its sheerest and most forbidding facet. In 1936 a pioneering assault spearheaded by Paul Petzoldt managed to link the 2500-foot face's most obvious features, a parallel network of massive diagonal ledges, before exiting onto the North Ridge. Subsequent parties cobbled together a more challenging and direct finish, so that today's complete North Face is a highly-prized classic—and not without Eiger-like aspects, including aspirants like me who, despite repeated thumpings, return to it again and again.

The reasons I've taken such an ass kicking on the Grand Teton's *Nordwand* are not complicated. I'm pretty sure I'm good enough to get up it; I've climbed mountains higher, harder, and more dangerous. But good and smart are different things, and there are definitely times when I'm more the one than the other. My early failures were largely due to discounting the importance of acclimatization. It is all too easy to sit in my home nearly at sea-level and plot a commando-style assault on the Tetons, reasoning that altitude will not be a factor or that I will simply "suck it up." The grim reality has been that my head and gut have been sledgehammered by the folly of climbing too high too fast, and so the only thing that sucked was the plan.

Lousy conditions are the other bane of my obsession with the Grand's North Face. Despite warnings from the park rangers and other climbers that stonefall was raking the face, or that waterfalls were streaming down key pitches, I've humped my load to the base "just to have a look." And when these reports have inevitably turned out to be true (or even understated), instead of shifting to a more reasonable objective, I've elected to squat like a glowering prisoner chained to the bottom of the dank wall, gambling my entire holiday on the hope that conditions might improve. Of course, they never have.

But last summer it looked as though the failures might all be coming to an end. The weather, climbing conditions, and lessons learned from past mistakes suddenly meshed. Two years of drought had all but eliminated ice, snow, and even water from the ledges of the North Face, and transformed the nasty 'schrund at the bottom of the face (normally a crux) into little more than a shrug. Moreover, before arriving in the Tetons, I had already been at altitude in the Wind River Range, sleeping and climbing above 10,000 feet for the better part of a week. I'd never been more prepared, the face had never been more benign—this time, nothing short of a bullet in the brain was going to stop me from ticking the Grand.

Two strategies for climbing the North Face hinge upon the fact that the descent is on the opposite side of the mountain, making it impractical to cache anything below the face. In other words, any bivy gear must be toted up the route. For this reason, some parties attempt the climb as a single marathon push: approaching through the dead of night, arriving under the face at dawn, climbing up and over the top by late afternoon and, they hope, arriving back at the trailhead again not long after dark. Needless to say, this kind of assault is only contemplated by the very fit and the very fast. The more moderate tack is to hike up into the moraine-choked gulch beneath the face in the afternoon, bivy on or near the glacier that occupies the head of this basin, and launch up the route at first light, well rested, but with a heavier pack.

Neither of these, however, was good enough for me. I wanted it all, the best of both worlds, all the good without the bad: to hike in leisurely, camp comfortably, and climb unencumbered. The linchpin of this scheme was not some new-fangled ultra-light and warm sleeping system. It was my wife.

My wife, Dina, is not a mountaineer. She'll play around on both ice and rock, cragging with me or friends, but she has little passion for the sport.

She loves the mountains to be sure, and like me, goes to them to revel in their beauty, to drink in the alpine environment. But while I climb, she is content to hike, scramble, or sketch. There is one other reason that she goes to the mountains: I *do* need to stand on top, and she would do anything to help me get there.

Essentially, my plan for the North Face was to capitalize on her goodwill: Dina would hike the approach with me, helping me carry enough food and gear for a cozy bivouac. The added bonus of snuggling in with her rather than some hairy lump of XY chromosomes meant that I could anticipate one of my finest mountain nights ever. And the next morning, while I tackled the climb, she'd break camp at her leisure and hike back down with the overnight stuff. In this way I would be outfitted for decadence, yet still enjoy the luxury of climbing with an almost empty pack.

It never occurred to me that there might be a degree of selfishness to these logistics; I rationalized that Dina would enjoy the hike and the night out, she'd get to see some spectacular scenery, and have a little adventure of her own. Indeed, her response to the proposal was enthusiastic, although tempered with some reservation about the off-trail scrambling required to reach the wall. But it was easy to allay her concerns. Easy because I'd been up there before. And easy because I really didn't give it much thought. It was, after all, just a hike.

Even now, after the fact, the reality of the trail leading up to the North Face barely registers with me. The mindless treadmill slog from the Lupine

Meadows trailhead to Surprise and Amphitheater Lakes is about as inspiring as three hours on the Stairmaster. I vaguely recall leaving the main trail and contouring around the approach gulch that leads to the bivy site via a series of loose, exposed ledges and traverses. But I was so preoccupied with anticipation and excitement over my forthcoming climb that I paid very little attention to the terrain—until I looked back.

Pausing to catch my breath, I finally glanced at Dina, and in that split second, everything changed. Instead of a cog in the machinery of my Grand plan, I saw a woman quietly enduring terrain that for her was absolutely terrifying. Fighting back panic with every step, she was slowly picking her way through the treacherous moraine, cheeks streaked with silent tears, but moving nonetheless steadily upward, motivated not by adventure or ambition, but by the honest desire to help me succeed.

I turned around right then and there. And failure has never felt so awful, or so right.

Maybe I'm not smart enough to get up this mountain. Or maybe now I am, finally. Because on that hike I gained the wisdom to recognize the hidden costs of blind ambition. But I still feel like crap. I didn't get to climb my nemesis, again. It wasn't due to any of the usual causes, rockfall, bad weather, or altitude. This time, in the end I *was* stopped by a bullet—not in the brain, but through the heart. One I never saw coming, and for reasons I never even considered. And this haunts me, even more than the North Face of the Grand.

Originally published in CLIMBING, *No. 210, 2002.*

*Author's note: After this piece ran, I received a range of feedback. Most readers appreciated my confessional on short-sightedness and mutual sacrifice; one flattered me greatly by calling it, "*Gift of the Magi*-esque." But a few felt this story was demeaning to my wife, painting her as weak, eager to please—even subservient. Let me set the record straight: Dina is one tough cookie; an athletic force of nature (a marathon runner) with an even stronger sense of self-assurance that she wields like a mallet whenever one of my balls needs a little help finding the wicket. The woman is a middle-school English teacher, for God's sake. It goes without saying that she is more than capable of taking care of herself.*

LET THE BUYER BEWARE
Can a "Have" and a "Have-Not" Rope Together?

"HO...LEE...SHIT!" I mumbled. From our vantage on the rim of the wintry, boulder-choked canyon, Chas and I stared slack-jawed at the fat ice smeared across the opposite wall. Like the contrail from a Crayola missile, the massive, mineral-stained formation billowed from the depths into a waxy, aquamarine taper streaked with hues of burnt umber and maize.

Chas expressed himself according to his pedigree by striking a Christopher Columbus pose: hands on hips, eyes glittering, his teeth bared with the triumphant grin of a conqueror. In this case, however, the blank on the map was a vast tract of Canadian wilderness, our New World was the promise of undiscovered, unclimbed ice, and our Santa Maria was a banana-yellow Skidoo snowmobile.

Unlike Columbus, we hadn't needed a royal patron to finance our expedition. As the ruler of a successful business empire worth millions, Chas was practically a king himself. And like many young, successful entrepreneurs, he had seized upon adventure sports such as ice climbing as a way to keep the adrenaline pumping after the markets closed. The fact that he'd been reduced to slumming with the likes of me is an illuminating commentary on the stratification of modern society and proof that climbing makes strange bedfellows. As the Yosemite climber/philosopher Eric Beck once postulated, "At either end of the social spectrum there lies a leisure class." Chas and I were the bookends of that theory.

Thus it was Chas who had procured the snowmobile that was essential for penetrating the wilds of backwater Ontario; it was Chas who'd towed it north behind his battle-tank SUV until the roads were not just unplowed, but unimagined. And it was Chas' innate drive to seek and plunder—along with his GPS—that had led us deep into uncharted territory, and, finally, to this remote canyon overlook, quite literally the brink of success.

Now it was time for Gunga Din to earn his billet. "I'll fix a descent line," I announced, eager to press the assault and contribute to the cause.

As far as the eye could see in both directions, the chasm presented a formidable barrier...but not to us. Thanks to an extra rope and ascenders, we were well outfitted for a short bit of canyoneering. As I spooled out the rappel line, however, Chas' enthusiastic grin eroded into a skeptical pucker. Following his gaze, I peered over the edge and saw that the end of our rope had come up short of the talus. How short? That was the Million Dollar Question. For one of us, though, this was chump change.

"It doesn't look too far," Chas announced. "I think you'll be able to down-climb from there."

It was my turn for skepticism, not to mention alarm at his choice of pronouns, but in deference to my king (and the royal bankroll that had gotten me here), I clipped on my rap device and lowered off. By the time I was within spitting distance of the rope's end, I realized we'd been bamboozled by the smoke-and-mirrors of foreshortening—this canyon was more Grand than gulch: The ground was at least another full rope-length away, and the wall below was sheerer than honeymoon pajamas.

The only possible anchor was a single, stunted tree, and while I waited for Chas to join me at this precarious stance, I had a bird's-eye view of the icy colossus cascading from the northern rim. Fate had led us to it, but by placing us on the opposite side of such a moat, Fate had also buggered our chances of climbing the thing. We were burning daylight—a precious commodity in the Canadian winter, but absolutely *priceless* at the moment, this being the last day of our expedition. To my mind, we had two choices: throw in the towel and jug back up, or sacrifice another rope—one of our twin 8mm lead lines—in a desperate bid to reach terra firma. The first option would be admitting defeat, and the second was a kamikaze gambit that would leave us to attack at least 300 feet of vertical ice armed with a single, half-ass cord.

Despite the cruel anguish of walking away from such a delectable plum without even taking a nibble, I was inclined to cut our losses and bail. Of course, the Emperor would have none of it. Upon arriving at the stance, he eyed the scrubby anchor, gave it a couple of heart-stopping jerks, and announced: "We'll rap again and pull the ropes."

I'd always envied Chas, and not just his fortune. I can't order breakfast without flipping a coin (and I still end up wishing I'd gotten the waffles), so I admire people who have the ability to make decisions, especially ones that incur risk, and never look back. It's no wonder they rise to become captains of industry. I suppose the two go hand-in-hand: unwavering commitment and fabulous success. But one could argue that "courting disaster" is also part of the equation.

Pulling our ropes would essentially maroon us at the bottom of this bear-pit gorge: Even if we managed to top out on the north side, the next road in that direction was in Siberia. The only choice, then, would be to drop back into the gorge and, without any rock gear, search for a way back to the south rim—almost certainly in the dark. The idea Chas was proposing was reckless, foolish…and utterly thrilling. This was the stuff of great generals, princes, and kings. This was Caesar leading his legions across the Rubicon. This was *grit*, and for once, I was determined to impress upon someone of Chas' stature that I too possessed it, and in a form unrelated to personal hygiene. With no further discussion, we rigged another rappel and slid into the unknown. When our ropes finally rattled down at our feet, the die was cast.

THE CLIMB WAS magnificent: two long pitches of steep, virgin waterfall ice—a five-star classic by any measure. Belaying Chas up, I had ample time to bask in the glow of such glorious victory snatched by simple resolve from the jaws of defeat. Like Alexander after crushing the Persian armies, I swept my hand across the vista of the canyon and shouted into the void, "I weep, that there are no worlds left to conquer!" And then I saw the Santa Maria. Like a tiny sail upon a vast ocean, the snowmobile was little more than a yellow dot on the opposite rim of the canyon—a jarring reminder of the precariousness of our situation, and a wake-up call that although the battle may have been won, the war was unresolved.

"...the promise of undiscovered, unclimbed ice."

An hour later we were back on the ground and on the march, although it would have taken time-lapse photography to prove it. In the same way we had botched our initial assessment of the canyon's depth, we had also underestimated the difficulties of traversing its floor. From above, the talus had looked to be a size that would yield to simple boulder-hopping—which was true if one happened to be the Statue of Liberty. Chas and I, however, were floundering among rocks the size of small cottages. Sliding into the dark, snowy recesses in between, we labored like plow horses to the summit of each block, where we lay panting in the gathering gloom, desperately scanning each new section of the rampart overhead for some hidden gully or climbable weakness.

At one point Chas lagged behind, and when he finally reappeared something was missing.

"Shit, Chas," I exclaimed, "you've lost the rope!" Sure enough, a spanking-new lead line had disappeared from the back of his pack. The lashings must have come loose, and I groaned at the thought of having to retrace a single step of this infernal terrain. But the truth was even more disconcerting.

"I chucked it," Chas said, then, flinging his pack to ground, he began unstrapping his ice axes. "I can't carry this stuff any farther," he panted. "I'm leaving it here."

I stared incredulously. Chas' pack was a treasure chest of state-of-the-art equipment. Clearly my King had gone mad, but I also saw this as a defining moment for myself: another opportunity to raise myself beyond the level of a lowly squire by demonstrating my true mettle. Despite my heavy burden, I asked, "Can I carry anything for you?"

"No," he insisted, "I'll leave it here." And then he paused. "Unless..." he whispered. And what was it then that I saw in his eyes, some flickering of raw emotion—deference? Respect?

"Do you want to buy any of this?"

That was the moment when the pennies fell. My Captain—oh, my Captain!—was, in fact, just a capitalist. And apparently, I was just another mark. Nothing could have disappointed me more, except perhaps my own reaction. Maybe when the going gets tough, we all revert to our basest instincts. Whatever the reason, I suddenly found myself pawing through his hoard, mumbling, "How much?"

WE EVENTUALLY got out of that canyon. And it wasn't due to any great display of leadership or grit, just blind luck. As darkness enveloped us, we discovered a shallow cleft filled with enough trees and bushes to scramble up. But like the whole of our expedition, it was a Pyrrhic victory. We arrived on top, not as a team, not as warriors, not even as a wealthy monarch and his loyal footman. The dictum had shifted from "Carpe Diem" to "Caveat Emptor."

Chas and I don't hang out together anymore. In fact, he's quit climbing, although I have no doubt that he's still moving up in the world. These days, the only way I'm likely to mix with a person of his caste is by hanging out at a stoplight with a squeegee. But at least I know now that there's grandness and commonalty on both sides of a luxury windshield. The proof can be found in a remote northern canyon, where the boulders are strewn with cast-off axes, an expensive parka, and the rest of the Emperor's new clothes.

Originally published in CLIMBING, *No. 223, 2003.*

Author's note: As a writer, it feels like I'm always down to my last nickel, but there have been fleeting moments of high living: My first rack of cams was purchased with winnings from a poker game; I financed at least one trip to the Alps with a windfall of savings bonds that fell out of an old dictionary. Still, none of this was money I really earned, but I'm not complaining—after traveling to places like East Africa and India I'm well aware of the fact that in terms of privilege, I've won the lottery. Shame on me if I ever gripe about money because I don't know the meaning of the word poor. So this essay is not intended as a whine about wealth or largesse, but a commentary on the broad social strata within the climbing community and resulting strange bedfellows. Nevertheless, I find wisdom (and comfort) in the words of poet and writer Dorothy Parker: "If you want to know what God thinks of money, just look at the people He gave it to."

Oblique view of the Eigerwand; the prominent diagonal snow feature is the First and Second icefields

INTRODUCTION TO ARTHUR ROTH'S
*EIGER: WALL OF DEATH**

DEATH IS NO STRANGER to the mountains. From the earliest days of human intercourse with the high peaks, a grim toll has been exacted upon the ranks of the unwary or the unfortunate. Grisly evidence in the form of Stone or Bronze Age corpses is, even today, periodically disgorged from the snouts and eddies of alpine glaciers. During Europe's Age of Enlightenment, when crystal prospectors and chamois hunters failed to return from forays up into the strange and terrible world of ice and rock, the cause of death was as likely to be attributed to dragons or griffins as avalanches, crevasses, and other less fanciful mountain perils. Apparently, when it came to the mountains, enlightenment also went missing.

But it was during the late eighteenth and nineteenth centuries, when the first mountain tourists began to arrive in the Alps and mountain climbing purely for the sake of adventure came into vogue, that the casualties really began to mount. Each time disaster struck, headlines trumpeted the news, and level heads clucked their tongues and wagged their fingers at such folly. As the cemeteries of Chamonix and Zermatt began to fill, the mountains, and climbing in particular, came to be regarded as the province of the deranged. Curiously, the sport also enjoyed unprecedented popularity.

The most famous of these incidents was Edward Whymper's doomed conquest of the Matterhorn—perhaps the defining example of defeat snatched from the hands of victory. During the descent from the peak, four of Whymper's six rope-mates—a young aristocrat, a clergyman, a teenager, and one of the most celebrated mountain guides of the day—plunged to their deaths. The hue and cry over such appalling loss of life caused Britain's Queen Victoria to consider outlawing the practice of mountain climbing among her subjects. Perhaps believing that the notoriety of such a

---

*Eiger: Wall of Death by Arthur Roth was first published in 1982; this new introduction was written for a special edition of the book printed in 2000.

terrible accident would be sufficient to discourage anyone from repeating a climb of this severity, she never issued such an edict. Among climbers, the Matterhorn promptly became "the peak to do" during the Victorian era.

The examples go on and on: Mallory and Irvine's enigmatic vanishing act on the slopes of Everest; the bizarre death of Maurice Wilson who hoped to crash an airplane into that same mountain in a misguided attempt to achieve the first ascent; the German bloodbath on Nanga Parbat that spanned two decades, encompassed six expeditions, and claimed 26 lives.

But despite all the other mountain catastrophes both past and present, all the dark footnotes in alpine history written in blood, no mountain has come close to supplanting the Eiger for the degree of ominous foreboding it conjures among climbers or its unequivocal association with death. The history here is simply too chilling ever to be forgotten or ignored. Dramas that have played out on the North Face of the Eiger, diligently researched and adroitly narrated in this volume, challenge the imagination. Like Shackleton's epic saga, the life and death struggles of Kurz, Heckmair, Longhi, and Harlin would make poor fiction—they are too unbelievable. That they really happened is the foundation of the Eiger's enduring mythology. Other mountains may be bigger, harder to climb, even more deadly, but, by virtue of its sensational history, the Eiger remains the great headstone of mountaineering.

It seems only natural that Arthur Roth should have been drawn to write about this mountain. Best known as an author of adventure novels for young adults, Roth's themes often centered around capricious tragedy and the subsequent struggle for survival. Titles like *Avalanche, Snowbound,* and *Two For Survival* seem natural segues to a history of the Eiger. The irony is that through the writing of *Eiger: Wall of Death,* Roth experienced a rebirth of sorts.

In his youth, Roth would have made a good candidate for the Eiger. Hardened by a childhood of being passed between orphanages and relatives (his mother died when Roth was five, and his father was confined to a mental institution even earlier), Roth early on developed the willful determination and utter self-reliance of an adventurer. Like many of the climbers who were fighting and dying on the Eiger, Roth's early adulthood during the late 1940s and '50s was a hard, primarily blue collar existence: Military service, prospecting, forestry and factory work were among his rough-and-tumble vocations. And while men like Hermann Buhl, Claudio Corti, and the other Eiger North Face petitioners looked to the mountains for their salvation, Roth found his with a pen.

It was nearer the end of his life, during his research for this book, that Roth discovered the personal rewards of mountain climbing and pursued it with all the enthusiasm and passion his advancing years would permit. A surprising turn of events, one might speculate, for a man whose introduction to the sport was an immersion in the study of mangled and dismembered body parts, rope stranglings, brutal stonings from rockfall, and excruciatingly prolonged and unmerciful deaths from exposure. What possessed Roth (at an age when most men are contemplating retirement) to tie himself into a climbing rope and deliberately venture into harm's way is an enigma that emerges time and again from the pages of this book. Knowing the truly dreadful fate of some who have gone before, what motivates any person to climb a mountain—much less the Eiger? It's the million-dollar question and one each climber can only answer for him or herself.

My own obsession with the Eiger began the way so many obsessions begin: I read a book. Not this book because it didn't exist at the time. My catalyst was Anderl Heckmair's *My Life as a Mountaineer*. Not wanting to reveal any crucial plot points in that book or this, let me just say that Heckmair—a brilliant climber and adventurer—figures significantly in the history of the Eiger's North Face. As a teenager, painfully ungifted at any form of traditional athletics, I found Heckmair's book a revelation. In mountaineering, no one chooses sides (hence no one is chosen last), the playing field is the mountains (an environment full of exotic fascination), and the game is adventure (what teenage boy couldn't be seduced by that one?). Again, as with so many aspiring mountaineers, my initial introductions to the sport were self-taught. I found a rope, found a friend, and found a cliff. Managing somehow not to kill myself, or anyone else, in those early stages, I found the rewards to be immensely satisfying, and I progressed quickly. For the first time in my life I felt special, privileged, and skilled. Climbing became the axis of my world: My reading, my friends, my future plans, all revolved around climbing. And because Anderl Heckmair had been my inspiration, my ambitions were consumed by one mountain in particular.

Eventually, I went to the Eiger. Naturally, luckily, the weather and the climbing conditions were terrible and I left empty handed. But I went back again. And again. Each time with more experience and confidence. Until finally, over three unforgettable days in the autumn of 1989, my climbing partner and I—to borrow a phrase from Sir Edmund Hillary—"knocked the bastard off." As we emerged from the shadows of the North Face, a place haunted by so many ghosts, into glorious sunshine, my soul seemed to undergo a similar transition. All the insecurities of youth, all the uncertainties of adulthood, any lingering doubts about self or the future, were left behind forever. I had found, by successfully running this notorious gauntlet, a shortcut to the peace of mind, confidence of purpose, and utter delight with the world that some people search for their entire lives. For myself, and I suspect for Anderl Heckmair, for all the men and

Emerging into "glorious sunshine;" the Author (left) and Roger Volkmann on the summit of the Eiger

women who have climbed this face, and even for Arthur Roth who never did, but discovered the joys of climbing because of it, the Eiger was a wall of life.

Of course, many were not so fortunate. Among those who climb mountains, the early attempts and fatalities on the Eiger are generally recognized as being far more impressive and inspiring than any latter-day success. What I achieved by repeating the climb in late 20th century bears little resemblance to what the pioneers faced. The advantages of time and hindsight are huge: Knowing where to go, what to expect, having access to modern equipment, accurate weather forecasts, and the possibilities of modern rescues—any one of these might have saved any number of the casualties described in this book. Where I climbed, these men truly adventured. In those early days, venturing onto the Eiger North Face was akin to stepping onto an alien world. The isolation, sense of the unknown, and level of commitment were total. Climbers went, essentially naked by today's standards of high-tech clothing and gear, into an utterly hostile and uncharted wilderness. That some never returned is predictable, that many did is remarkable. Either way, my tremendous respect for those with the audacity and the courage to undertake a climb like the Eiger in little more than canvas clothing and golf shoes is the single greatest impression I carry with me from my own climb. Perhaps this is why Eiger stories are among the most popular and oft-repeated among mountaineers. They encompass our best hopes and our worst nightmares. The climbers are who we want to be, in situations we don't ever want to be in. Heroes and horrors: the classic elements of mythic tales.

So if Roth lingers upon the doomed, if he occasionally resorts to hyperbole and sensationalism, who can fault him? This is the mountain synonymous with such things. And modern super-climbers doing extreme climbs on the Eiger only reinforce its legendary status. When an Austrian climber vaulted up the North Face in an astounding four-and-a-half hours just a year after this book was originally published it was a stunning achievement, but it made headlines because it was the Eiger. Similarly, the fact that the Eiger has now been soloed as one-third of a twenty-four hour helicopter-assisted enchainment of alpine north faces, or that an ascent has been broadcast on live television, have not diminished its reputation one iota. That the Eiger is still the focus of such mountaineering and media extravaganzas is proof enough: Although the killing may have halted, the Eiger is still the Wall of Death.

Originally published in EIGER: WALL OF DEATH, *The Adventure Library Edition, 2000.*

Author's note: There is a host of classic books dedicated to the climbing history of the Eiger North Face—in this regard the mountain is perhaps second only to Everest. In terms of a gripping narrative with broad appeal (a good read for climbers and non-climbers alike), Roth's book is generally considered top of the heap.

DOWN AND OUT

Contemplating My Return to a Sport That Has Moved On Without Me;
Or Is It the Other Way Around?

*C*LIMBER, *INTERRUPTED*

"Oh, *no!* Climbing." Not even a question mark. It was the natural reaction, repeated time and again, by all who knew my passion. After all, here I was, a mountaineer of indeterminate skills and judgment, void of other athletic interests or talent, now hobbled upon crutches and clamped below the knee in a Goliath-sized walking cast. What could it be other than evidence of some epic mountain disaster? I'd like to think my situation conjured images of a magnificent fall, a stoic collision with unforgiving stone, capped off by a heroic crawl over talus and ice back to civilization. Never mind that those who knew me doubtlessly envisioned a stumble in the dark while peeing from an unplanned bivouac. Either way, a tale of mountain adventure was what people expected to hear, and what I longed to tell. The truth, however, was the antithesis of glorious injury, and demanded a shameful confession:

"Gardening."

Blank looks, then a cautious brightening: "You mean cleaning out a crack?"

"No. Digging a hole."

More perplexed expressions. A final stab at context: "Ah, a snow cave! Or a deadman anchor?"

"Um, no. Digging. In actual dirt. To plant…plants."

In fact, the deadman reference wasn't far off the mark because although I didn't know it at the time, in terms of climbing, I'd also dug my own grave.

Instead of an ice axe, a shovel was literally the implement of my destruction. Hammering my heel repeatedly behind the blade had transmitted blunt, concussive impacts throughout the foot's musculature, eventually rupturing a sinew deep within the ankle. At first I felt only a burning discomfort, like a mild sprain, and so I kept at it, stomping and chipping at the rocky clay with blind determination, ultimately planting myself deep in a depression of my own making.

For weeks, months and then years afterwards, the vertical tear hiding within the tendon eluded diagnosis; meanwhile, every step I took ground the fibrous gristle, exacerbating the damage. I deteriorated from limp, to crutch, and even wheelchair. Eventually, I abandoned any form of ambulatory exertion and took to the couch, no longer even an armchair mountaineer.

By the time the surgeon finally deduced and repaired the injury, years of inactivity and unburned calories had accumulated over me like a lead blanket. Any thoughts of climbing had long ago been routed to dead-end sidings of the brain, abandoned in isolated pockets of hazy memory and impracticable dreams. In a bloated, sedentary gloom, I could imagine no path leading back to the mountains. Objects at rest tend to remain at rest.

Finally, badgered by family and friends, shamed by my own reflection, and with the fear of god put in me when my slimmer and more active father suddenly clutched his chest and dropped dead in my arms, I turned off the TV, pried myself out from between the sofa cushions, and ate an apple. Training had begun.

I walked roads, then trails, ever faster, finally running. Slowly the pounds began to melt away, muscles firmed, and the ankle held. I saw light at the end of the tunnel, even began day-dreaming about possible trips and routes to mark my return to mountaineering. For the first time in years I bought a climbing magazine. And that's when the needle skated off the record:

5.15b. Really. *Really?!*

STRANGER IN A STRANGE LAND

I never expected the merry-go-round to stand still, but until I got bucked off, I guess I never appreciated just how fast it was spinning. Sure, I've got a dusty box in my basement full of T-tons and Peck nuts and other relics of mountaineering archeology that no climber born after the Reagan administration has ever heard of. But the evolution from those bits of antiquated chockery to the state-of-the-art gear I had been snagging into cracks right before I kicked that garden spade had seemed measured and logical, like the little finches of the Galapagos Islands gradually developing slightly different beaks or minor variations in plumage in response to their changing world. Now, judging from the pages of the magazine, during the time I'd been away from climbing, everybody had turned into flamingos.

In particular, the current high-water standard of mid-range 5.15 seemed absolutely trippy. Not that the upper fringes of climbing were ever my bailiwick—even in my prime, I was elated whenever I managed to untangle a 5.11 ball of twine. Long ago, however, when mountaineers were still

"Comically preposterous" advertisement, circa 1981

clucking over the fact that the Yosemite Decimal System for rating fifth-class climbing (5.7, 5.8, 5.9, etc.) had necessarily popped its top to accommodate the mathematically nonsensical 5.10 and beyond, I saw a magazine advertisement that poked graphic fun at the grades. In it, some guy had posed for a photo by backing his ass and legs beyond the lip of a jutting horizontal overhang, the underside blank and smooth as troweled concrete, his rope dangling freely through empty space. The caption read, *Leading a 5.15 pitch!* At the time, we all chuckled because the number, like the photo, was so comically preposterous. In those bygone days, when the best in the world were poking at the lower fringes of 5.13, the likelihood of 5.15 ever becoming a reality seemed on par with printing the Bible on a pinhead. Of course, I should have seen it coming: Even in my heyday, 5.13 was thoroughly mastered, even passé, as the elite hammered away at what they snootily termed "hard 5.14." Nevertheless, in my mind, because of that one memorable spoof ad, the notion of 5.15 climbing had remained the height of absurdity. Then, in the midst of my convalescence, scientists announced they'd managed to etch the entire Old Testament on the head of a pin.

So here I am, Gripped van Winkle, wide awake again at last, blinking in the strange dawn of an unfamiliar and unsettling reality. Or perhaps, because of my absence, *I'm* just seeing things through fresh eyes. Whatever the case, climbing seems to have turned upside-down. It's a world gone mad: Little kids are climbing Everest, Greg Mortenson is the Devil, and shares of Black Diamond are publicly traded on NASDAQ.

The question isn't when I will ever climb again, it's whether I even want to.

GEAR UP OR GET OUT

"Dammit, dammit, *dammit!*"

It was 1991. My buddy R. and I had just come off a miserably taxing winter aid climb, part of a youthful ambition to establish the first grade VI wall climb in the Midwest, a lateral series of linked pitches and traverses across the half-mile face of Palisade Head. Humping our mountain of equipment back to the car had exhausted our reserves of strength and patience—not to mention the last minutes of daylight. Then, just as our eager push for hot food and warm beds seemed all but done, my car planted its heels, resisting all efforts to reverse out of the snug little pullout like a bull that only knows one direction out of the chute. Bucking and shuddering, the engine bellowed, the tires pawed, but the vehicle stubbornly refused to back up more than a few inches.

"Maybe there's a rock under one of the wheels," R. suggested. "You want me to check?"

"Hold on!" I screamed, working the gas like a pump organ, parlaying a frenzied rocking between forward and reverse toward escape velocity. Suddenly the entire rear end of the car rose up a foot or so, and the vehicle broke loose, bouncing and lurching wildly as if backing over a dead horse.

The stark light of the high beams illuminated a scene of even more chilling carnage: a lumpy debris field of mangled ropes and shredded packs. It was all there, despite having been brutally raked and strewn beneath the spinning tires and oily undercarriage of the car; every bit of our climbing gear, right where we'd left it.

"Fuck!" I bellowed at R. "Didn't you load the stuff into the trunk?!"

"I thought *you* did!"

So you see, I know first-hand that even the idea of having to replace one's entire accumulation of climbing equipment is enough to conjure extreme notions (Do I really need *two* kidneys? Do I even need one?), even throwing in the towel. And today, after being left to molder, most of my kit belongs in a museum or a dumpster. The ropes, webbing and other soft goods have turned as brittle and funky as my grandmother's wedding dress, and much of the hardware is hopelessly outdated. Compared to the latest-and-greatest ice tools, bristling like rose stems with wicked-looking grips and pinkie rests, my axes are a couple of Neanderthal shin bones. Re-outfitting myself with new, state-of-the-art gear has real potential to break me, both mentally and financially. Even before the Great Car Disaster, I'd already been forced to replace all my equipment once. That was after some miscreant managed to snatch a bulging, monster pack from right under my nose in Paris (City of Light Fingers). And after I crushed the whole lot under the car? Oh, I continued to climb on that stuff for another decade. Like I said, the prospect of losing everything can short-circuit the neurons of judgment and light up the lobes where crazy runs the show.

So what will I do this time around—that is, if I decide to rack and roll? Pony up, at least in part. Even I have to admit that by now my ropes are beyond salvage (a little motor oil is one thing, but actual decomposition really can't be ignored). Likewise, I'll concede to shelling out for new tools. I'm not sure if the latest configurations represent a progress of form, function, style or marketing hype—I really don't care; when you're the only turkey in a flock of flamingos, you'll grab at anything just to fit in. In terms of my boots, jackets and other clothing…perhaps there I'll be more patient. They say that if you hold on to anything long enough, it eventually comes back into fashion. I do know this: For over a hundred years, every mountaineer from Whymper to Hillary went into battle wearing woolen long johns. Then, around 1980, wool abruptly fell out of vogue, usurped by a new crop of pricey synthetic fabrics made from spun petro-chemicals that were hydrophobic (apparently fibers so fierce they are literally rabid) and warm as a bear's armpit—an apt analogy, considering that's exactly what they smelled like after a day or two in the field. There's always room for improvement. And so today I see the ads and catalogs are touting an even more expensive miracle fabric heralded as the end-all for odorless warmth and insulation: merino wool.

BECAUSE IT IS BARE

Of course, it's impossible to speculate about getting back into the game without reflecting on why I ever wanted to climb a mountain in the first place. "Because it is there"? With that oft-quoted quip George Mallory took the prize for brevity, and maybe being kind of a dick, but Mallory is also credited with a lengthy and eloquent explanation that only a complete asshole would consider abbreviating, so here I go: "There is something in mankind which responds to the challenge of a mountain and goes out to meet it…[I]t is the struggle of life itself, upward and forever upward. What we get from this adventure is sheer joy…and that is what life is for."

Maybe. But for me, it was also about girls.

In the beginning, I was a bookish little spud, athletically inept, introverted, literally disconnected from my world—my favorite pastime was sitting outside all night in a lawn chair sketching the constellations. Climbing is also fundamentally a question of connecting the dots, and so when a middle-school Phys Ed instructor forced me onto the 30-foot woody he'd nailed up the gym wall, I stunned myself and everyone else by intuitively unlocking the sequence and being the first one up. The whole class cheered. Even the girls. A future decided, then and there.

Of course, the notion that climbing mountains will make someone more attractive to the opposite sex is complete rubbish. The exact opposite is true. Even *Mountain* magazine, that now-defunct vessel of unbridled masculinity that pumped air month after month trying to keep the ideal afloat, lamented, "What female will ever be impressed by the fact that a man would rather spend the night on some frosty ledge, spooning with another stinky dude, rather than cuddled up with her in a warm bed?" Nevertheless, it remained my dream to one day partner up with some gorgeous rock groupie. Ironically, that's precisely what it took to finally point me in the right direction:

The rain in the Mont Blanc massif had been so persistent that my climbing partner flew home in a desperate bid to rise above the clouds and see the sun again. I, on the other hand, sought refuge at En Vau, an idyllic cove along the French Riviera, famed for its pocketed limestone walls and towers. When I arrived, the place was teeming with sunbathers and other day-tourists, but throughout the afternoon, as the canyon's inevitable shadow gobbled up more and more of the beach, the crowds dwindled until all that remained along the margin of the azure lagoon were a few small tents: my own and two more that belonged to other climbers—Americans, to boot. One housed a pair of grim-faced guys from the Seattle area, who despite a high tolerance for wet and dreary weather had also fled the sodden valleys of the Alps like rats from a drain. The other tent belonged to S., a sunny and athletic young woman from Colorado who was also flying solo, and just happened to be looking for a climbing partner.

Bingo.

I introduced myself.

S. smiled. She asked if I had any interest in hooking up with her for a few days.

This didn't mean what it does now; nevertheless, hopeful to the end, I winked—*way* too slowly.

She told me she had a boyfriend at home.

And from that point on, we got along famously. To her credit, once the ground rules were established, S. gave me the benefit of the doubt, accepting without prejudice that what may have seemed a creepy, innuendo-laced advance was in fact an unfortunate congenital tic. We spent several lovely days together cragging along the sun-kissed fringes of the Mediterranean, where any further tendency for eye spasm was masked so completely behind my sunglasses that it was all but forgotten, almost as if it never existed at all.

There's more to the story, however, and in the end, it represented a turning point for me. Like any significant epiphany, this was forged in a

The idyllic cliffs and beaches at En Vau, on the French Riviera

gauntlet of internal conflicts and external pressures (including stratagems that would cause Machiavelli to blush).

After we worked our way through the classic routes at En Vau, S. surprised me by suggesting that we journey on together to the Verdon Gorge, a massive canyon and the premier climbing destination for European rock on a grand scale. She'd taken to the French limestone and was eager to extend our partnership in order to sample what the soaring walls of the Verdon might offer.

It was an invitation no sane man would refuse: a holiday in sunny Provence with a delightful and attractive female companion. Unfortunately, over the past few days, I'd gone a little crazy—thanks to the two brooding palookas camped just up the beach.

The truth is that in the evenings, after bidding S. sweet dreams, I'd taken to relieving any niggling carnal frustrations by drowning them in late-night lager-fueled bonding sessions with the ill-tempered gorillas from the Pacific Northwest. There was a reason why these guys were so grumpy: They were alpine to the core, and since the environment here wasn't beating them up, they were left with having to torture themselves. They endlessly second-guessed their decision to abandon the mountains, but spoke of it in terms of a "retrenchment" rather than retreat, and were already planning a counterattack. Their thinking was pretty messed up; we'd all just come from the Alps, where only a fish could argue that the season wasn't a wash, but as a thwarted mountaineer myself, I found their dark rhetoric and manly grunting infectious. It wasn't long before recalling me to active duty had become a new brick in their quixotic road. They convinced me that in fact it was *this* place—the beach—that presented the greatest peril; the danger here was in going soft, losing my edge and my self-respect…seduced by simple pleasures and—they thumbed darkly toward S.'s tent—a feminine influence. In the end, I swore an oath to return with them to the Alps, to attempt one of the great Swiss Nordwands, the notorious north faces. Never mind that these walls were typically regarded as alpine death traps, even in good conditions. We would kick some ass or go down swinging.

But first I would have to break with S., and it wasn't going to be easy. She made sure of that.

"No…no," I told her firmly, while kneading tanning oil between her shoulders, working it underneath the edges of her sports bra, per her request. "I've got unfinished business in the Alps!"

She was killing me; lazily sunning herself on a foam pad, but clearly working to undermine my resolve by pressing an unfair advantage. And so I added, rather meanly, "I simply cannot *waste* any more time rock climbing."

"But why not?" S. pouted. Sitting up, she leaned conspicuously in my direction and smiled prettily. "Haven't we had a good time?"

"We spent several lovely days together cragging along the sun-kissed fringes of the Mediterranean…"

"Well, yes, of course. It's been awesome," I admitted, before clinging to focus. "But try to understand that I'm an *alpine* climber—mountains are what I do. For me, the rest of this is just…training!"

S. breathed out an unimpressed sigh. "Well, I don't get it. All that cold and ice, instead of this?" She massaged another squirt of oil into her thigh. "And *Switzerland?*" She raked her tongue against her teeth with disgust. "I mean, the Swiss are *so* uptight. I just can't believe you wouldn't rather stay here in France, with me, where everyone is just so…free!" And with that, she suddenly peeled off her top and stretched out like a leopardess along the length of her pad, her skin a dizzying study in contrasts: bronzed contours along sun-burnished shoulders and arms, while elsewhere touched for the very first time by the dazzling and glorious light of day.

Vive la France! So began the communication with which I tendered my resignation (in my defense, I did leave a note): *Sorry, lads, change in plans—off to Verdon! Hate to disappoint, but c'est la vie, right? Best of luck vis-a-vis Nordwands. Drop me a line after (if you're not too broken up. Ha!). Cheers!*

Here's the thing: In the years that followed, I actually did climb a Swiss death trap or two, but I find that now, with the perspective of time and after a period of forced retirement, I can honestly say that I have as clear and satisfying memories of that magic trip to Verdon with S. as from any significant or hard-won alpine contest. She and I lit it up. Climbing mind-blowing rock by day; dancing in the streets of La Palud and strolling moonlit lavender fields by night—I'd always dreamed that climbing would lead me to romance, and then it did. And it had nothing to do with sex (though my companion continued to take perverse delight in pulling my strings). Rather, we experienced that other definition of romance: a spirit or feeling of happy adventure, excitement and the exotic.

Bliss. Mallory's "sheer joy."

But do I even need climbing to find it? Absolutely not. I know this because my wife and I recently shared an equal experience exploring the misty cliff-side monasteries and ancient pathways of Bhutan. I don't know which is more remarkable, that we found a way to wander freely through this notoriously closed kingdom, or the fact that I actually have a wife (at long last, a female companion who doesn't point me to a separate tent at night). I only know that together, we encountered one of the few remaining pockets of unspoiled Asia, the Himalaya of forgotten time and lost dreams, and I never once missed my ice axe.

This isn't to say that I'd never consider climbing another big mountain. In fact, there's always been one that would send me scrambling back into the saddle faster than snakes in the sage. I even have a plan…

THE HIGHEST LOSER

As an adolescent, I made a list of all the summits I dreamed of visiting one day. Foremost was the mountain that reigned supreme over all others by sheer virtue of its size. Even then I could appreciate that it would not offer the steepest or most technical terrain, but there is something irresistible about ticking the ultimate, and for a budding climber, nothing carried a greater thrill than the prospect of scaling the highest mountain ever measured. I'm referring to Olympus Mons, a volcano that rises 14 *miles* in elevation on the planet Mars.

Of course, I now know that most of the truly exciting developments the futurists keep saying are just around the corner will never come to fruition—innovation is driven by profit potential, not science fiction. (It's why I was able to clap out the lights on my dream of climbing via personal jetpack.) Commerce, however, may be my ticket to achieving another ambition—a sort of consolation prize, a mountain of lesser elevation but more gravity than the Martian colossus. I'm talking about that relatively insignificant high point on the next planet over toward the sun: Mount Everest, the Kosciuszko of the solar system.

While I was still climbing, I never put much serious thought into attempting Everest. If the opportunity had suddenly fallen into my lap, I would have jumped at it, but left to my own devices, I found the challenges of costs and logistics too daunting. And since nobody ever did offer me a slot *gratis* on a packaged trip—despite my willingness to pen a bestseller about the ensuing disaster—I joined the haters, denouncing commercial

The Author, in training mode

expeditions for having turned Everest into the clown car of mountaineering (once they opened the door, the bozos just keep coming and coming). But these past few years on the couch have given me an opportunity to view the world through a new lens—a whole bunch of lenses actually, and I've changed my tune. Reality television may mark the advent of human devolution, but it could also be my salvation; a way for me to get back in shape again, plus hitch a free ride to Everest. To this end, I'm pitching my own show, and trust me guys, it'll kill.

It's part survival game, part weight-loss competition; the ultimate endurance race meets a "gumbies in the death zone" documentary. The contestants are a bunch of morbidly out-of-shape climbing has-beens, but instead of a fat camp, we (attention, casting director: note pronoun) are sent to the northeast ridge of Everest. From there, it's an all-out race for the summit, but with a twist: no food allowed. That's right: outwit, outplay and out-*fast*. The gamble is that we're already packing enough stored lipids around our guts and thighs to get us to the top. Hilarious high jinks ensue: We waddle around falling into crevasses a lot, but, like corks in a bottle, we don't drop very far. Drama unfolds: Who gets voted off the glacier for crapping his pants on the Chinese Ladder (*solid* evidence of contraband rations)?

There's a ton of cross-promotion and product-placement opportunities: We're all outfitted with the logos of our personal corporate sponsors (e.g. family-style restaurant chains), whose goods and services are instrumental in getting us all well-marbled pre-climb. Eventually, however, the field thins as the mountain literally eats us alive, burning off the flab, trimming all the white from our bacon, until—like a butterfly exiting a chrysalis—one honed Adonis emerges from his quadruple-XL expedition suit and plants his ass alongside his Waffle House flag on top of the world! Besides summiting Everest and getting a temporary reprieve from type 2 diabetes, the winner receives a lifetime supply of climbing swag (updated every time styles or ethics evolve, or if anything gets lost, stolen or driven over with a car); he also receives freedom from ridicule at the crags for his outdated techniques and his wool (not merino) knickers; he's granted the authority to cap the Yosemite Decimal System once and for all, so there are no more reminders that everybody except him seems to be getting better, and he's given the power of life and death over anybody who even *thinks* about uttering the numbers "5.16."

OK, time for me to stop. I swear it was never my intention to preach. I don't want to be that guy…the cranky old man who lives in the past, thinks his answers are the only ones, and spends all day guarding his turf against the kids on their newfangled bikes.

I'm just trying to figure out where I go from here.

Will I ever climb again?

Maybe not. I know I can get what I really want and need out of life without risking life and limb.

But maybe. Despite the bewildering spectacle of the constantly evolving climbing scene, the mountains offer rich experiences and relationships that just aren't the same on paper or on screen—even in high definition.

Originally published in ASCENT, *2012.*

Author's note: I have indeed returned to climbing, with recent trips to the Tetons (no, I still haven't climbed the North Face of the Grand) and Mount Rainier under my belt (along with a waistline that is back in fighting shape—merely size XXL again). I've even been showing up regularly at the local climbing gym, a development my friends say is far more dumbfounding than the advent of 5.15.

Summit of Mount Rainier; May, 2014

Verse

Parody—that's my deal: life imitating art beneath the Matterhorn

HERE STANZA MOUNTAIN POET

A Preface to This Collection of Verse and a Nod to the Masters

MANY PEOPLE—including, I would wager, the lion's share of magazine editors—will argue that the audience for climbing poetry is pretty much limited to colicky babies and nervous cats who may be soothed by its meter, and therefore the form has little place or relevance in mountain writing. Well, argue till you're blue, it's just not true. The fact is, poets have been composing celebrated verse inspired by lofty peaks since the book of Psalms (*I will lift up mine eyes unto the hills...*). Climbing, in particular, has birthed its fair share of well-regarded bards and troubadours including John Menlove Edwards and Wilfrid Noyce—perhaps there is something in the English air or diet that incites poetic abandon? The literary pre-war British mountaineer Geoffrey Winthrop Young published entire books of crowd-pleasing mountain poetry, including many poems specifically about climbing. Among these are the haunting reflections of "The Cragsman," in which a climber clinging to a mountain wall considers the consequences of simply letting go:

In this short span
Between my finger-tips on the smooth edge
And these tense feet cramped to the crystal ledge
I hold the life of a man...

Meanwhile, in North America, Robert Service (another Englishman!), enjoyed popular success composing rollicking, rhyming verses ripe with satirical humor. Unlike the earnest romantic poets of the Victorian period, Service steadfastly refused to take himself or his craft too seriously—in fact, he insisted that it *not* be called poetry—an approach that made his work highly accessible, not to mention commercially successful. Although Service never wrote about climbing per se, his characters were hardened prospectors, part of an unruly gold rush subculture and pitted against the untamed wilds of the Yukon—themes that resonate with mountaineers.

In this same whimsical vein, the climber/poet who arguably has had the most impact and success writing specifically for and about climbers is the

Reading from Tom Patey during the Gentlemen's Ascent (p. 354)

Scotsman Tom Patey (and *finally*, someone from north of the wall). Patey's poetic oeuvre, published posthumously in 1971 with his other classic writing as *One Man's Mountains*, is marvelously irreverent, exceedingly clever, and utterly hilarious. Whether lampooning the notable climbers of his day (e.g., "Onward Christian Bonington" to the tune of "Onward Christian Soldiers") or the climbing scene (as in the unhappy plight of a girl seeking romance among climbers, depicted in "The Squirrels' Song"), Patey never pulled his punches. His aptitude for smart, skewering satire was undiminished by the fact that he often chose to flex his poetic muscle creating droll send-ups of popular songs.

Anyone who is familiar with Patey's work will instantly recognize that he has had great influence upon my own tendencies for parody and rhyme, but I am not a parrot—I came by these things honestly. Throughout my formative years, the mocking humor of *Mad* magazine, Tom ("The Elements" song) Lehrer, and Monty Python was profoundly affecting. As a bit of a smart-ass myself, the biting and socially provocative aspects of satire appealed to me and quickly found a place among my favorite forms of literature and comedy. Not surprisingly then, shortly after I first started writing, I began experimenting with climbing-themed parody. (One of those early exercises, "The Ballad of the Green Belay," was included in a guidebook I authored in 1984.) But when I discovered Tom Patey I knew somebody had gotten there first and done it better than I could ever dream of doing. This didn't discourage me, but it meant that in terms of my own compositions, I could cross conceit and hubris off the list of things I was ever going to have to worry about.

One thing Patey and I do share is the problem of having co-opted outdated or quirky songs with melodies known to only a few people who may themselves be a couple beats short of a measure. (If you can spontaneously summon the tune to "Barrett's Privateers" or "A Hymn to Him" you should probably apply to be on a game show, then use the winnings to move out of your parents' attic.) In Patey's case, his ability to turn a phrase makes the issue moot, his songs can be read as poems and they still work brilliantly. With my stuff, contemporary readers at least have the option of instantly calling forth these tunes (and poems*) from a host of media resources—a crutch I have leaned upon for discerning the melodies to some of Patey's songs.

So consider this never-before-published *Verse* of mine an homage to Tom Patey—mere shadows of what might have been had he not fallen from an ocean spire at the age of 38, prematurely dousing a candle that still had a lot of creative wax left to burn. And while this sampling of my poetry, songs and satire may not appeal to everyone, for readers who appreciate Patey, Robert Service and other masters of these forms, my hope is that there is something here to lend a smile or two.

Author's note: "Never-before-published"—a warning bell if ever there was one. It seems only right to apprise the reader that, just as Tom Patey wrote mainly about the climbing scene in his native Scotland, my verses are heavily colored by my own experiences as a Midwesterner. Poetry by and about a middling climber from the Great Plains—how are editors not clawing one another over this?

---

*Unlike Winthrop Young, Service or Patey, I lack what it takes (e.g., ambition) to create much in the way of original poetry. With few exceptions, my compositions hang upon a framework of preexisting songs, poems, or well-known poetic structures. Parody—that's my deal.

Because It Isn't There

One day I'll sit by the fire and write
Of my much envied life as a brave alpine knight.
With a glass at my elbow that's brimming with port,
I'll gather the chapters to file my report:
Accounts of the Tower, El Cap and the Eiger,
Of a boy from the plains—then a man—then a tiger!
Who prowled the crags like a beast on the stalk,
And bagged mighty routes tho' he never used chalk.
But when I review all my mountains and glories
I'll sigh 'cause there's one thing that's not in these stories;
Though my climbs are diverse, my résumé's shy—
There's a hole in my list nearly six miles high!
Despite all the summits I've set down in print,
The one people want is the one that I didn't…
And that's why the Public won't give me a look,
The fact that Mount Everest is not in my book.

"But wait!" I will say, "I've got rats on the *Nose*!
I've got falls on the Matterhorn, canyonland woes!
There are tales of Alaska, Scotland, the Alps,
Of ropes that yank teeth and climbs that take scalps!
I've partnered with doubt, known fear in excess,
Shed tears on the Grand—and the Eiger? Oh yes!
Been bombed on the Dru without getting scratched,
Escaped from a canyon (with both hands attached!),
Nearly trampled by elephants, drowned on a wall,
I've survived forest fires and a ninety-foot fall.
I've had climbs melt away while I'm miles o'er the scree,
Did I mention the Eiger? Twice before? Now it's three!
And here's something else: I've chummed with Steve House,
Petzoldt, MacInnes and Heckmair and spouse.
Shaken hands with Bonatti, belayed other Greats,
It's all in these pages—and more here awaits!"

"Well that sounds impressive," the Public will say,
"But who is Bonatti? And what is 'belay'?
And where is the stuff that we love to hear?
'Bout a team that's assembled from folks far and near,
Some are ex-models and some are just jerks,
But you're all very rich or you've mortgaged the works
For a two-month ascent of the ultimate tower
(Tho' the Sherpas fix ropes to the top in an hour),
And your Guide calls the shots from Camp Mission Control
Where a fistfight breaks out with some climbers from Seoul
Who keep jumping the queue on the route to the Col,
But you all work as one after somebody's fall,
Then finally, up top, sucking gas in a swarm
It all goes to hell when you're slammed by a storm!!
These are the stories that thrill and amaze,
We can't get enough of this Everest craze!"

"Now look," I will counter, "You really must see
That there's more to this sport than is shown on TV!
Great mountaineering is not just the highest,
The fact is, the media's Everest-biased!
There are other hot climbs that could sizzle a Geiger,
For example, a peak that the Swiss call the Eiger—"
"No thanks," says John-Q, my entreaty is nixed,
There's a news-alert flashing! Attention is fixed
On breaking reports coming out of Nepal:
Our reporter is live at the scene of the fall!
…And so I will sit with my wine by the fire
And a stack of rejections from publishers higher
Than all of the pages 'bout mountains I've penned,
Without Chomolungma 'twas moot in the end,
Despite all the years and the effort it took,
F***ing Mount Everest is not in this book!!

SONG OF THE ALPINIST
(To the tune of "Do You Hear the People Sing?" from *Les Misérables*)

Do you see the climber's grin?
It is a mask of alpine pain,
Etched with the hollow stress of hunger
And the toll of mental strain.
When all hell breaks loose above
Where will the splintered fragments fall?
There is a mind coming apart
On a mountain wall.

Will his helmet end in shards
Or will he dodge the cruel debris?
The mountain deals the cards
And he will gamble what will be...
But losing the bet
That is no way to set a brain free!

Do you see the quaking boot?
It is but one step from the grave,
Beneath a crumbling wall of courage—
Maybe too far gone to save.
Through the currents of the mist
He can hear the Boatman's call,
There is a mind coming apart
On a mountain wall.

He came seeking mighty deeds
And planting seeds of youthful hope,
But his garden sprouted weeds
With the first tying of the rope.
Now all of it's rotted,
His wits too unknotted to cope!

Do you hear the mournful notes?
It is the symphony of dread,
It is the taunting of the tempest
And it swells inside his head.
As the winds begin to shriek
And the clouds begin to bawl,
There is a mind coming apart
On a mountain wall.

Two concrete (visual) poems; with apologies to E. E. Cummings:

FLUX

A
damp
and steaming
mountain up there
wreathed in morning mist
friends probably on top here I sit
wracked with cramps backside against a log
praying for death crouched over a damp and steaming mountain

CRUX

the end
is near
just a few more feet
to the belay anchors
but still
no gear
sketchy
r u n   o u t
and holy crap
this climb is
really hard
really thin
and now
getting
even
!!!!
crux
panic
pumped
just move
shit shit shit
key hold missed
botched seqeunce
but somehow holding on
wild lunge *thank god* bomber jug
back into your holes hungry worms not today

HIGH-KU

A selection of short poems in the traditional Japanese form—17 syllables divided into three phrases of five/seven/five respectively:

the first time we met
you *belay on,* me *climbing*
you had me at *climb*

yosemite sam
that dude never climbed el cap
so maybe just sam

ober gabelhorn
zermatt's other peak, eclipsed
but more fun to say

hey wet sleeping bag
I'm the one freezing to death
so why are you down?

day six still storming
one more snore and I'll kill you
this tent smells like ass

messner bonington
combined, higher than the moon
that's a lot of books

*k2 you're so great
so cool so desirable*
sucks to be k1

fucking dumb question
that's what he meant when he said
because it is there

THE BALLAD OF THE GREEN BELAY
(To the tune of "The Ballad of the Green Berets")

We drive old cars into the West,
Soaring granite is our quest,
A thousand miles we'll cross today
For a thousand feet of vertical play.

And though the rule upon the walls
Is that the leader never falls,
Gravity can't be denied,
A Sticht* in time can turn the tide.

A probing shoe explores the cliff,
The toe skates off—we're ready if!
For the duration of the flight
Our practiced grip is iron tight.

To catch these falls, defines our task,
"Who are these lads?" the locals ask,
"Where are they from, what do they seek,
These masters of belay technique?"

And from our rigging in the skies
We hear these questions as they rise,
Our voices echo from on high,
"Belay is off!"—*then* we reply:

"In northern climes we were born,
A fabled land of endless corn,
At Palisade, upon the Lake
We delve the art of the friction brake.

When at a stance we lace each crack,
We feed the rope with little slack,
We shout our signals clear and bold,
Our slings are new, our anchors hold.

And ever braced to make arrest,
To drop one hand would fail the test,
So lest we slack or feel the urge
We grimly chant this solemn dirge:

---

*A 1980s-era belay plate.

'There lies our friend, his body wrecked,
Climbed with a greenhorn, then he decked,
One hundred feet he fell that day
And all because of a green belay.'

So should the leader peel and drop,
The rope may stretch, a piece may pop,
But not an inch of line will run,
For when we second, we're second to none!"

LAMENT FOR THE BASTILLE
AKA THE CRABBY OLD CLIMBER SONG
(To the tune of "Northwest Passage")

Oh, if one more time,
I could scale the *Northwest Corner*,
To follow in the steps of Layton Kor and Pat Ament,
And not wait in line
Behind groups and kids and foreigners—
I'd revel in the thrill of that event!

Just up the road from Eldorado Springs there stands a rock,
A monolithic sentinel of sandstone stained with chalk,
These white cracks and handholds speak to passage over time
Of the multitudes that muster here to climb…

Oh, if one more time,
I could scale the *Northwest Corner*,
To follow in the steps of Layton Kor and Pat Ament,
And not share that climb
With the groups and kids and foreigners,
Who'll dog me every inch of the ascent.

How they throng the mountain is a scene that sinks the soul:
Like how insects swarm a carcass or a python eats one whole,
They flock upon its ledges, they mob the noble walls
Like shoppers on Black Friday at the malls...

Oh, if one more time,
I could scale the *Northwest Corner*,
To follow in the steps of Layton Kor and Pat Ament,
But not lose my mind
At the groups and kids and foreigners,
And the teeming gridlocked climbs they represent.

Below the *Bastille Crack* the next in line depart the queue,
Nearby on the *Northcutt* there's a party launching too,
Now they race to claim the space and stance both pitches share
Tho' three groups gone before them are still there!

Oh, if one more time,
I could scale the *Northwest Corner*,
To follow in the steps of Layton Kor and Pat Ament,
But instead now I'm
Wedged 'tween groups and kids and foreigners,
Packed wall-to-wall where once nobody went...

Back then no eyes were witness if I stepped upon a peg,
No one there to chuckle at the shaking of my leg,
Now they grab my footholds even as I lift my feet,
Leaving me with no place to retreat!

Oh, if one more time,
I could scale the *Northwest Corner*,
To follow in the steps of Layton Kor and Pat Ament,
Sans the pressing bind
Of groups and kids and foreigners,
Who mock that I'm so slow I should pay rent!

Reprise:
I spend all my time,
Staring up the *Northwest Corner*,
Pining for the "good old days" of Kor and Pat Ament,
Days like in my prime,
Without groups and kids and foreigners,
Instead I'm just alone in my lament!

WHY CAN'T A WOMAN CLIMB MORE LIKE A MAN?
(To the tune of "A Hymn to Him" from *My Fair Lady*)

Why would she abandon such a specimen as me,
And *willingly* become my climbing ex?
She—on purpose—left the thrill
Of bearing witness to my skill,
To partner with another of her sex!

Of course, Nature gifted her with some advantages,
Not just the ones upon which I obsess,
But lower mass and balance that she manages
To muster without bluster to combust her
And then thrust her via something called *fin*-esse?!

But...why can't a woman climb more like a man?
Men are like apes,
We're born robust,
Genetic behemoths
With bones you can trust!
Who, when we climb, plow like oxen through the tricky stuff,
Why does a woman...have to make it so tough?
She ponders every crux like she's Pythagoras,
Like it's something to be solved inside the head,
Can't she see that thinking is a drag for us?
Why use brains...when you've got muscle instead?

Why don't the women climb just like us men?
Where's the show?!
The poses of strain...
The expletive howls...
The flaunting of pain?
Why does every woman move with fluid tendency?
Like water flowing backward up a hill,
It's unnerving and unnatural for us to see,
Why not *attack*...and go for the kill?

Sure, she may be supple as an acrobat
With muscles that astonish for her size,
But propose to me I swap my brawn for this and that?
No thanks—it's the build of Samson I prize!

(NEXT PAGE)

(CONTINUED)

Why can't the women take a page from us boys?
Men are rock solid,
Unyielding and dense,
Wired for hunting,
For bagging ascents.
A man is always focused on the task at hand
By keeping track of every little win,
Being first or fastest is what we demand,
Whereas most gals…they act like bragging's a sin!

Why aren't they *eager* to rope with a lad?
Men are so helpful,
So quick to advise,
So free with opinion
That shows we are wise.
Ready to slap your back while telling you what *we'd* have done,
Why can't the women…have that kind of fun?
And God forbid we try to help the ladies out
By yelling constant beta as they twirl,
Or offering a compliment like when we shout:
"You're pretty strong—for a girl!"

So why can't a woman just climb like a man?
If I was a woman,
I'd hit the gym,
Forget being clever…
Climb more like *him*.
I would learn to heave my body like gorillas do,
I would train myself to boast and spray and cuss,
I would swagger 'round the crag seeking guys to screw,
Why can't women…think like us?!

Author's note: Satire is risky, self-parody doubly so. Easily viewed as presumptive or pandering, it can fall flat as an Iowa mile. Nevertheless, after watching female friends endure these attitudes over the years (and, on occasion, being guilty of them myself) I decided we boys might benefit from a little self-reflection…this ditty is my way of holding up the mirror. Ladies (there I go again!), forgive me if I've come up short—I can only pretend to know your frustrations. Men, I have two words for you: Lynn Hill.

PENDING WALL
A line-for-line reworking of "Mending Wall," with apologies to Robert Frost:

Someone there is that doesn't love a wall,
Who feels a frozen-fear-swell under it,
And spills the lower boulders with his spew;
And as the mental gap widens, prepares a defense—even two.
The work of the weather is one angle:
We have come after it and found despair
Where it has left not one dry stone on a stone,
But still my partner would have us starting up!
Despite my yelping dogs... my blisters I mean.
No—no one mentioned *them* before, or even felt them made,
But this morning I find them excruciating.
I let my partner know below the hill,
Then and there, I draw the line,
And a wall—not just cliff—is between us. Again.
For my side, I voice this defense:
"We each have the stones we were born with,
Some have loaves, and some so nearly balls—"
He needs no spell to upend the balance:
"You've made the decision to stay where you are? Behind my back?!
(I worry that he will wear his fingers rough handling me)
You think this is a *game?!*"
One on a side, little remains to be said,
Except, who needs this stupid wall...
He is all tree and I am soft fruit.
My excuses mean nothing to him,
What gnaws at me cannot uproot him, I think,
But still I say what is not true: "Good defenses make good climbers."

ODE TO THE GENTLEMEN'S ASCENT

Some years ago, two gentlemen—admirers of old-school climbing tradition and Scottish poetry—joined on Robert Burns Day (January 25th, the birthday of the illustrious 19th century poet) to ascend Nightfall, *a classic two-pitch ice climb in northern Minnesota. What made this expedition unique is that the pair was outfitted head to toe in century-old clothing. Several years later, this tomfoolery was repeated by four gentlemen, an outing enshrined in memory (and preserved in a jar of alcohol!) after one of the party sacrificed part of a digit to frostbite. Before the originators knew it, the "Gentlemen's Occasional Ascent" had become something of a tradition itself, occurring every few years, attended by ever-swelling numbers—including a woman who stepped right out of her oversized leather boot mid-climb!—and featuring a raucous Scottish Ceilidh (talent show/drinking party) the night before the ascent, for which the following song was composed:*

(To the tune of "Christmas in the Trenches")

The month was January and though memory is poor,
'Twas likely in the fast-paced year of 1994,
Technology was booming, invention was the thrill,
But in northern Minnesota time stood still.

In a cold and shadowed river gorge two figures could be seen,
Shod in leather, cloaked in tweed, they trudged the dark ravine,
They'd come to make a statement, make a climb and make a stand,
By cleaving to traditions old and grand.

354

Their jackets and their waistcoats were stitched with nature's threads,
Woolen fabric swathed them from their socks up to their heads,
On each hand a boiled mitten, scratchy knickers 'round each thigh,
And 'round each neck a gentlemanly tie.

In due course the destination for the pair was reached:
A massive ice-filled gully where the canyon had been breached,
They roped together, tipped a flask and said a little verse,
Then made an antiquarian traverse.

This was the humble starting of the Gentlemen's Ascent,
A wool and leather, whiskey-soaked occasional event,
Half birthday jubilation for the Bard of "Auld Lang Syne,"
Half chance to dress like gentlemen and climb.

The original intent was that this be a one-time feat,
But just a few years later it was destined for repeat,
And, in truth, this second coming was twice what had come before,
As the number in the party now was four.

The stage was set, that brave quartet attacked the ice with zeal,
Again the hoary pillar felt the kiss of tweed and steel,
The air was thick with spindrift and the brogue of Highland prose
As up the frozen Beastie they all rose.

And it wasn't just the poetry of Rabbie Burns they maimed,
As polar winds cut through the glen, a casualty was claimed,
All great expeditions must exact a price, and so
Their ice-nipped leader offered up a toe.

This is the lore and history of the Gentlemen's Ascent,
A wool and leather, whiskey-soaked occasional event,
Part birthday celebration for the Bard of "Auld Lang Syne,"
Part chance to dress like gentlemen and climb.

We hold that modern textiles are no match for sheepy clothes,
Thus as the years move forward, this backward movement grows,
The woolen ranks upon the flanks of *Nightfall* have increased,
With all those in attendance duly fleeced.

And with each incarnation we have seen a thing or two:
We've watched a lassie top out in the dark without her shoe,
She showed us bigger stones than in the wall the Romans built
And that a gentleman is more than meets the kilt.

(NEXT PAGE)

(CONTINUED)

Lads in skirts have also shown their mettle on the hill,
Dangling Scot-free they've shown us more than that, and still
Their tartan insulation saved their bacon *and* their ham,
And warmed them like a golden highland dram.

So raise a cup o' kindness to the Gentlemen's Ascent,
This wool and leather, whiskey-soaked occasional event,
Half Burns Day celebration and half climb from days now gone,
And may the Lord protect us in the dawn!

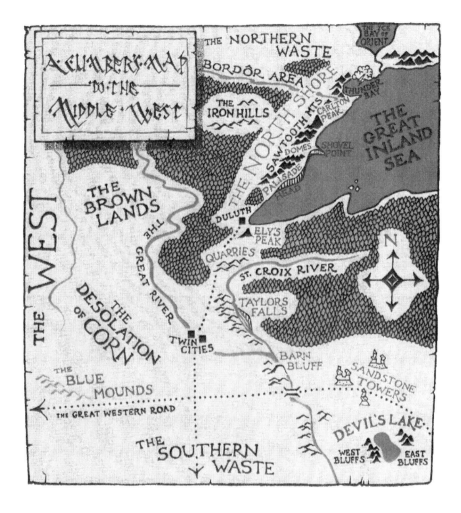

HOARD OF THE RINGS

AKA CARABINER INVENTORY FOR GOING WEST

With apologies to J.R.R. Tolkien:

Three rings for some longer slings, should need arise,
Seven pairs for fixed gear (for which I'll be praying),
Nine for the trad rack draped to my thighs,
One with a locking gate for raps and belaying
Beyond the border where Colorado lies…

One string of shiny links, one string to bind me,
One string that I will bring to clip the rope behind me,
Beyond the border where Colorado lies.

357

THE WHISKEY SONG

Composed after a third winter trip to Ben Nevis (route total: one) to explain what could compel a person to keep going back. Note: a few of the more dialect-infused distillery names have been written phonetically to facilitate pronunciation.

(To the tune of "Hallelujah")

Scotland's where my heart remains,
The winds are fierce, it always rains,
So loving it might seem a contradiction,
But not by choice—it's not my fault,
The thing they do with barley malt!
'Tis a miracle, a gift, and an addiction…

Golden treasure,
Royal pleasure,
For the bourgeois!
Hal-le-lu-u-jah!

From Glencoe to the river Spey
Like Highland winds I nipped my way…
I think you get the picture now (or do ya?)
The friends I made there kept me warm—
At least the ones in liquid form,
To them I sing this song of Hallelujah…

Hallelujah!
Glad I knew ya,
"Here's to ya," (raise glass)
Hal-le-lu-u-jah:

Acken-toshin, Cragganmore,
Boona-hav'n, Edradour,
Talisker, Glen Farclas, The Balvinnie,
Bru-ich-laddie, Aberlour,
Cardhu, Tamdhu, Mannochmoor,
Highland Park, Ben Nevis and Dalwhinnie…

Lagavoolin!
I'm not foolin'—
Hallelujah!
Hal-le-lu-u-jah!

Glen Gar-i-ock, Banff, Bowmore,
Arran, Oban, Convalmore,
Loch Dhu, Gnoc Dhu, Deanston and Glen-allecky,
Springbank, Rosebank, Inver House,
Laphroaig, Loch Lomond, Famous Grouse,
Ardbeg, Ardmore, Aultmore and Glen-morin-gee...

Isle of Jura
I'm not sure of...
Shoots right through ya,
Hal-le-lu-u-jah!

Tully-barden, Little Mill,
Tamnavoolin, Old Dunhill,
Speyburn, Millburn, Coleburn, Caperdonick,
Glens: Kinchie, Roth-es, Goyne and Spey,
Glen Scotia, Ord and Glen Moray,
Glenfiddick and Glenlivet and Glendronick!

The Macallan?
By the gallon!
Hallelujah!
Hal-le-lu-u-jah!!

The mountain and the cure

REFLECTIONS OF A RUN-OUT LEADER
(To the tune of "Barrett's Privateers")

Oh, a child once climbed to a lofty bough...
(*I wish that I was dreaming now!*)
From that glorious thrill, the seeds were sown
And a vertical life was set in stone.

Chorus:
God *damn* this wall!
I was told
I'd cruise my way from hold to hold,
But the pro is shite!
The rock is slime...
Now I'm losing grip on a run-out line,
The last, I swear, I'll ever climb!

So the boy read books that would teach him how...
(*I wish that I was dreaming now!*)
To ascend sheer rock, high peak and hill,
Tho' at home on the plains these things were nil.

(Chorus)

He climbed what ground wasn't fit to plow…
(I wish that I was dreaming now!)
But he longed for the glory of the greater test
So he coiled his ropes and journeyed West.

(Chorus)

He scaled every tower, peak and prow…
(I wish that I was dreaming now!)
And he learned protection must not be vague
And the "R" and the "X" should be shunned like the plague!

(Chorus)

Thus a laced-up pitch was his solemn vow…
(I wish that I was dreaming now!)
But he could be betrayed by a sandbagger's guile
Or the guidebook description that's off by a mile!

(Chorus)

That boy was me, and I'll allow…
(I wish that I was dreaming now!)
That youth is a thing that I'd have back
Here to steel my nerves far beyond the crack.

(Chorus)

I'm staked for slaughter like the fatted cow…
(I wish that I was dreaming now!)
But a stake's wishful thinking and the nightmare's real,
The butcher is a mountain and off I'll peel!

(Chorus)

Reprise:
So *damn* this wall!
And damn my fears,
That have plagued me for so many years,
I'll pull like hell,
Shed no tears,
And send this prayer toward the Heavenly Ear…
That He's a god of mercy—not a bombardier!

WE DON'T MAKE THE RULES
(To the tune of "We Didn't Start the Fire")

Edward Whymper, alpenstocks, roped protection on the rocks,
Woolen slacks, ice axe, artificial aid.
Wooden ladders: Devils Tower, Shiprock: David Brower,
Lassos, first bolts, "fair means" crusade.

Patriotic expeditions, British climbers on a mission,
Front points—what they spawn: Heckmair on the Eigerwand.
Iron pins, hip belay, Sentinel, Salathé,
Bolt ladders—doubt shatters—it's a slippery slope we're on!

We don't make the rules,
But the game keeps shifting
And the lines keep drifting,
We don't make the rules,
But the laws of style
Are changing all the while…

Annapurna amputations, British back with innovations:
Nylon sewing, O-2 flowing, Ev-er-est won!
Nanga Parbat and K2, Vibram has a new shoe,
Hermann Buhl is superman—favorite son.
Dru solo, *Thimble* free, Harding in Yosemite,
Fixed ropes, siege style, more bolts, more bile,
Royal Robbins: dismay, *Dawn Wall*—no way!
Wheels coming off the cart, compressor on the Torre!!

We don't make the rules,
But the game keeps shifting
And the lines keep drifting,
We don't make the rules,
But the laws of style
Are changing all the while…

Pin scars, clean freaks, modern "hammerless" techniques,
Bonington: big win—up where the air is thin.
Alpine style, Hidden Peak: Messner starts a winning streak,
George Willig's on TV, but George Lowe's making history!

Whillans harness, chalk bags, painter pants, climbing mags,
Ray Jardine, camming pro, 5.13—here we go…
Worked routes, freed climbs, sticky shoes and speed climbs,
John Bachar: no slacker, climbing hard and solo!

We don't make the rules,
But the game keeps shifting
And the lines keep drifting,
We don't make the rules,
But the laws of style
Are changing all the while...

Hangdogging, French-free, Bosch drill—*mon ami!*,
Fixed anchors, New Day: sport climbing's here to stay.
Climbing gyms, competitions, retro bolting—sans permission,
Chipped holds, bolt wars, fisticuffs, crowbars,
Greased cracks, cheater sticks, "stolen" routes, dirty tricks,
Cliffhanger's bolting gun: that thing looks like *lots* of fun!

We don't make the rules,
But the game keeps shifting
And the lines keep drifting,
We don't make the rules,
But the laws of style
Are changing all the while...

Lynn Hill, Alex Lowe (where did all the heroes go?)
Painted rocks, closures, Internet, posers.
Seven Summits, cell phones, clients in the Death Zone,
Big dollars, Krakauer, Mallory in living color.
Fast and light, BASE jumps, stunt climbs, garbage dumps,
Hire a guide, hitch a ride, never venture outside,
Media that never rests, children climbing Everest,
Wing suits—can't miss! How do we climb out of this?!

We don't make the rules,
But the game keeps shifting
And the lines keep drifting,
We don't make the rules,
But without them drawn
Can we still climb on?
And on,
And on,
And on...

MONT-BLANC DAWN
In the style of "Kubla Khan," with apologies to Samuel Coleridge:

In Chamonix is high Mont Blanc,
A stately pleasure-dome of snow,
Where Arve, the milky river, is,
And granite *aiguilles*, so 'tis
Where alpinists must go.
From every nation comes this rabble,
A clinking, stinking Tower of Babel,
Like Noah's beasts, two by two,
But single file they funnel
Onto the ridge, this purposed crew,
Beyond the Midi tunnel.

Oh *Merde!* A soldier fallen prior the battle,
Not from some wall or stellar peak
Nor gully where the loose bricks rattle,
But here among this herd of cattle
Outside the *téléphérique!*
Unfazed, the masses trudge the blade,
Shuffling past the victim splayed,
Then like a Phoenix o'er the flame
The casualty lifts up his frame!

An alpine Lazarus? Not so—
Just one who's gorge now marks the snow,
Not first nor last to stain this hummock
With the issue of his stomach.
Whether 'tis fear or merely liquor,
He vows 'twill not cull him from the ranks,
And so rejoins the march upon these storied flanks!
While all 'round the headlamps flicker,
In bobbing lighted pools they pass:
The candled acolytes of this high Mass,
Processing shadowed glacier alley,
Between the frozen rocky pews,
To where spidery couloirs loom o'er the valley,
Then grit their teeth, shrug off the booze.
They've glimpsed their fate, white fangs drawn:
The Tacul awaits, and they lurch on.

Upon high Mont Blanc 'tis much the same,
On icy dome and snowy bridge
Dawn kindles hope to forge a name,
So pity those late to the game
Forestalled upon the ridge.
Where those upbound meet chest to chest
With those just off a summit dance,
A standoff on the Bosses crest!
Who then takes the dreadful step toward Italy or France?
But oh! The coming light envigors the faint-hearted,
And so, throughout the range, these rays
Spur them on—the race has started!
Tho' few embrace the sun because
In minds and guts a question gnaws,
Like Saint George marching to the fray,
Upon the Dru or Grand Jorasses
Dragons lurk to smoke their asses:
Will they live to climb another day?

ABOUT THE AUTHOR

David Pagel is a technical and creative writer with a degree in geology. He is a former Senior Contributing Editor and columnist for *Climbing* magazine; his mountaineering writing has also been featured in *Rock and Ice* magazine, the *American Alpine Journal* and *Ascent*. He is the author of *Superior Climbs: A Climber's Guide to the North Shore* and *The First Chinook*. David lives with his wife, Dina Post, in Duluth, Minnesota.

13249651R10212

Printed in Great Britain
by Amazon.co.uk, Ltd.,
Marston Gate.